What Every Parent Needs to Know

What Every Parent Needs to Know

Love, nuture, and play
with your child

MARGOT SUNDERLAND

DK INDIA
Senior Art Editor Ivy Roy
Art Editor Jomin Johny
Managing Art Editor Navidita Thapa
DTP Designers Manish Upreti
Pre-production Manager Sunil Sharma

DK UK
Senior Editors Jemima Dunne, Victoria Heyworth-Dunne
Project Editor Martha Burley
Project Art Editors Mandy Eary, Vicky Read,
Alison Gardner
Senior Jacket Creative Nicola Powling
Senior Producer, Pre-Production Tony Phipps
Senior Producer Stephanie McConnell
Managing Editor Stephanie Farrow
Managing Art Editor Christine Keilty

First published as *The Science of Parenting*
in Great Britain in 2006 by
Dorling Kindersley,
A Penguin Company
80 Strand, London, WC2R 0RL

A CIP catalogue record for this book is available
from the British Library

ISBN: 978-0-2412-1656-9

Reproduced by Media Development Printing,
Great Britain
Printed and bound in China

A WORLD OF IDEAS:
SEE ALL THERE IS TO KNOW

www.dk.com

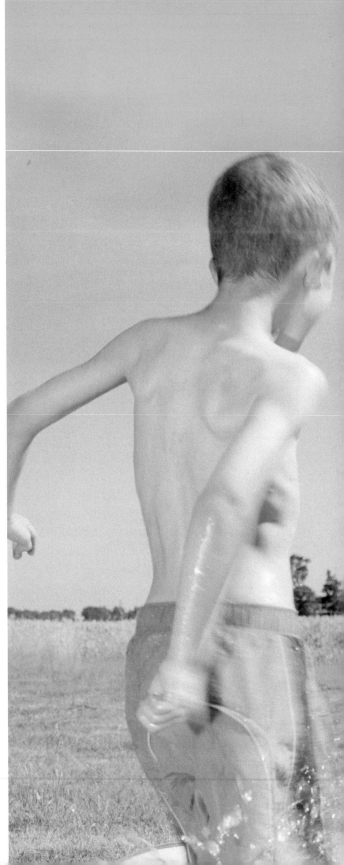

Contents

Forewords

If we act upon what science can tell us about parenting, we can develop more benign societies.

There was a moment of shock when I first realized how much impact the everyday interactions between parent and child can have on a child's developing brain. Yet the mass of scientific research on this subject was not getting through to parents or to the public arena. This is what fuelled my passion to write a book that would not be just one more opinion on parenting (we have quite enough of these already), but would rather empower parents to make informed choices for their children based on what we can learn from these scientific studies.

This book would not have been written without the ground-breaking research of Professor Jaak Panksepp in the US, who has been studying the emotional brain for more than 30 years. His findings are not only significant within the world of neuroscience, but also have major implications for humankind. His work, and that of others, offers us joined-up thinking about why so many children grow up to be adults who suffer from depression, anxiety, or problems with anger.

If we are prepared to act upon what science can tell us about parenting, we can push forward to develop more benign societies with greater compassion, capacity to reflect, and respect for difference. Perhaps, too, society will begin to see that by nurturing parents, children will be empowered to thrive.

Margot Sunderland
Director of Education and Training,
Centre for Child Mental Health, London

This second edition of this superb manual for optimal child rearing practices describes how healthy minds emerge from emotionally well-fertilized brains. The affective and cognitive qualities of childcare – even before birth – can have lifelong consequences for mental health. Children whose emotional feelings are cherished and respected will live more happily than those whose early passions are not acknowledged and soothed. Excessive distress and loving care have lasting negative and positive consequences on the emotional circuits and cognitive abilities of developing brains.

Modern neuroscience has illuminated how brain structures and neural-chemistries elaborate emotionality in animals, which has direct implications for infant and childhood mental health. As we better understand the nature of social emotional urges within children's brains, we will be able to open more doors to children thriving. The pre-school years are especially critical for the future success of every child. Margot Sutherland has brilliantly updated the abundant scientific evidence of our ever-increasing knowledge of developing brains and minds. She shares a scientifically informed secure base for child-rearing practices that can help make this a better world.

" Here we have a scientifically secure base for child-rearing practices in the 21st century. "

Jaak Panksepp, PhD
Professor and Baily Endowed Chair of Animal Well-Being Sciences,
Department of Integrative Physiology and Neuroscience, Washington State University
Distinguished Research Professor Emeritus,
Department of Psychology, Bowling Green State University
Head of Affective Neuroscience Research,
The Falk Centre for Molecular Therapeutics, Northwestern University

Introduction

I have written this second edition of *What Every Parent Needs to Know* from the standpoint of a professional who for 17 years has been studying the long-term impact of parenting decisions on the child's developing brain. I am all too aware of how much harm has been done to countless children over the generations as a result of opinion-based parenting (or "nanny knows best"). With this edition of the book I am also writing from the perspective of a working parent who is extremely familiar with the joys, the anxieties, the stress, and profound feelings of fulfilment of parenting children.

I am thrilled that now, because of the recent advances in our knowledge of the brain science of human relationships, we don't need to repeat the mistakes of the past. However, so much of this vital scientific knowledge has not been getting through to parents. Also, significant advances have been made in the ten years since the first edition of this book. In writing this new edition I want to bring the most up-to-date research to parents so they can make informed decisions – to give them evidence-based parenting skills. Parents have a right to know the impact of their parenting choices and ways of relating to each other and their children on a child's developing brain; it's as much a right as knowing about their nutritional needs. I have drawn on over 2,000 scientific studies from laboratories, medical departments, and universities all

*“*Now we have a greater understanding of how to help children thrive, things can change for the better, in the family and in society, too. *”*

over the world. But rest assured I am also committed to communicating in a jargon-free, accessible language.

Research shows that parent–child relationships change brains, not just minds. The evidence is overwhelming that our childhood experience with our parents also dramatically impacts our later physical and mental health, for better or worse. It can affect whether children are likely to go on to lead deeply rewarding lives, or whether they might have stress-related blood pressure problems, suffer from dementia, have a compromised immune system, or experience anxiety. In addition,

❝ To experience a warm world inside your head depends very much on special 'one-to-one' moments with your parents. ❞

"So many grown-ups can't manage stress well. Because no one helped them enough with stress and distress in childhood, they never set up effective stress-regulating systems in their brains."

since the publication of the first edition there have been new findings: we now know that parenting can even turn on or off key genes, protect against cancer, help a person enjoy longevity, and a lot more. So with the evidence-based parenting practices described in this book, you can give your child the very best gift of quality of life, stacking the cards the right way for better long-term mental and physical health. Without it, it's too easy to choose some commonly accepted child-rearing practices, which can damage a child's brain and body. This book is here to help ensure you don't do that!

The latest brain science brings with it the need for a real paradigm shift by parents. Rather than simply thinking about the immediacy of whether to sleep train or not, use controlled crying or not, co-sleep or not, ignore tantrums, use the naughty step, or let toddlers play on tablets, we need to ask ourselves the following questions: "How are my parenting choices now likely to affect the long-term chemical balance and higher human functions in my child's brain? How are the ways I relate to my child on a daily basis going to affect her physiology, her ability to make good decisions under stress, the likelihood of her suffering from anxiety or depression later, or capacity to go on to thrive in the world of work and personal relationships?". Neuroscience does not provide the solution to the jigsaw in our understanding of what children need to be able to thrive, but it is a vital jigsaw piece.

Some people say, "Look, we don't need to be told how to parent. All you need to do is love them! Children grow up just fine without parenting experts!". If good parenting comes naturally, how come we have this statistic: in 2014, there were over 57 million medicinal items dispensed in the UK for depressive illness and anxiety disorders. There are only 53 million people in the country![1] This speaks so loudly about the fact that parenting practices in the past have not supported the best quality of life for our children. We now know the parenting practices that change children's brains in such a way as to protect against depression and other mental health problems in later life. And the good news is that it's never too late to change how you parent to bring about these wonderful results for your child.

So why does parenting have such an impact on a child's brain and body? The answer is that when a child is born, her brain is still forming – it's not finished. Some of the brain cells are still in the process of moving to the right place (a process called migration). In the first year of life, genes key for emotional well-being are still being expressed. In addition, vital regulatory systems are being set up in the infant's brain and body. All these acutely

" Some children grow up with hearts big enough to feel the suffering of humankind; not just people in their close circle but those with different views, cultures, and beliefs to their own. **"**

❝ Parenting power means that your child will not lose her awe and wonder about the world as she moves into adulthood. **❞**

sensitive processes are very vulnerable to adverse change from stress in the infant's life. So your relationship with your child in these early years is a massively impactful experience. Furthermore, your child's brain is like an unwired computer. Whether it will be wired up for "calm" or "alarm" will depend again so much on your relationship with your child.

You might think that surely it's genes that count, not just parenting style. In terms of mental and physical health, yes it is. We have vulnerability genes and protective

genes. But the picture is no longer as simple as nurture versus nature. In recent years, scientists working in the field of epigenetics have found that genes can be turned on or off by external and environmental factors – and this includes parenting style. The right sort of parenting will turn off vulnerability genes and turn on protective ones and the wrong sort of parenting will do the reverse.

In short, we have now entered a brand new era of parenting, where for the first time we have the scientific evidence, not just opinions, that explains how to enable a child to thrive. In this second edition of my book I will show you this evidence. I have revisited the contents of each chapter and included the latest research in every section. I have reorganized the chapters, too. There is one that focuses on how to help your child to develop a capacity for fun, humour, and spontaneity, and another that looks specifically at how parenting can ensure your child fulfils her potential. Special relationship times are vitally important for you both so I have added a new chapter full of practical play ideas backed up by brain science that help you have the best relationship. There are still chapters that look at sleep, behaviour, and crying, and, as well looking after you. Overall this book provides you with key evidence-based skills to support you in the enormously important task of being a parent.

> **"** Experience can change the mature brain... but experience during critical periods of childhood organizes actual brain systems. **"**
> Bruce Parry

your child's brain
in your hands

Parents are not magicians. They can't guarantee their children happiness in later life, or protect them from loss and rejection. But they can dramatically influence systems in their children's brains that are key to the potential for a deeply fulfilling life, as we shall see throughout this book. Before we start it is important to understand a few facts about the human brain.

The evolution of the brain

About 300 million years ago, reptiles had evolved on Earth. Mammals and finally humans followed much later. Amazingly, the structure of our human brain still bears witness to this history. Around six to seven million years ago, the earliest of our human relatives (hominids) had a brain about half the size of our own.

BRAIN STORY

Our lower brains are very like those of other mammals, but our higher brains, or frontal lobes, are much larger, so we can think more deeply than any other animal.

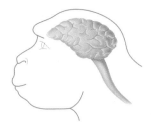

A chimpanzee has small frontal lobes (shown in blue), so it thinks mainly in the present.

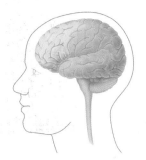

Our large frontal lobes (blue area) allow us to imagine, reason, and solve problems.

How our brains grew

The brain remained small in the first upright man, *Homo erectus* (about 1.5 million years ago). By around 200,000 years ago the brain of our direct ancestor, *Homo sapiens*, had grown massively, matching our own modern brain in size and showing a connectedness that suggests an advanced ability to generate new ideas. Some 50,000 years ago, humans were painting, making ornaments and jewellery, and adopting religion, but it still took a long time for humans to develop the capacity for sophisticated thinking that we enjoy today.

So what are our brains like today?

Our brains are made up of many interconnecting structures, which include our early reptilian brain, a lower, or mammalian, brain, and – the crowning glory of evolution – a higher human brain. Each region of the brain is connected to the others by a network of nerves, yet has its own functions.

Sometimes the brain regions work together in a beautifully coordinated way and, with the activation of some pro-social brain chemicals, this brings out the best in humans. At other times, the brain's alarm systems are in the driving seat, even when there is no physical or psychological threat. This can make people act in ways that cause all manner of misery to themselves and also to others. The incredible thing is that, as a parent, you can influence both the development and the activation of key functions and systems in your child's brain and the way that these systems interact.

Basic instincts

Humans might feel superior to other animals because they have the most developed higher thinking brain. But we are not superior in terms of the old reptilian and mammalian regions of our brain. In fact, these parts of our brains are very similar in overall organization (relative to size) to those of other mammals. These more ancient brain regions have mostly stayed the same over millions of years. As one scientist said, "It's like carrying around an ancient museum inside our heads."[1] What's more, our higher, rational, brain can easily be hijacked by these lower regions. When we feel unsafe, physically or psychologically, impulses from the reptilian and mammalian parts of our brain can hijack our higher human functions, and we can behave like a threatened animal. We can experience impulsive "fight-or-flight" reactions that make us lash out with rage or move into anxious behaviour.

As a parent, you can have an impact on your child's brain so that his higher brain will be able, for most of the time, to manage the primitive lower brain reactions. Parenting will influence your child's higher brain (in particular the frontal lobes), lower brain (mammalian/limbic system), and the brain stem, which includes the mid-brain.

> **"**The world is very old and human beings are very young.**"**[2]

The reptilian brain evolved around 300 million years ago. It is instinctive, controlling body functions such as breathing and digestion, and has functions based on survival.

The mammalian brain evolved 200 million years ago, and with it came new brain programmes for social behaviour – such as care and nurturance, playfulness, and bonding.

Humans have been around for 200,000 years and have developed highly sophisticated powers of reasoning, but we still have reptilian and mammalian areas in our brains.

About the brain

The brain is made up of key areas: the largest is the cerebrum, consisting of four regions, or lobes. The cerebrum is also in two halves, or hemispheres, often referred to as the right and left brain. One of the regions, the frontal lobes, is also known as the higher brain. This area is affected by parenting as are the corpus callosum, which links the right and left brains; the mammalian, or lower, brain; the brain stem; and the cerebellum, an area behind the brain stem.

How you raise and respond to a child has a powerful influence on how the different parts of the brain are activated. At birth, higher human functions are not "on-line" and the connections between the different parts of the brain are not fully formed. Nurturing parenting instead of stress-inducing parenting can help optimal development of these functions and connections.

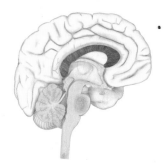

CORPUS CALLOSUM

This structure (shown in green) is a complex band of fibres that joins the left and right hemispheres of the brain, acting as the main information pathway between them. The right and left sides process the world in very different ways. The language centres are largely on the left, so the left brain processes verbal communication and attends to detail. The right processes the world more in terms of overviews, emotional atmospheres, and through images and metaphors. Unlike the left brain, it has strong links to the lower, or mammalian, brain and the body, so has a far more embodied take on the world.

THE FRONTAL LOBES

The largest of the four major lobes of the higher brain, these are located at the front of the brain. Frontal lobe functions include the ability to learn, attend, and concentrate; plan and problem solve; manage stress; and control impulse. There are several regions each with a different function: the dorsolateral prefrontal cortex, the ventromedial prefrontal cortex, and the orbitofrontal cortex (see also page 22).

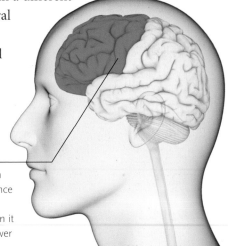

This part of the higher brain is involved in emotional and social intelligence and can lead to the greatest achievements in humans when it works in harmony with the lower (mammalian) brain.

THE LOWER BRAIN

Also known as the mammalian brain, limbic system, or even the emotional brain, this region has the same chemical systems and structures as in other mammals, such as chimpanzees. The area contains seven huge hormonal forces – the genetically ingrained emotional systems (see page 29). There are three alarm systems – RAGE, FEAR, and PANIC/ GRIEF – and three calm and well-being, or pro-social, systems – CARE, SEEKING, and PLAY – and, finally, LUST.[3] These systems are like muscles. The more we activate one of them, the more it becomes part of the personality. The way you parent dictates which of these systems is in the driving seat in your child's life. There are key structures within the lower brain that are connected to particular emotions.

BRAIN STEM AND THE MID-BRAIN
This part of the brain (coloured blue) is essential for regulation of key body functions – heart rate, breathing, eating, arousal and consciousness, and the sleep cycle. It also includes both reward centres and alarm systems. Alarm systems include the locus coeruleus, which releases noradrenaline when we are stressed, often interfering with clear thinking, and the periaqueductal grey, or PAG, which triggers very defensive behaviour such as fight-flight-freeze. It also plays a key role in all the seven genetically ingrained systems (see left). Sleep apnoeas in sudden infant death syndrome are caused by failure in arousal in this part of the brain.

The anterior cingulate is a key region of the CARE system. It triggers well-being chemicals when we feel loved or loving, but withdraws them when the PANIC/ GRIEF system is triggered.

The caudate nucleus plays an important role in higher human functioning, goal direction, action and approach, and attachment behaviour.

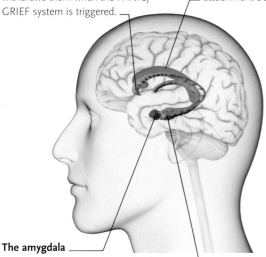

The amygdala is an important structure involved in the RAGE and FEAR systems. It works out the emotional meaning of everything that happens to a person. It can trigger the release of high levels of stress hormones.

The hippocampus is a key memory system in the brain. This and the prefrontal cortex hold autobiographical memory.

CEREBELLUM
Situated behind the brain stem, scientists used to think that the cerebellum (coloured pink) only helped with motor coordination, control, and postural balance. It is now known that this part of the brain is also associated with emotional intelligence.[4] Pathways between this region and the higher brain are key for social intelligence, skill learning, and emotional regulation.

Parenting the brain

For centuries we have been using child-rearing techniques without any awareness of the possible long-term effects on a child's developing brain. This is because, until now, we couldn't see the effect of our actions on what was going on inside a child's brain. However, we now know that the way parents interact with their child can have long-term effects on his brain functions and on the chemical balance in his brain.

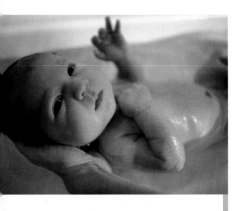

CONSIDER THIS...

Loss of brain cells (neurons) is part of the brain's natural "sculpting process", which continues throughout life. In the strengthening of key connections in the brain, unnecessary or under-used pathways are pruned away. At birth we have around 200 billion brain cells, but by the age of one we have already lost some 80 billion of them. By the teenage years we have lost about 90 billion brain cells; by the age of 35, about 100 billion brain cells, and by the age of 70, about 105 billion. This is all because of what is known as "synaptic pruning". It's just the same as pruning back a rose bush to make it grow well.

With the advances of neuroscience, brain scans, and years of research on the brains of primates and other mammals (whose emotional brains have virtually the same architecture and chemical systems as ours), we now have vital information about the impact of different ways of parenting on a child's brain. Your approach can determine whether or not your child's brain systems and brain chemistries are activated in such a way as to enable him to enjoy a rich and rewarding life.

Parenting style has so much influence over how your baby's emotional brain develops

You as parents have great influence over how the emotional brain develops, in particular because there are critical periods of brain growth in the first years of life. The infant brain starts to form new brain pathways at a very rapid rate during this time. In fact, 90 percent of the growth of the human brain occurs in the first five years of life. Over these crucial years, millions of brain connections are being formed, unformed, and then re-formed, directly under the influence of your child's life experiences and in particular his emotional experiences with you.

By the age of seven, this massive sculpting activity slows down because more and more brain cells are being myelinated. (Myelin is a whitish material made up of protein and fats that surrounds the brain cells in sheaths, like a form of insulation.) Myelination enables better communication between brain cells and strengthens brain pathways, fixing them in place. Hence there is some scientific truth underpinning the often quoted Jesuit assertion, "Give me a child until the age of seven, and I will give you the man."

The parent–child connection

Everything your baby experiences with you will forge new brain pathways in his higher brain (frontal lobes). The human brain is specifically designed this way so that it can be wired up to adapt to the particular environment in which it finds itself. This adaptability works for or against the well-being of a child. If, for example, a child has a bullying parent, his brain can start to adapt to living in a bullying world, with all manner of changes in brain structure and brain chemical systems, which may result in hypervigilance, heightened aggression, or fear reactions, or heightened attack/defence impulses in the reptilian part of his brain. With emotionally responsive parenting, however, vital connections will form in his brain that enable him to cope well with stress in later life; form fulfilling relationships; manage anger well; be kind and compassionate; have the will and motivation to follow his dreams; experience the deepest calm; and be able to love in peace. So the way you listen to your child, play with him, cuddle him, comfort him, and treat him when he is being naughty are of real significance.

Setting up higher human functions

Much of the infant brain is developed after birth not before, so it is open to being sculpted by both negative and positive parent-child interactions. At birth, your child's higher brain (see page 18) is very unfinished, so much so that a newborn baby is often referred to as an "external fetus" (see page 36). Babies are born with in the region of 200 billion brain cells, but they have very few connections between these cells in their higher brain – so it's not "on-line". Some of these

BRAIN STORY

Brain wiring from birth These diagrams show how a baby's higher brain forms connections at a very rapid rate as it is sculpted by experiences in the first years of life. At the beginning, brain cells are unconnected, like dangling wires in a computer.

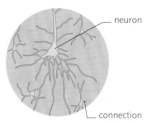

neuron

connection

A newborn baby has around 200 billion brain cells, but few connections.

In a child of about one year, cells in the higher brain have developed many more connections.

In a child of about two years, the brain wiring has become more complex and synaptic pruning has begun.

BRAIN STORY

Different parts of the frontal lobes (shown as coloured areas on the diagram below) can develop wonderfully in your child's brain with emotionally responsible parenting, but may remain underdeveloped with other sorts of parenting.

• Orbitofrontal region (pink): plays a key role in the effective management of strong feelings and the inhibiting of primitive impulses from the lower brain. It also helps a child to respond sensitively to other people, and to read their emotional and social cues.

• Dorsolateral prefrontal region (yellow): involved with our ability to think, plan, and reflect and make choices.

• Ventromedial region (blue): involves a child's ability to think about emotional experiences and calms the mammalian/reptilian parts of the brain when they go into a state of alarm.

• Anterior cingulate region (green): helps us to focus attention and tune into our own thoughts (self-awareness).

The two brain hemispheres are split apart here to reveal the structures of the mammalian brain deep inside.

connections will be largely responsible for the emotional and social intelligence of your child, and it is over these connections that you have so much influence.

Good parenting has a dramatic effect on a child's higher brain. The frontal lobes are often referred to as the social organs because their optimal development is so dependent on having really good relationship experiences. When these happen, vital frontal lobe functions come on-line and your child's emotional and social intelligence develops, and with it his ability to learn, concentrate, reflect, plan, and control his impulses to lash out or run away, and to empathize, stay stable under stress, and problem solve.

The brain's alarm systems are on-line at birth

Because your child's higher rational brain is so unfinished at birth, initially his lower brain, which is already on-line, will be in the driving seat. When babies and toddlers have primitive explosive outbursts it is because the alarm systems in their lower brains have been triggered. Your child's brain is awash with stress hormones, which tells him that there is a terrible threat – hence the explosive outburst. A baby simply can't calm himself down because his frontal lobes are not on-line yet.

There are many alarm systems in the lower and reptilian parts of the brain: in particular the amygdala in the limbic system, the periaqueductal grey (PAG) in the midbrain, and the locus coeruleus in the brain stem (see page 19). One of the main functions of the amygdala is to work out the emotional meaning of everything that happens to you. If it senses that something threatening is happening, it communicates with another structure in the brain called the hypothalamus (see page 41), which actions the release of stress hormones, to prepare the body for fight or flight. To a young child, a "terrible threat" might be that he's lost his dummy, you have put the baked beans too close to the ham on his plate, or you are putting him into his car seat! These massive

"I love my Mummy"

There is an amazing flow of emotional energy and information from your brain to your child's brain and from your body to your child's body. This is also true with other adults who play an important role in your child's life. Your emotional state, and what's going on in your frontal lobes, will have a direct and powerful impact on key emotional systems in your child's brain and key arousal systems in your child's body.

BRAIN STORY

When we experience feelings of fear, rage, or sadness, brain scans show large areas of activation (red) in the lower and mid parts of the brain and deactivation (purple), largely in higher brain areas.

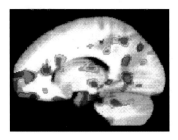

Fear produces activation in ancient structures in the lower and mid-brain.

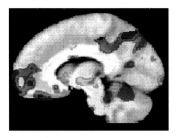

Anger produces activation deep in the brain stem.

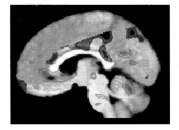

Sadness activates part of the lower brain's CARE (attachment) system (see page 91).

"over-reactions" occur because he can't calm the amygdala through thinking, coupled with the fact that he does not have a working backdrop of years of life experiences to know that he is sweating the small stuff. Such outbursts are never naughty, but normal in terms of his stage of brain development. Hence he should never be punished when he's like this; instead, soothe and empathize with him.

You are your child's emotion regulator

When the alarm systems have triggered in your child's brain, you are his absolute lifeline to helping him regulate his states of high emotional arousal and bodily arousal (the autonomic nervous system, see pages 44–45). He simply cannot manage these states on his own. If his crying is not responded to he will eventually stop crying, but this is a desperate closing down, known as dissociation (the "freeze" part of fight–flight–freeze). It should never be confused with feeling calm. Times of quiet and silence like this often generate far higher levels of stress hormones than when the baby is crying. Not knowing this leaves too many parents still using "cry-it-out sleep training" and other such stress-inducing interventions (see Crying and separations, pages 34–63).

Emotionally responsive parenting will enable your baby to establish effective stress-regulatory systems in his brain. By soothing your baby's distress, particular brain pathways form that naturally quieten stress. If you do this day after day you are literally helping to establish the stress-regulating systems essential for his IQ (intelligence quotient) and EQ (emotional intelligence) and his ability to thrive in the future at work and in personal relationships.[5] There is a mass of research that shows that lack of effective stress regulatory systems is at the core of mental illness and much of the violence in our society today. Drug addiction, alcohol abuse, sex addiction, self-harm, eating disorders, and smoking are desperate attempts to change very painful chemical states in the brain. Brain scans reveal that violent adults are still driven, like infants

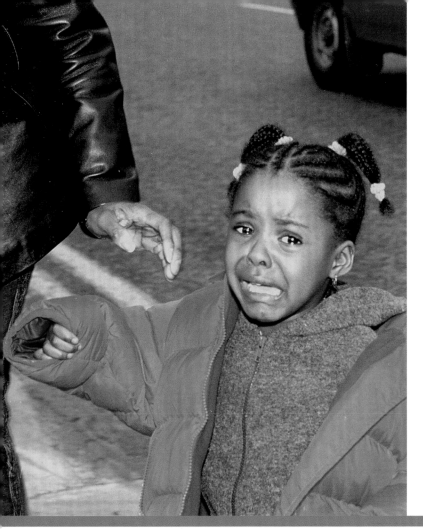

"I need to be calmed"

A distressed, upset child needs your compassion, soothing, and physical comfort to bring her dysregulated (see page 267) body and brain systems back into balance.

and toddlers, by the rage/fear, defence/attack responses deep in the lower (mammalian) brain.[6]

As a parent, you can prevent your child from having to live like this

You cannot save your child from life's inevitable sufferings, but you can have a dramatic impact on his quality of life by parenting in such a way that effective stress-regulating systems and anti-anxiety chemical systems are firmly established in his brain. Consistent emotion regulation is challenging, but brings enormous rewards. If you have two or more under–fives, you may find meeting your children's every need can feel relentless at times; a young child has an emotional regulatory need every 20 seconds.[7] These demands do ease significantly from the

"Because your child's higher brain is so unfinished, his lower brain will be in the driving seat."

❝ The developing brain, in the crucial first years of life, is highly vulnerable to stress. ❞

age of four, but in the meantime you will definitely need breaks and to bring in other willing adults as emotional regulators. That said, put the work in during these early years and you give your child one of the best gifts possible – the ability to handle stress well. It's at the very core of resilience and being able to thrive in relationships.

Your child's body is in your hands, too

There are stress regulatory systems in the body, too – the autonomic nervous system (ANS) is also known as the bodily arousal system. Again, emotionally regulating parenting helps develop a well-balanced autonomic nervous system, in turn influencing vulnerability to or protection from health

❝ Be excited with me ❞

In helping your child to establish effective stress-regulating systems in her brain, she needs to be deeply met in joy as well as in emotional pain. This is because joy is a stressful high-arousal state, too. So meet her exuberance with your own. When children are not helped with the "stress" of joy, they can be frightened of the bodily arousal of excitement in later life.[8]

problems across the lifespan, and also longevity. Research shows that when comforting your child's stress and distress, you are also regulating his autonomic nervous system and so positively affecting his digestive and elimination systems, his temperature control, his breathing and heart rate, as well as strengthening his immune system.[9]

When a parent, often quite unwittingly, moves into stress-inducing rather than stress-relieving parenting, the child's autonomic nervous system is thrown out of balance, which can result in a heart rate of up to 140 beats a minute in dysregulated children (the same as children who have been abused or neglected, see page 267). These children can then develop weight control issues; gastrointestinal disorders; breathing problems such as asthma; migraine; skin problems, such as eczema; or immune system deficiencies – now and/or in later life.[10]

But many of us never got this gift of emotional regulation in our childhood

We have only known fairly recently just how important empathic response is for children in setting up effective stress regulatory brain systems and lots of us didn't get that sort of response ourselves as children. Many of us got an irritated or "get over it" response, or were ignored. Many of us were disciplined with anger, not with empathy, which, as we will see, strengthens the primitive "fight-flight" parts of our brain.

So as an adult what can I do?

If you suffer from stress, anxiety problems, or depression, it's never too late to establish effective stress-regulatory systems in the brain. The best thing is to go and get the stress regulation you never had as a child in your adult life through psychotherapy or counselling. With repeated attuned emotional responsiveness from a therapist it is possible to establish these vital systems in your frontal lobes.

ANIMAL INSIGHTS

All mammals have alarm systems, designed to protect them from danger. Even today, the lower human brain shares very similar anatomy and chemistry to that of other mammals. In ancient times, these alarm systems were very useful and protected humans from predators. Today, these systems register alarm when we feel psychological stress. We can feel irrationally frightened or anxious when, in fact, there is no real danger (physical or psychological).

"You can have a dramatic impact on your child's quality of life.**"**

"I'm learning so fast"

There is a major growth spurt in the frontal lobes of a child's brain in the first two years of life. This period is a great window of opportunity for establishing brain pathways that underpin learning and language development, and also for establishing anti-anxiety chemical systems in the brain.

"There are genetically ingrained systems in the lower brain for the most wonderful feelings of well-being, but whether these potentials get expressed depends largely on the parenting you get."

Parenting can directly affect your child's brain chemical systems

We can be both splendid and terrible – the brain carries the potential for both. Deep in the lower, or mammalian, brain, is the limbic system where human passion resides – both passionate love and passionate hate. There are systems here that trigger intense feelings of fear, hate, or rage, while others trigger the loveliest warm, compassionate, and generous feelings. This part of the brain fuels the most amazing acts of courage and kindness and the most terrible acts of cruelty. For over 35 years, leading neuroscientist Professor Jaak Panksepp has studied the alarm systems and well-being systems in the limbic system. His findings are now accepted and deeply revered. He found seven genetically ingrained emotional systems in the limbic system. Each has a particular brain chemical profile. There are three alarm systems that trigger high levels of stress hormones: RAGE, FEAR, and PANIC/GRIEF. There are three calm and well-being systems, CARE (attachment), SEEKING, and PLAY systems known as pro-social systems, that trigger well-being chemicals such as opioids. The seventh system is LUST, which is not part of our discussion in this book.

Just like a muscle, the more we activate one of these systems, the more developed as part of our personality it will become. So of course we want parenting that activates the calm/well-being systems and not the alarm systems. Throughout the book I will come back again and again to these systems to empower you as a parent to modify the RAGE, FEAR, and PANIC/GRIEF systems in your child's brain and strengthen his pro-social systems.

Some forms of parenting (such as being frequently shouted at or criticized; parents rowing, even mildly; verbal or physical aggression; traumatic separations from parents in the early years) repeatedly activate the child's RAGE, FEAR, and PANIC/GRIEF systems. These systems trigger stress hormones, which ultimately can make us act like frightened or angry animals or become withdrawn or depressed. In contrast, some forms of parenting repeatedly activate the child's CARE (attachment), SEEKING, and PLAY systems, which trigger pro-social chemicals. The good news is that it's never too late to change a family culture so that the pro-social systems come to the fore. If not activated, these lovely systems stay dormant, waiting for someone to wake them up.

More about the calm/well-being systems

These are genetically ingrained systems for the most wonderful human capacities: tenderness, creativity, play, gentleness, kindness, and concern for others. Whether these potentials are expressed depends so much on how you are parented. Some of the key chemicals triggered by these

CONSIDER THIS...

If you don't consistently comfort and calm a child who is experiencing a stressful amygdala trigger, it can lead to adverse changes in his brain. These include triggering of too high levels of stress hormones. Over time this can bring about cell death in the parts of the brain associated with memory and emotional and social intelligence.

When any of the alarm systems – RAGE, FEAR, or PANIC/GRIEF are triggered in a child's lower brain, he will be in a state of emotional pain and intense bodily arousal unless an adult helps him to calm down. This is because once one of the alarm systems is triggered, neurochemical and hormonal forces will be activated, which can overwhelm the mind and body.

systems are opioids. If the way we parent repeatedly activates these lovely well-being chemicals in a child's brain, they will increasingly become part of his personality and the brain will habituate to optimal levels of these and other calming chemicals (opioids often work in combination with oxytocin and prolactin). Hence, neuroscientists refer to "emotional states becoming personality traits" or in shorthand: "states become traits".[11] The whole feel of the world changes when these chemical systems are in dominance in the brain. We do not want to fight and we don't feel anxious because these chemicals are anti-anxiety and anti-aggression molecules. Establishing optimal levels of these chemicals in your brain in childhood is a vital component of what we mean by resilience. It is no surprise therefore that neuroscientists refer to these chemicals as "nature's gift to us".[12]

What does parenting that triggers the child's PLAY, CARE, and SEEKING systems look like?

• **The PLAY system** Repeated playful interactions between parent and infant, particularly physical play and attachment play (see Chemistry of love & joy, pages 84–125 and The best relationship with your child, pages 242–59).

• **The CARE (attachment) system** Parenting with emotional responses that make a child feel safe (not on-off, shouty one minute, warm the next). A parent who can say sorry when he or she gets something wrong; who consistently soothes a child who is distressed; and helps regulate all the child's feelings including anger (See Chemistry of love & joy, pages 84–125). Parents who discipline in ways that don't shame or frighten, and give consequences where appropriate in ways that maintain dignity (see All about discipline, pages 220–41).

• **The SEEKING system** Parenting that models an energized engagement in life – a "let's do" attitude. These parents model exploration, curiosity, and creativity by accompanied play, and know how to prevent stress hormones blocking their child's system (see Chemistry of drive & will, pages 126–43).

More about the alarm systems

Stress-inducing parenting will keep activating the RAGE, FEAR, and PANIC/GRIEF systems in the child's brain until emotional states that induce anxiety, aggression, or depression become personality traits. Key chemicals triggered through these systems include cortisol and corticotrophin releasing factor (CRF). If these are injected at high levels into animal brains, the animals become depressed, anxious, and aggressive. The myth that the infant brain is resilient to stress has resulted in millions of children not reaching their potential.[13]

What does parenting that triggers a child's RAGE, FEAR and PANIC/GRIEF systems look like?

It's any parenting that triggers prolonged stress states in the child. For the sensitive parent, it's easy to hear when this has happened; the pitch of the child's scream or his crying shifts to a higher intensity, a more dreadful note of pain. This can happen for example from certain forms of sleep training, controlled crying, or verbal aggression between parents. Research shows that even mild tension between parents or lack of communication between family members can result in a smaller cerebellum due to cell death caused by emotional stress.[14] Regular shouting can damage the auditory processing parts of the child's brain.[15] It can also follow if a mother is not emotionally available enough to a child (because she is depressed) and doesn't get help from people who can emotionally regulate the child until she is able to do so again.

But isn't all of this relevant only for children who have suffered abuse or neglect?

No, the studies that underpin this book are not about abuse or neglect, they are about common child-rearing practices and the effects of common stressful parent–child interactions. We all need cortisol – we would be dead without it! When cortisol is within normal levels, it helps us cope with normal everyday stress. But cortisol at too high levels, for too long

CONSIDER THIS...

Research shows that if your child has an over-reactive stress response system, he or she will be vulnerable to suffering from depression in later life, as a reaction to life's hard knocks. In 2014, there were 57 million prescriptions given out for medicines to treat depressive illness in the UK alone. The country only has a population of 53 million.

Seeking counselling or therapy in later life can be a real second chance to develop effective stress-regulating systems in the brain, but it can take a long time. It's so much better to avoid problems with good parenting in childhood.

becomes toxic in the child's developing brain and can adversely affect brain cells, brain pathways, and organs. Parenting that triggers a child's RAGE, FEAR, and PANIC/GRIEF systems results in prolonged activation of these stress hormones. Stressful experiences in the early years alter the developing brain.[16] A child's brain is acutely sensitive and if you put it through excessive or prolonged stress states it can malfunction on a long-term basis.

Good stress and bad stress

• **Good stress** (or stress inoculation) This occurs when optimal levels of adrenaline, noradrenaline, and other stress hormones are triggered. It happens for example when you take your baby swimming for the first time; it's a challenge for him, so he clings on to you at first then loves it. In this instance, the stress hormones trigger in combination with other positive arousal chemicals such as serotonin and dopamine.

• **Bad stress** This is when the stress hormones cortisol and CRF trigger at too high levels and stay around in the brain and body for too long. Such stress can cause cell death in the child's brain in key areas associated with learning and emotional and social intelligence.[17] It can also lead to depression, anxiety, and stress-related illness in later life. It can even turn off key genes for emotional and physical health; prevent the release of calming chemical systems in the brain, the formation of new neuronal connections, and the birth of new brain cells; cause accelerated ageing; disrupt the immune system; and result in a higher incidence of cancer.

But let's not finish on a gloomy point

The good news is that your parenting can strengthen the pro-social systems in your child's brain and it's never too late to start! This book focuses on ways of parenting that do not trigger the child's alarm systems. If you relate to your child in ways that keep triggering the care/well-being systems, your child is likely to grow up warm, empathic, and with a love of learning.

Key points

• Human brains contain primitive emotional alarm systems deep in the lower regions. Without emotionally responsive parenting, our higher brains can easily be hijacked by these systems.

• As a result of certain forms of child-rearing, some adults remain stuck with the emotional development of a child.

• Every positive experience with a parent forges important new pathways in a child's higher brain.

• It is essential to help a child with his "big" feelings, to avoid future problems with stress and over-reaction.

• Your child needs to feel you are an emotionally strong parent who can teach him how to be calm.

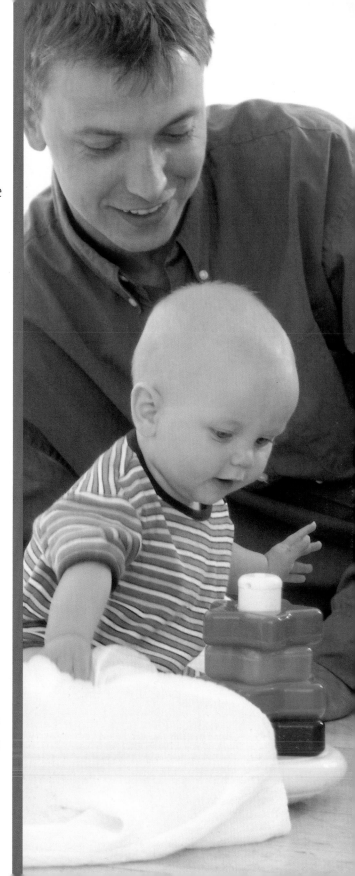

crying &
separations

Over the years, there have been many advocates of leaving babies and toddlers to cry. Mothers were told their babies were just "exercising their lungs" or that continually picking up a crying baby would "spoil her". More recently, spells of crying have been used to train babies to go to sleep and establish clear bedtime routines. There is no denying that these techniques work!

An uncomforted child will stop crying eventually if there is no response. But there are real costs. In this chapter we'll explore the research that reveals how stress from prolonged crying and separations can affect a baby's developing brain. We will also look at the wonderful long-term investment you make when you comfort your crying baby consistently.

All about crying

Babies are genetically programmed to call out for comfort when distressed.
Crying is your baby's intense bid for you to help her with her overwhelming
feelings and frightening bodily sensations because her brain is not yet developed
enough for her to manage these on her own. Babies do not cry to exercise their
lungs, to control you, or just for the hell of it. They cry when they are unhappy
and need to alert you because something is really bothering them, either physically
or emotionally. They are crying for your help.

ANIMAL INSIGHTS

All infant mammals, not just the
human species, are genetically
programmed to cry as a way of
communicating their need for help
with their painful separation distress.
Research has shown that if a puppy
is taken away from her mother, she
can cry 700 times in 15 minutes.[1]

Why babies cry

Four million years ago, humans walked on two legs for the
first time. Because this led to the freeing up of their arms to
accomplish complex tasks, over time intelligence increased.
The bipedal shift meant the human pelvis became narrower
and, as intellectual capacities increased, the brain grew bigger.
The evolutionary solution regarding childbirth was for the
human infant to be born very immature because otherwise
the enlarged head would never get through the mother's
narrowed pelvis. So of all mammals the human is the most
immature at birth. In fact, it has to complete its gestation
outside the womb. Sigmund Freud was right when he said
the human infant comes into the world "not quite finished".
You need to think of your newborn as an "external fetus".

Yes, she is that raw. Yes, she is that sensitive.
Yes, she is that vulnerable to stress

Your baby will cry for many reasons. She will cry because
she is tired or hungry or over-stimulated by too much adult
fussing. She also moves easily into fear of threat and shock –
the shock of the too bright, too harsh, too cold, too hot, too
sudden. The amygdala in the lower brain (see page 19), which
functions as a detector of potential threat, is perfectly on-line
at birth. Imagine her world. How can she know that the noisy

liquidizer is not a predator that will come and attack her? How can she cope with the shock of being undressed and immersed in water when you lower her into a bath?

At first it can be hard to work out what her crying means

But over time you will be able to read her cries more and more accurately. You will learn, for example, to tell a hungry cry from a tired cry. That said, there will be times when you will not know what the crying is about. This doesn't matter. What matters is that you calm her down and that you have the mental and emotional space in your mind to really hear and take seriously her panic and her pain.

How long does all this crying continue?

The first three months are often the worst. Crying usually peaks when the baby is three to six weeks old and then abates at around 12 to 16 weeks. Sheila Kitzinger suggested that crying lessens at this time because, by then, babies are more mobile and can grasp and play with things, so they no longer cry from boredom or frustration.[2]

Older babies and toddlers will still cry when cold, hungry, tired, or ill, although the shock of the world has dramatically lessened. But they are awash with new feelings. They suffer from states of panicky separation distress and are increasingly clear about likes and dislikes, what frightens them or displeases them. In the pre-verbal child, crying often means "no". "No, I don't want you to put me down; it makes me panic." "No, I don't want to be put on a stranger's lap; I was so settled in your arms." "No, I hate the feel of that jumper."[3]

All this panic response means high levels of stress chemicals washing over a baby's brain

These chemicals are not dangerous in themselves, but as the following pages will show, it's a different story if they are left swirling round her brain for long periods in bouts

"Help me cope with the world"

If you consistently soothe your child's distress over the years, and take any anguished crying seriously, highly effective stress response systems can be established in her brain. These will enable her to cope well with stress in later life. [4]

of prolonged crying, and no one takes her panic seriously and comforts her. Distancing yourself from her distress, whatever some sleep training books may tell you, or even worse, an angry response to your baby's crying (although sometimes you may feel like it) is never appropriate.

Prolonged crying

Let's be clear at the outset – it is not crying itself that can affect a child's developing brain. It doesn't. It is prolonged, uncomforted distress that affects the brain. So, I'm not advocating rushing to your child as soon as her bottom lip starts to wobble or after a short burst of protest crying that lasts a few minutes (perhaps because she couldn't have her favourite toy).

Prolonged crying is the type of crying that any sensitive parent (or, for that matter, anyone sensitive to the despair of others) will be able to recognize as a desperate calling for help. It is the type of crying that goes on and on and on, and eventually stops when the child is either completely exhausted and falls asleep or, in a hopeless state, realizes that help is not going to come.

If a baby is left to cry like this too often, a stress response system in her brain may be affected for life

There is a wealth of scientific studies from all over the world showing how early stress can result in enduring negative changes in a baby's brain. As we will see on the following pages, a child who has experienced periods of prolonged crying can develop an over-sensitive stress-response system that may affect her throughout life. This can mean that all too often her perception of the world and what is happening to her will be coloured by a sense of threat and anxiety, even when everything is perfectly safe.[5]

CONSIDER THIS...

When a baby is left howling in her room:
- High levels of toxic stress hormones wash over her brain.
- There is a withdrawal of opioids (chemicals that promote feelings of well-being) in her brain.[6]
- The brain and body's stress response systems can become hardwired for over-sensitivity.
- Pain circuits in the brain are activated, just as they would be if she were hurt physically.[7]

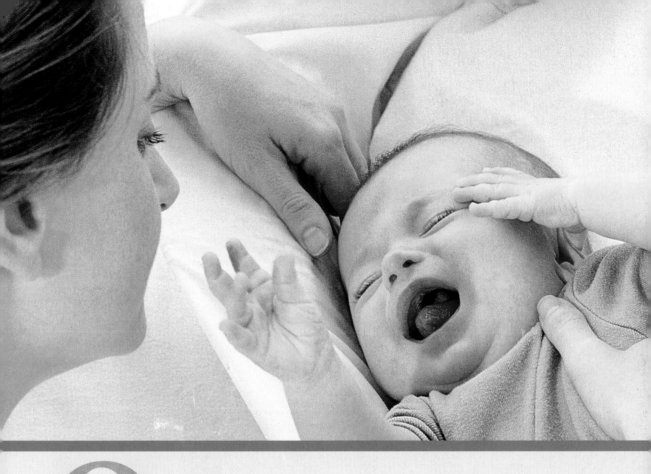

Can a baby manipulate or control a parent through crying?

- Parents may wonder if their baby is using crying to manipulate them, especially when they hear comments from well-meaning friends and family such as "Just leave her. She's just trying to control you. Give in now and you will suffer later." We now know this is neurobiologically inaccurate.

- To control an adult, a baby needs the power of clear thought, and for that she needs the brain chemical glutamate to be working well in her frontal lobes (see page 18). But the glutamate system is not properly established in a baby's brain, so that means she is not capable of thinking much about anything, let alone how to manipulate her parents.

- Some parents cut off from their child's pain, and hear it as "just crying". This can be a result of their own upbringing. Because no one responded when they were babies, they are now unable to feel their child's distress.

What's happening in your baby's brain?

Parents would never dream of leaving their baby in a room full of toxic fumes that could damage her brain. Yet many parents leave their baby in a state of prolonged, uncomforted distress, not knowing that she is at risk from toxic levels of stress chemicals washing over her brain.

Earlier generations of parents let their babies cry because it "exercised their lungs", having no idea how vulnerable the infant brain is to stress. In a crying baby, the stress hormone cortisol is released by the adrenal glands. If the child is soothed and comforted, the level of cortisol goes down again, but if the child is left to cry on and on, the level of cortisol remains high. This is a potentially dangerous situation, because, over a prolonged period, cortisol can reach toxic levels that may damage key structures and systems in a developing brain. Cortisol is a slow-acting chemical that can stay in the brain at high levels for hours, and in clinically depressed people, for days or even weeks.

This micrograph shows the structure of cortisol, a hormone produced in response to stress.

GETTING STRESSED

As distress levels build up in a crying baby, a hormonal chain reaction is set in motion. It starts deep within the lower brain, in a structure called the hypothalamus: the body's general hormone controller. The hypothalamus produces a hormone that triggers the nearby pituitary gland to release another hormone called ACTH (see opposite). This, in turn, stimulates the adrenal glands (just above the kidneys) to release the stress hormone cortisol. Cortisol then washes over the body and brain. This stress response system is known as the hypothalmic-pituitary-adrenal (HPA) axis.

A distressed baby has a highly activated HPA axis that pumps out cortisol. This can be compared to a central heating system that can't be switched off.[8] Comforting the baby triggers the off-switch. Brain scans show that early stress can cause the HPA axis to become permanently wired for over-sensitivity.

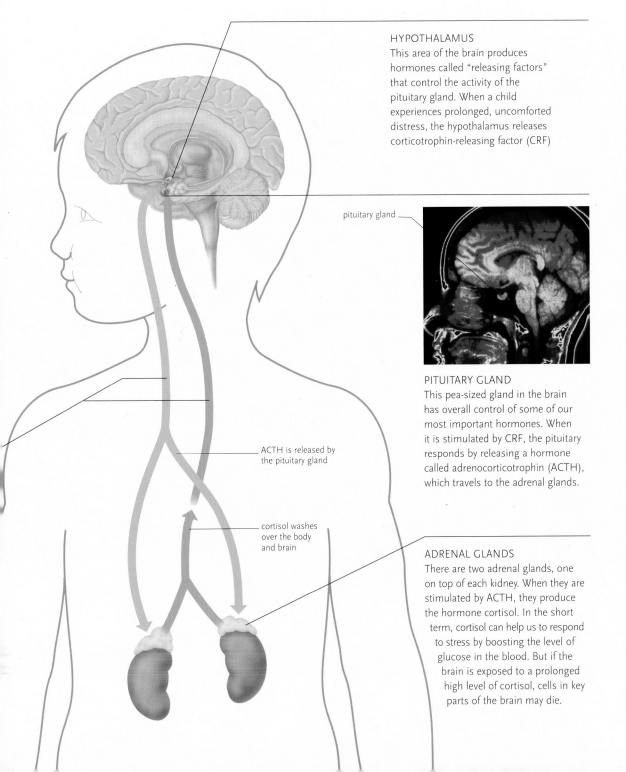

HYPOTHALAMUS
This area of the brain produces hormones called "releasing factors" that control the activity of the pituitary gland. When a child experiences prolonged, uncomforted distress, the hypothalamus releases corticotrophin-releasing factor (CRF)

pituitary gland

PITUITARY GLAND
This pea-sized gland in the brain has overall control of some of our most important hormones. When it is stimulated by CRF, the pituitary responds by releasing a hormone called adrenocorticotrophin (ACTH), which travels to the adrenal glands.

ACTH is released by the pituitary gland

cortisol washes over the body and brain

ADRENAL GLANDS
There are two adrenal glands, one on top of each kidney. When they are stimulated by ACTH, they produce the hormone cortisol. In the short term, cortisol can help us to respond to stress by boosting the level of glucose in the blood. But if the brain is exposed to a prolonged high level of cortisol, cells in key parts of the brain may die.

Storing up problems

Increasingly, scientists are linking stress in infancy and childhood to the soaring numbers of people suffering from anxiety and depressive disorders from adolescence onwards. Integral to these disorders is an over-sensitive stress system in the brain. We have seen from the research how early stress can cause long-lasting changes in the stress response system in a child's brain.

Wired for stress

What does an over-sensitive stress response system mean for a child as she grows up? It's a bit like having a faulty burglar alarm in her head, which keeps going off with the smallest thing. Her brain can react to small stressors, that other people take in their stride, as if they were big and threatening. Also, being wired for stress in early life can leave a child vulnerable to depression, anxiety disorders, stress-related physical illness, and alcohol abuse in later life.[9] This is particularly the case with children who were left to cry as babies and then experienced a childhood of strict discipline with little warm, physical affection to compensate.

Early stress can cause cell death in a very important structure in the brain

This structure is the hippocampus, which plays a role in long-term memory and it's found deep within the lower mammalian brain (see page 19). In the brain scans of children who have suffered intense uncomforted distress, the hippocampus appears somewhat shrunken because of cell death within its tissues. We don't know exactly how much this cell death affects a child's working memory. However, adults with a shrunken hippocampus score lower on memory and verbal reasoning tasks.[10] Brain scans have also shown that the hippocampus of a very stressed child resembles that

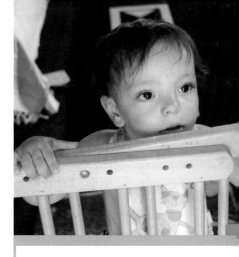

of an aged person. Some neuroscientists regard stress in early life as a risk factor for accelerated ageing of this part of the brain.

Are all children affected the same way?

Science does not have a precise answer to this. Because each child is unique, the effects of prolonged crying cannot be predicted with any certainty. Some children may get away with developing a mild neurosis in later life because early stress has altered key systems in their brain, while others with genetic vulnerability and additional life stresses, such as suffering loss or being bullied, may later develop a full-blown anxiety or depressive disorder.

Studies on other mammals with lower brain structures and chemical systems like ours show that early stress can leave an infant's brain in a highly disrupted biochemical state. Essential systems involving the emotion chemicals opioids, noradrenaline, dopamine, and serotonin, which are still being established in an immature brain, may be badly affected, resulting in chemical imbalances in the brain.[11]

When dopamine and noradrenaline levels are low, this can make it more difficult for a child to focus and concentrate; this can lead to learning difficulties in comparison with other children. Low serotonin levels are one of the key components in many forms of depression and also in violent behaviour. Opioids are vitally important for diminishing feelings of fear and stress, which is why deactivation of opioids in parts of the brain can lead to increases in negative feelings and stress, and decreases in positive feelings.[12]

CASE STUDY

Sleep training Billy

Bedtime had always been difficult for Billy and when he was ten months old, his mother was keen to try sleep training.

When she left him each night, Billy cried for her desperately, but she decided to tough it out for a week or two. Sure enough, over time, Billy stopped crying when he was put down and his mother counted this as a success. "He never cries now when I leave him," she said. Billy was also separated from his mother for much of the day, as she was at work. At his nursery, he had very little physical contact because the staff did not pick up the babies very often.

Billy has become less responsive during the day and other relatives now worry about his quietness. One family member has even commented that "It's as if he isn't really there any more." Some people think babies and children are not capable of depression, but they are.

The science of comforting

In the stress of intense crying, your baby's autonomic nervous system, which automatically regulates the internal workings of the body, is thrown off balance. The result is physical and emotional upheaval. A young child cannot control her bodily arousal – but your love and comfort will.

BRAIN STORY

There is a key anti-anxiety chemical in the brain called gamma-aminobutyric acid (GABA) that inhibits high levels of cortisol (see page 40) and calms the lower brain's threat-detection system (amygdala). Research shows that if young mammals are left alone or in a prolonged state of distress, this can have a marked influence on how the GABA genes unfold in the brain. This can alter the brain's sensitivity to stress, resulting in an agitated attitude to life. Long term, an altered GABA system can lead to anxiety disorders and depression. Without an effective anti-anxiety chemical system, humans may feel:
- psychologically fragile
- more prone to fear or anger than is appropriate to the situation
- less able to calm themselves
- easily thrown by minor stressors.
An altered GABA system, caused by too much uncomforted distress in childhood, may make adults prone to using alcohol for stress relief because this artificially regulates the brain's GABA system.[15]

What happens when your child cries

When your child cries in an intense, desperate way, her bodily arousal system, the autonomic nervous system (which is still maturing after birth), is way out of balance. While she is distressed, the aroused (or "sympathetic") branch of this system is overactive, and the calm and centred (or "parasympathetic") branch is underactive. This means that your baby's body is primed for action, "fight-or-flight", as high levels of adrenaline are released. She is experiencing an increased heart rate; higher blood pressure; sweating; tense muscles; faster breathing; and suppressed appetite (because the digestive system is conserving blood and energy to prepare the muscles for action).[13]

It is up to you to bring everything back into balance. Your comforting activates the vagus nerve (see opposite), which belongs to the "slow down and relax" parasympathetic branch of the autonomic nervous system. The more responsive you are, the greater your regulation of her body arousal systems will be, and the more long-lasting the effects.[14]

The dangers of hyperarousal

When you soothe your distressed child, you regulate her autonomic nervous system. Research shows that if a child's need for comfort is not met with emotional responsiveness and soothing, this system can, over time, become wired for bodily hyperarousal.[16] This can make life a stressful and exhausting affair. It can also result in all manner of physical ailments in later life: for example, problems with breathing (such as asthma), heart disease, eating and digestive disorders, poor sleep, high blood pressure, panic attacks, muscular tension, headaches, and chronic fatigue.[17] There is also a wealth of research material (known as brain–gut studies) linking uncomforted stress in early life with irritable bowel syndrome in later life. In one survey, fewer than 50 percent of the men and barely 30 percent of the women who took part in it had regular bowel habits.[18]

Many parents are simply not aware that a child's bodily arousal system is still developing after birth and that it is supersensitive to stressful experiences such as being left to cry. So leaving your baby "to settle herself" can have long-term adverse consequences for her body and brain. She cannot bring her autonomic nervous system back into balance; only you can do that.

> **"**Many parents are simply not aware that their child's bodily arousal system is still developing after birth...**"**

BRAIN STORY – THE VAGUS NERVE

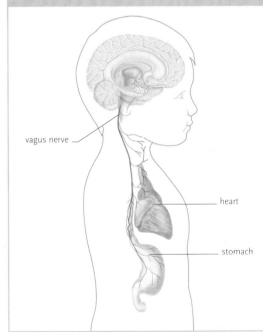

vagus nerve

heart

stomach

Comforting a screaming child activates her vagus nerve, which originates in the brain stem. This nerve, which is known appropriately as the "wanderer", regulates the function of major organs all over the body. As your soothing takes effect, the vagus nerve will rapidly restore order to key body systems disrupted by distress – rebalancing the digestive system, heart rate, breathing, and the functioning of the immune system.

One of the greatest gifts you can give your child is to help her establish good "vagal" tone. This means that the vagus nerve works well in all its calming, regulating functions. Research shows that good vagal tone is linked to better emotional balance; clear thinking; improved powers of attention; and a more efficient immune system. People with good vagal tone tend to be nice to have around.

How to soothe your baby

In order to activate the calm and centred branch in your child's autonomic nervous system, you need to quieten yourself down first. Breathing techniques are great. As soon as you do some effective deep breathing, your whole system will calm, and your body will start to send messages to your brain, telling it to stop pumping out high levels of stress chemicals. If you find this difficult, it's worth going to a meditation class that teaches breathing techniques.

Don't try to calm your baby at the same time as doing something else. For emotional and bodily regulation to take place, she needs to feel that her distress is the only thing on your mind.

If your crying baby is not in need of physical attention such as a feed or nappy change, then being next to your calm body will soothe her. Sometimes this works immediately, or it may take a while to happen. In effect, you are using your mature bodily arousal system to help regulate her very immature one.

Do things that stimulate the anti-stress chemical systems in her brain

Three key comforts release the calming chemical oxytocin in a baby's brain in a way that can drop levels of stress chemicals back to base rate. These are touch and massage, sucking, and warmth.

• **Touch and massage** Most babies will stop crying if they are picked up. Close bodily contact regulates their bodily arousal system, activating the calm and centred branch, as well as releasing oxytocin.[19]

If you want to use baby massage (see opposite), it is worth going to a class to learn more about it. The wrong sort of touch is dysregulating and over-stimulating and will make your baby cry more.

• **Sucking** Help your child to find her fist or thumb to suck. You can also offer your fingers. If your child is absolutely inconsolable, then, and only then, use a dummy. Never use it as a plug when she is not distressed. This is because the mouth is vital for communication and the forming of sounds pre-speech. It's also vital for oral exploration (such as putting toys in her mouth). You can end up feeling ruled by the dummy because your child won't go anywhere without it.[20]

• **Warmth** Keep the room temperature at about 21°C/70°F. Hold your baby cuddled close to your body or snuggled in a flannelette sheet and the warmth will trigger oxytocin release. You could get in a warm bath with a stressed-out newborn.

Other strategies you can try

• **Movement and rocking** Babies love rhythmical movement, particularly being carried around, being pushed in the pram, or being in the car. It is thought that the rhythm triggers associations of being carried around in the security of the womb. Make sure that you do not rock too hard, however, as this can have the same effect on the brain as shaking, which can cause burst blood vessels.[21]

• **Low sound** Let your baby listen to the washing machine

"Most babies will stop crying if you pick them up. Close bodily contact regulates their bodily arousal system."

"Your touch helps to soothe me"

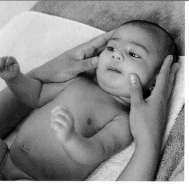

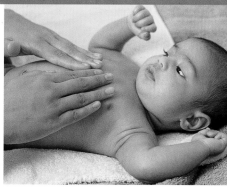

You can massage your baby from about two weeks old. It is a good way to comfort and calm him and to help strengthen the bond between you. Choose a time when he is awake and alert and you are both relaxed.

Lay your baby on a soft towel and make sure he is warm and comfortable. Starting at the crown of his head, massage very lightly across his cheeks and down to his shoulders.

Massage gently down his body using a downwards motion. Talk to him as you massage, and engage in lovely eye-to-eye contact. If your baby loses interest, then try again another day rather than persist.

or spin dryer, as the sound is evocative of the security of the womb. You could also play a recording of your heart beat, but this is often only effective if used from the start after birth.

• **Provide novelty** This activates dopamine in the brain. If your baby is screaming with sheer boredom, think of ways to provide novelty. Keep small toys, such as a finger puppet, in your bag to amuse her on a journey.

• **Avoid overstimulation** If you think your child is over-stimulated, take her with you into a quiet, low-lit room.

Hard-to-comfort babies

About one in five healthy babies is highly sensitive in the first few weeks. These hard-to-comfort babies can be like this due to genetic make-up, stress in the womb, or a difficult birth. Research shows that if a mother is repeatedly stressed in the last three months of pregnancy, high levels of the stress chemicals cortisol and glutamate can be transmitted through the placenta into the brain of the unborn child. So it's vitally important that you get as much soothing and comfort as you can in pregnancy. If you have lots of stress in your life once your baby is born, this can also result in a baby who cries more. If you have a hard-to-comfort baby, she will need a lot of soothing and comforting, and to do that well you will need soothing and comforting, too, from family and friends.

Make sure that you're not left in a desperate, isolated state with a screaming baby

Put your baby in her pram and go to the park, café, or a group with other parents. Isolation is extremely bad for brain chemistry. It can result in a dramatic drop in levels of serotonin (a key mood stabilizer), leading to aggressive impulses. It can also lower levels of dopamine (a positive arousal chemical), so you can feel awful over and above the distress you feel about your baby's screaming.[22]

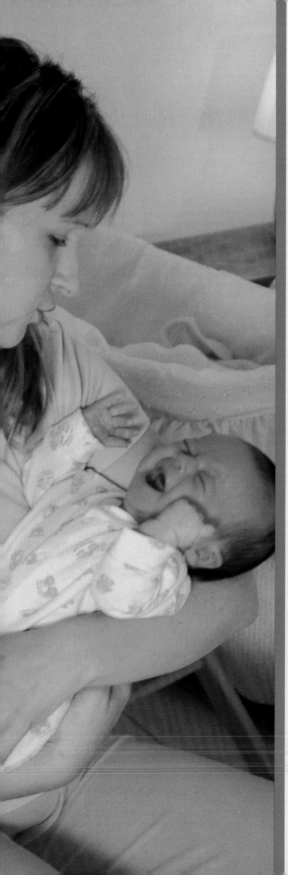

I have tried everything and I feel demoralized – what do I do now?

Let's be really clear. No one is disputing the fact that it can be totally exhausting when you are endlessly comforting a distressed child who just won't stop crying. When you have tried everything, you can feel impotent and demoralized, and want to burst into tears. The following may help:

● Remember that "this too shall pass". This phase usually lasts for only the first three months, yet many worn-out parents think that it will be a life sentence.

● Remember what a long-term gift you are giving your child when you calm her. All that calming time is an investment for the future, regulating her emotional and physical systems, which means that later she will have the ability to manage stress well.

Why do I feel like screaming when my baby is screaming?

Your baby's emotional states are so raw and primitive that they can easily trigger one or more of the three alarm systems in your lower brain: RAGE, FEAR, or PANIC/GRIEF. At the same time, your high levels of stress chemicals can block the release of your positive arousal chemicals, such as dopamine and opioids. You need emotional regulation. Ring a health visitor, join a parents' group, cry in your partner's arms, or get support from a counsellor or therapist (see pages 281–85).

Separations and time apart

When your baby reaches six to eight months of age, separation anxiety starts to kick in and often continues in some form until she is well over five years old. Early on, your baby will start to panic if you are out of her sight. Take her intense feelings seriously. You are her world, her everything, you represent her very safety.

ANIMAL INSIGHTS

Eight-year-old Flint, one of the chimpanzees observed in the wild by biologist Jane Goodall, became depressed and lethargic after the death of his mother. Within three weeks he too was dead. Jane Goodall found that after the death of a mother, an infant chimpanzee, even though nutritionally independent, might be unable to recover from the pain of grief and so may die. The PANIC/GRIEF system in the chimp's lower brain has virtually the same neuroanatomy and chemical systems as that in a human brain.

A little bit of understanding

Your baby is not being "needy" or "clingy". The PANIC/GRIEF system in the lower brain (see page 19), is genetically programmed to be hypersensitive. In earlier stages of evolution it was very dangerous for an infant to be away from her mother and if she didn't cry to alert her parents to her whereabouts, she would not survive. The development of the frontal lobes in the higher brain naturally inhibits this system, and as adults we learn to bring it under control with cognitive distractions, such as reading a book or watching TV.

If you are not there – how does she know you have not gone for ever?

You can't tell her that you will soon return, because the verbal centres in her brain aren't on-line yet. When she learns to crawl and toddle, let her follow you – yes, even into the toilet.

Prising her off you and shutting her in a playpen is not only very cruel, it can also lead to long-term adverse effects. She may move into panic, which means a dramatic and dangerous rise in those stress chemicals in her brain. This can lead to the wiring of an over-active FEAR system that may affect her later in life, resulting in phobias, obsessions, or fearful avoidance behaviour. Gradually, she will become more secure with you in the house, particularly as she becomes verbal. She will learn that if you go on your own to the toilet, she is unlikely to never see you again!

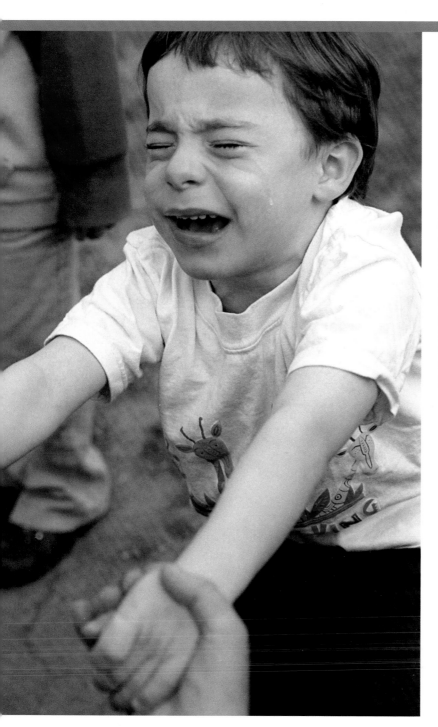

"When you leave me, it hurts so much"

When a loved person isn't there and a child is too young to understand, it can be extremely painful. You can't just say to a child who is missing his Mummy – "look, don't feel like that", yet adults often give that sort of message to small children. When we prise a distressed child away from his parent and urge him "not to be silly", we entirely underestimate the power of the massive hormonal reactions in his brain and body.

BRAIN STORY

This brain scan of a child from a Romanian orphanage shows what can happen to the brain when a child receives basic physical care, but is deprived of love, affection, and comfort.

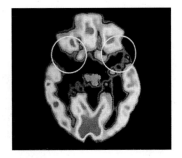

The black areas in this brain scan show inactive areas in the temporal lobes – part of the brain that is vital for processing and regulating emotions. Temporal lobe inactivity can result in poor social and emotional intelligence.

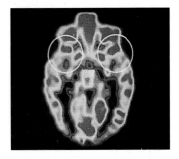

This is the brain scan of a child who has received loving parenting. In contrast to the brain scan of the Romanian child there are few black areas, meaning that the temporal lobes are fully active.[25]

Separation hurts small humans in much the same way as a physical pain

When a child is suffering because of the absence of a parent, the same parts of the brain are activated as when she is feeling physical pain.[23] So the language of loss is very much the language of pain. It does not make sense to comfort a physical pain, say from a cut knee, but not feel that it is necessary to address an emotional one such as separation distress. Yet, sadly, that's what many parents find themselves doing. They are reluctant to take on board the fact that the emotional pain of their child is just as real, but this pain is a neurobiological fact that should be respected by all.

We sometimes push our children to independence long before they are ready

Perhaps fuelled by a fear of our own dependency, our parenting traditions can push children into early separations. Sending children to boarding school at a young age is an example of this. A child aged eight can still be hypersensitive to separation distress and find it difficult to be away from parents for a long time. A child's emotional pain should always be taken seriously in key decisions about how long times apart should be, and how often and with whom the child should be left. The brain's GABA system (see page 44) is sensitive to very subtle environmental changes, such as separation from a parent. Studies link separation in early life to alterations in this anti-anxiety system.[24]

Even short-term separations may do harm

Some studies have found long-term changes in the HPA axis (see page 40) in a child's brain from even short-term separations, when the child was left with an unfamiliar carer. This stress response system is instrumental in how well we manage stress in later life. It is very vulnerable to being adversely affected by early stress.[26] Other studies link separation in early life with depression. Studies with higher mammals reveal that infants separated from their mothers stopped crying but then moved into a depressed response. Play with friends ceased and objects in the room were ignored. At the time of going to sleep, there was an increase in crying and agitation. If the separation continued, there was further withdrawal, leading to lethargy and a more entrenched depression.

In the 1960s, research showed that some children who were left with unfamiliar people for several days went into a full-blown bereavement response, which left them reeling from the trauma years later. The children in the study had been left with well-meaning adults or placed in a residential nursery for several days while their mothers were in hospital. Their fathers would come to visit, but basically they were left with adults whom they did not know.

One little boy, separated from his mother for just 11 days, stopped eating, cried endlessly, and repeatedly threw himself on the floor in despair. Six years later, he was still very angry with his mother. The researchers observed countless other children who had been left for several days and were in a state of yearning without end. Many would stare, for hours at a time, at the door through which their mother had left. They did not want to play; they just wanted to watch the door. This research, much of which is on film, changed attitudes throughout the world towards children visiting parents in hospital.[27]

But isn't moderate stress good for a child?

Some people justify leaving a child uncomforted (for instance, during sleep training) by calling it "stress inoculation". But stress inoculation involves introducing a child to moderately stressful situations to help her to handle stress better. For example, you might gently introduce a baby to a big bath for the first time – at first she's scared, then she loves it. People who say that a child screaming for a prolonged period is only experiencing moderate stress are deluding themselves.

"I'm addicted to Dad"

The brain chemistry of loving relationships is naturally addictive. When you hold your child, love her, soothe her, rock her in your arms, delight in her time after time, a very strong bond will develop between you. The bond will then mean that any tender loving contact with you will release natural opioids and oxytocin in your child's brain. When this happens, your child will be in a wonderful state of oneness and contentment.

The childcare question

There is a great deal of recent research showing improvements in cognitive performance (IQ) of a child who has attended a nursery before the age of five. Sadly, these positive changes have not been found to extend to emotional health and intelligence (EQ). Here we find that the opposite is true.

CONSIDER THIS...

I believe all nurseries should have "emotional nurses", chosen for their calmness and emotional warmth.

These need to be people who frequently have opioids and oxytocin in dominance in their brain, probably because they were on the receiving end of warm parenting themselves, or good counselling or psychotherapy in later life.

In the UK, the almost phobic attitude to physical contact in schools (for fear of allegations of sexual abuse) is to the great detriment of children. We need a clear, well thought-out policy on touch that allows adults to comfort and hold young children in safe ways to activate their natural calming brain chemicals.

A problem with stress

Cortisol has its own natural peaks and troughs. It is naturally high in the morning and decreases as the day goes on. However, studies of children under five in nurseries have shown levels of cortisol rising rather than falling as the day goes on. What's more, as soon as these children were with their parents again, their stress levels dropped dramatically. In one study, cortisol rose in 75 to 100 percent of children when they arrived at nursery. This research is worrying because a key stress response system in the brain can become wired for hypersensitivity early in life.

However, researchers found that toddlers in nurseries who played more with other children had lower cortisol levels than those who tended to play alone. Research also revealed that with a minimum of a four-day settling in period in nurseries where one parent or an alternative attachment figure was allowed to stay, there was no worrying change in stress hormone levels in the child. So insist on staying! [28]

Some parents think their child is fine at nursery, but her stress hormone levels may be very high

We know that a child can look fine and not be crying yet still be distressed. A famous research study called "The Strange Situation Test" showed that one year olds who didn't cry for their Mummy when she left the room had equally high levels of stress hormones as those who did. In other words, the one year olds had learnt at such a tender age to bottle up their

"I don't want to be here"

Even a four year old may still be struggling with higher cortisol levels at nursery, so keep this in mind when you decide how long your child should spend there each day. Ideally don't lengthen the time away until your child has a good understanding of time frameworks and is confident that you will come back at the end of the session. Babies and toddlers can find long days at nursery particularly difficult because they have no sense of time and hence no notion of when or even if you will return.

feelings. This is worrying because when young children do not appear to be upset they are very unlikely to get the comfort they need.[29]

Nursery school children may become more difficult to manage later in childhood

The consequences of high levels of cortisol in nursery school children are becoming apparent. Evidence suggests that when children are cared for extensively in a nursery early on, this can be associated with an increase in difficult relationships between parent and child and more aggression and non-compliance in

"Toddlers who played more with other children had lower cortisol levels."

Q Sometimes I need to go away with work for a week or so. How will that affect my child long term?

It all depends on whom your child is left with. If your child is left with someone she knows and who is emotionally aware, such as a loving partner or family member, then your child will be fine. If this is not possible, there is worrying research to show that a child will react very badly if left with someone who is not able to provide emotional support.

the children.[30] It starts showing at age two. The findings were particularly significant for babies who had spent 20 or more hours per week in nursery care during their first year.

The emotionally aware childminder

Leaving a child with a very good childminder or nanny during the day is fine, as long as that person is able to give emotionally warm one-to-one attention. But it isn't enough to give this attention to a baby or a child only when they are overtly showing signs of distress. Researchers have found that when nannies got on with something else, thinking that the child was fine (because she wasn't crying) the child's cortisol levels shot up.[31] So choose a nanny or childminder who adores little children, who is great at responding to both joy and distress, and who would rather talk to your child than read a magazine! When interviewing, ensure you sit in the

> **"** Choose a nanny or childminder who adores little children and who is great at responding to joy and distress. **"**

"I need to be comforted"

Anna hates it when her Mum leaves and is still crying in spite of all her mother's attempts to reassure her that she will be back to see her again at the end of the day.

Anna's childminder, Joanne, is ready to help her recover from her distress. She moves in quickly and lifts Anna into her arms, giving her all the time she needs to cry and grieve.

As Anna's sobs subside and she starts to feel safe, her cortisol levels fall and she begins to relax and play. Joanne stays with her to make sure she stays happy and content.

ANIMAL INSIGHTS

Touch is very important when an infant has been separated from its mother. In a study with monkeys, researchers found that the infant animals would choose the comfort of clinging to a cloth dummy over taking food when their mothers were absent.[32]

background and watch the carer interact and talk with your child for at least 30 minutes. Your personal observations will be worth a million references. Is there laughter, delight, and a real feeling of warmth in the room between the prospective carer and your child? If so, then she is likely to be a source of opioid and dopamine activation, both of which are wonderful for the development of your child's social and emotional brain.

Your child needs to be held in familiar arms when you are not there

There is all the difference in the world between leaving your child with an unfamiliar minder and leaving her grieving for her "gone mummy" in the care of a calm, warm, loving person with whom she feels safe. If there are no loving arms for your little one, you are risking the activation of high levels of stress hormones in her brain. These hormones will deactivate the positive arousal hormones and your child will end up feeling awful. If your child is still crying when you leave, lift her into the arms of her minder. A good nanny or childminder should be able to soothe her painful feelings and amplify the positive ones. Holding and soothing will bring down her cortisol levels and activate a more positive chemistry in her brain.

Early separations and depression may be linked

The alarm response in the brain of a child stressed by separation from her mother is the same as that found in adults suffering from clinical depression – an illness reaching epidemic proportions in many parts of the world.[33] As we are not born with a gene for clinical depression, we need to look closely at the long-term effects of stressful childhood experience.

Amazing studies have been carried out into the brain chemistry of infant monkeys separated from their parents. Researcher Harry Harlow found that the unmothered infants became severely stressed and depressed. Many became abusive and neglectful mothers in their turn. In the worst cases, some failed to mother their own infants in later life.

"Mummy's gone, but I'm safe"

This little girl feels secure because the adults who care for her know that she needs help to manage separation from her mum and dad. When she is playing happily and seems fine, they give her the same attention as when she is crying or upset. They know that plenty of warm, emotionally responsive interaction and cuddles will help prevent her cortisol levels rising while she is separated from the people she loves.

The need to cling

Young mammals (animals and humans) cling to a secure adult whenever they feel unsafe. Some human parents get irritated about clinging, but animal parents don't. They don't have higher brains like ours, which question whether we should stop a child from doing it.

If a child clings to you, she is trying to bring down her high bodily arousal level and high levels of stress chemicals. She is also trying to activate the lovely brain chemicals that produce feelings of well-being (see page 86). She can't do any of this without you, as you are her secure neurochemical base. A child is not being naughty or "attention-seeking" by clinging to you; she is feeling unsafe, and needs your support. In clinging to you, she is trying to change the emotion chemical balance in her brain to a calmer and more positive chemistry.

What research tells us

Studies have shown that by the end of the first year, mothers who had attended promptly to their crying babies had children who cried much less than those whose mothers had left them to cry.[34] Although some people think that a child becomes clingy because he has been cuddled or loved too much, or "spoilt" by attention, there is no evidence that supports the theory that anxious attachment is a result of excessive parental affection or attention.

Prolonged clinging is far more likely where a parent has not handled the child's dependency needs well. The parents may have pushed the child to be more independent (often by literally pushing him away when he felt the need to cling to them) when he was still in this genetically programmed dependent stage of his development.

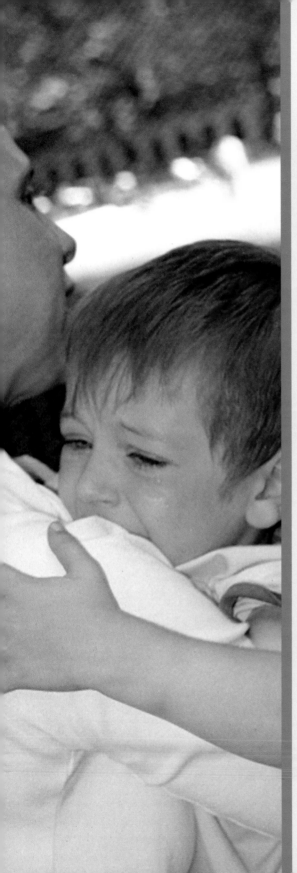

What should I do if my child clings to me at the school gates?

The best thing to do is to avoid a quick getaway when he's screaming for you to stay. Rushing off will make matters worse by sending your child's stress chemicals and stress hormones sky-high.

● Try to have quality time with him before you leave. Hold him really close. This will activate oxytocin and opioids in his brain and will make him feel calmer. It also means that he "finds" you before he "loses" you. When you leave, he will have a memory of a calm, soothing mother, rather than one who rushes away.

● Activate his SEEKING system (see pages 94–95), for example, by showing him the sandpit and encouraging him to start exploring. Take time to introduce him to a friend.

● Make an arrangement with a warm, kind teacher whom he knows, and whom he likes to pick him up in her arms, and use distraction to activate his frontal lobes; for example, by showing him a butterfly. Slip away quietly, knowing that you have given him that vital opioid fix in his brain before you go.

● If your child is repeatedly distressed when you leave, give him something to remind him of you, such as a scarf that smells of you, or record a loving message so that he can play your voice whenever he chooses.

❝ When children feel safe in the world, they will turn to it naturally. **❞**

CONSIDER THIS...

If you respond with compassion and patience to the clinging phase, it is a great investment for your child's ability to be independent in later life. If each time he has wanted to cling, you have picked him up and held him, he will start to feel very safe in his being-in-the-world. As he develops, he will then naturally start to turn away from you and explore the world for ever-increasing lengths of time. He will be just fine spending longer and longer times away from you with his friends, knowing that you are always there as a secure base, to which he will always return for emotional re-fuelling before going off again.

When the clinging stops

Parents often worry that their child's grief at partings and goodbyes will never end. But who ever heard of a teenager who bursts into tears when his parents announce that they are going to the cinema for the evening? As your child grows up, the PANIC/GRIEF system in her lower brain naturally becomes far less sensitive. This is largely because the development of the higher brain naturally inhibits this system. Then, in puberty, the increases in testosterone and oestrogen suppress the system even more. So when people say, "If I give into her clinging now it will never end", it is inaccurate in terms of a child's body-brain development.

Some children whose clinging has not met with an emotionally responsive reaction can move into a false independence. It is extremely shame-inducing for a child to be in a state of desperate need and meet with a rebuff or criticism, or to be told to be a big girl. As a way of dealing with the pain, some children take a "I don't need my Mummy!" stance, successfully hardening their hearts and moving into an emotional numbing against attachment needs. This can cause all manner of misery, loving in "torment", and fear of closeness in adult relationships (see Chemistry of love & joy, pages 84–125).

So when you have a clinging child, remember what an investment you are making in her long-term mental health if you respond with empathy and soothing. Remember the long-term anti-stress effects of repeated activation of oxytocin in the brain from all that physical affection. Remember the studies with other mammals that showed that if infants received loving touch, they were better able to handle stress, had a far less fearful response to life, were psychologically stronger, and even aged better!

Key points

• Parents can be trained out of their instinct to comfort a child, and a child can be trained out of his instinct to cry... but science is now showing us the costs.

• Prolonged uncomforted crying can adversely affect key systems in the brain and body, leading to a vulnerability to depression, anxiety disorders, and other physical and mental illness in later life.

• Being left to cry means a child learns that she is abandoned just at the time when she needs help.

• Early in a child's life separations must be considered carefully. When they are necessary, parents should always leave their child with an emotionally responsive, warm adult.

sleep &
bedtimes

Sleep training or co-sleeping? The debate has been raging passionately over the decades and the level of emotion it stirs up in people can be truly intense. Maybe a child's cry as the bedroom door closes contributes more than we realize to people not being able to reflect calmly on their options. This chapter presents the latest scientific thinking on the subject of where and how your child should sleep, and looks at current research into sudden infant death syndrome, or SIDS. I hope it will help parents to make an informed choice about what to do with their children at bedtime and during the night.

Getting your child to sleep

At bedtime, you should have one clear aim: to make your baby or child feel that all is well in his world. If you are successful, you will prevent stress chemicals being activated in his brain and leave him feeling very safe and loved as he drops off to sleep. There are things that can help you to achieve this, whether you choose to co-sleep or settle your child in his own bed.

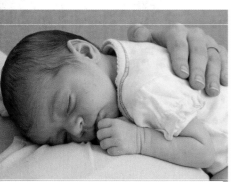

CONSIDER THIS...

If your baby has difficulty sinking into a blissful sleep, bodily contact with you will help her to relax, especially when she is very young. For an older baby, lie quietly next to her cot until she drops off or offer her calming contact by resting a soothing hand on her body.

The facts about children and sleep

First – babies are awful sleepers. When we accept this, maybe we will stop seeing a wakeful baby as some kind of parental failure. Research into the sleeping patterns of babies and young children has established that:

• **Babies are prone to wake far more than adults,** as their average sleep cycle lasts only 50 minutes, compared with our 90-minute cycle.

• **Persistent or recurring infant sleep problems** in the preschool years are very common.

• **Approximately 25 percent of children** under five years old have some type of sleep problem.

• **Up to 20 percent** of parents report a problem with infant crying or irritability in the first three months of life.[1]

Calming the brain at bedtime

Your primary aim at bedtime is to bring your child down from a super alert awake state, by activating the calming brain chemical oxytocin and the sleep hormone melatonin. The most likely way of achieving this is by establishing a soothing routine. Whenever this is repeated, there is a chance that it will activate the same calming chemicals in the brain.

Whatever you do, stay calm

If stress chemicals are being strongly activated in your own brain you can't expect to bring your child down from an aroused state. Your tone is everything, and if you are tense, uptight, irritated, or angry, your attempts to be calm will be false ones. All too easily, your stress and anger can activate the alarm systems in your child's brain, making him feel too unsafe to go to sleep. On the other hand, if your brain is strongly activating opioids, and your voice is gentle, quiet, and soothing, this can be deeply reassuring for your child and he is likely to respond brilliantly to you.

Snuggle up and read a story

While you read, your body contact with your child will activate oxytocin in his brain, which can make him feel sleepy. Listening to the story will engage your child's frontal lobes (see page 18), the part that naturally inhibits motoric impulses – such as the desire to jump about on the bed.

Try to set up a magical atmosphere. Dim the lights (the dark will activate melatonin) or use safe candles. You could also play soothing music, which can lower bodily arousal levels.

Don't give food that will keep him awake

Avoid giving your child protein food, such as meat or fish, in the two hours before bedtime, as it activates dopamine (a brain stimulant). Chocolate is not a good idea either, as it contains the stimulant drug caffeine. If your child is hungry, offer him a carbohydrate food such as a banana, as it activates serotonin in the brain, which can help to make him feel sleepy.

Avoid activating the FEAR system in your child's lower brain

If your child is frightened of the dark, keep a nightlight in the room. You could call it the "safe fairy" who will watch over your child as he sleeps.[2] Take his fears and anxieties seriously and reassure him. If you don't, his brain may keep triggering high levels of glutamate, noradrenaline, and CRF

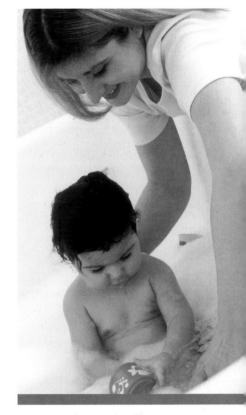

"I know it is getting close to bedtime"

A winding-down routine before bedtime, with a bath followed by a story, will help to regulate your child's bodily arousal system. He is also highly dependent on you to regulate his brain chemistry in a way that prepares him for sleep.

"Once his feelings are out in the open, you can find ways of soothing him."

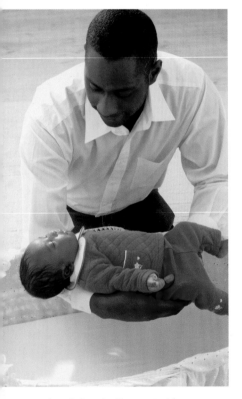

Having a baby with all her erratic sleeping patterns is hard work for a parent, but it is not true that you can never have an evening to yourself. Let her fall asleep in your arms, lay her in her basket or cot, and then quietly tiptoe away.

(corticotrophin-releasing factor), moving his body into a state of hyperarousal. When this happens, no human being will feel at all sleepy.

You may choose to lie down next to your child while he goes to sleep

If you do this, there should be no talking. Pretend to be asleep yourself; concentrate on your own deep breathing. The skin-to-skin contact will regulate your child's bodily arousal system and strengthen the bond between the two of you. The more calm you are, the more calm he will be. Consider the brain chemicals involved. Body contact activates the release of opioids and oxytocin – and oxytocin can promote sleepiness. Once your child is sleeping, you can leave to have your evening.

If your child is too anxious to let you go, it's worth asking him why

An anxious three year old who is suffering from the activation of the brain's FEAR and/or PANIC/GRIEF systems is likely to ask for another drink, a pee, or his dummy, when he is really trying to say that he is frightened. Ask him what he is afraid of, or what he thinks might happen when you leave the room. Once his feelings are out in the open and talked about, you can find ways of soothing him, such as giving him an item of your clothing to go to bed with, tucking him up in a special way, or reassuring him with words and cuddles. Use your emotionally warm presence to activate opioids in his brain, as these chemicals naturally inhibit PANIC/GRIEF activation.

I have to resettle my child continually, every night – what am I doing wrong?

If you are finding it difficult to get your child off to sleep night after night, you need to ask yourself some questions. First, are you being calm enough, still enough? The human brain is acutely sensitive to emotional atmospheres and to picking up emotions that you may be feeling strongly, but are trying not to show.

Is there an atmosphere of peace and safety in his room, with dimmed lights to activate the sleep hormone melatonin? Is your child tired enough? Has he recently eaten protein or chocolate, or had a fizzy drink, all of which will wake him up? Is he getting enough physical activity during the day? Make sure that he plays outdoors during the afternoon whenever possible; the more daylight he gets, the better he will sleep at night.[3]

Is something at home or school disturbing him, so that he doesn't feel safe enough to sleep? Do you tell him off a lot? Does he shout at you a lot? If he feels the relationship with you is wobbly, he can be scared to let you go.

Sleeping with your baby

Sleeping in close physical proximity to a parent provides a baby with a sensorially rich environment because of all the movement, touch, smells, and sounds. Skin-to-skin contact throughout the night has been shown to regulate a baby's immature body and brain systems, and can play a key role in maintaining his long-term mental and physical well-being.

ANIMAL INSIGHTS

All primates except humans co-sleep with their young as a matter of course. After all, infant mammals are tasty morsels for a predator if left in the dark, unprotected by their parents. Leaving a baby sleeping on its own (solitary sleeping) is only a very recent shift for humankind. For most of their two million years of evolution, humans have co-slept with their babies.

The history of co-sleeping

Ninety percent of the world's parents co-sleep with their babies. It's been going on since the beginning of humankind. No other mammal apart from humans puts their infants in social isolation to sleep. Parents in the Western world co-slept with their infants until about the 1850s. Putting babies away in another room coincided with a "germ myth" that breathing in another's breath caused illness.

Extensive scientific research shows that safe co-sleeping can be a real investment for your child's future physical and emotional health. Sleeping with your baby can positively influence his physiology, and all those extra hours of body contact can bring you together more, as bonding goes on at night at well as during the day.[4]

Close physical contact with you regulates your baby's temperature-control system

Skin-to-skin contact with the mother is the genetically programmed natural environment for a human infant. When a newborn baby is placed on his mother's chest, something amazing happens. If the baby is a little too cold, the mother's temperature rises two degrees to warm him; if the baby is a little too warm, the mother's temperature drops by a degree to cool him. This is called "thermal synchrony" and is just one of the extraordinary phenomena that result from close bodily contact between mothers and infants.[5]

" I feel so calm and safe "

Sleeping next to your baby can help to regulate his breathing. Studies have shown that sensory stimulation (such as the rocking of the mother's body as she walks, and the sounds she makes) keeps the unborn child "breathing" rhythmically using practice breathing movements that begin up to three months before birth. It is thought that the stimulation of sleeping next to a parent after birth keeps a child breathing regularly through the night.

Co-sleeping means hours of extra body contact

There is a mass of evidence to demonstrate that the more touch a child gets in childhood, the calmer and less fearful he is likely to be in adulthood. Physical contact helps to regulate the brain's stress response system and, without this regulation, this system can become hard-wired for oversensitivity. When this is the case, it can be very difficult for a child, as he grows up, to calm himself down when stressed.[6] Co-sleeping with a child in early life means an extra eight hours or so of stress-relieving skin-to-skin contact.

Psychological studies reveal that children who have co-slept with their parents in the first years of their life have a significantly higher self-esteem; experience less fear and anxiety; have a higher cognitive performance; suffer less mental ill-health in adulthood; and enjoy a greater feeling of

> " The more touch a child gets in childhood, the calmer he is likely to be as an adult. "

CONSIDER THIS...

Extra hours of body contact each night can bring about better bonding between mother and child. Mothers who maintain this prolonged skin contact have also found it easier to produce breast milk for an extended period.

" Even when asleep, mothers appeared to be aware of the baby next to them. "

satisfaction with life.[7] Studies also show that children who have never slept in their parents' bed are harder to control. Such children also tend to cope less well with being left alone, and are more likely to have tantrums and be fearful. This makes sense in terms of them getting less bodily and emotional regulation, and having less oxytocin and opioids released in their brains.

Are there risks with co-sleeping?

Some parents worry about co-sleeping because they have fears about suffocating their baby by lying on top of him. Research shows that these fears are unfounded, provided no one smokes and the parents are not likely to sleep so deeply that vigilance is impaired (see opposite).

In fact, in many cases, co-sleeping seems to bring a higher degree of maternal vigilance. One study of around 800 hours of video material showed that even when asleep, mothers appeared to be aware of the baby next to them. No mother rolled on her infant, however close they were to each other.[8]

Research has also shown that when co-sleeping, parents and babies spend most of the night facing each other. Babies don't just passively let themselves be smothered – even newborns will struggle and cry in response to something preventing them from breathing. That said, the safety factors listed opposite must be in place before you co-sleep.

What is sudden infant death syndrome (SIDS)?

SIDS (often known as "cot death") is associated with a problem with immaturity of heartbeat, breathing, or blood pressure during sleep. The heart–lung system of your baby matures only after birth. Until it matures, a young baby's respiratory system is not at all stable. In fact, the heartbeat of a perfectly healthy baby can be very irregular. This puts babies at risk of breathing problems, especially during sleep.[9] In the UK, 300 children a year die of SIDS, and most of these babies die before they reach the age of six months. Research makes it clear that certain sleeping conditions carry a significant risk, particularly in the first three months of life, which is the most vulnerable period (see Safety facts, right).

Research around the world shows very low rates of SIDS in countries where co-sleeping is common

Where and how a child sleeps raises very passionate feelings in some parts of the world. In many areas, it is not controversial – co-sleeping happens as a matter of course. This is largely to do with the fact that putting a baby or child in another room is not an option for many families around the world, because they simply haven't got a spare room. Solitary sleeping for babies is very much a Western middle-class phenomenon. One study showed that only four percent of Asian babies sleep alone.[10] In China, where co-sleeping is taken for granted, SIDS is so rare it doesn't have a name. One key researcher found that no one in China knew what he was talking about when he spoke about SIDS; they didn't understand his description of a young baby dying suddenly for no apparent reason.[11]

A recent international survey team, the SIDS Global Task Force, found that "cultures practising the highest co-sleeping and bed-sharing rates experienced ... the lowest SIDS rates of all".[11] As a result of such studies, many researchers think that higher rates of SIDS in Western populations may be the result of long periods of solitary sleep.

Key safety factors for co-sleeping

If you want to co-sleep with your baby, only do so if you are able to adhere to all of the safety measures (below and right) every night you sleep with your baby. This means that if one evening you are exhausted or have had a glass of wine, put your baby in a Moses basket or cot beside your bed. You can still have touch contact with him by reaching into his bed.

• **A baby must always lie face up** whether in a cot or in his parents' bed, and lie feet at the foot of the mattress in a cot.

SAFETY FACTS

To minimize the risk of SIDS, you should adhere to the common-sense safety rules listed here (whether the baby is in a cot or his parents' bed).

• A baby should always lie face up (never face down).

• A baby's head should not be covered while he sleeps.

• The room should be 16–20°C (61–68°F); 18°C (64°F) is ideal.

• A baby should sleep in your room for the first six months.

• If you or anyone in the house smokes, you should not co-sleep with your baby.

• If you have been consuming alcohol, medication, or drugs, or your vigilance is impaired by exhaustion do not co-sleep with your baby.

• Do not cover your baby with the duvet; use a blanket that comes no higher than the baby's shoulders.

• Do not let your baby sleep on or near a pillow.

• Do not let your baby sleep on a sheepskin.

• A baby should not co-sleep lying between two people.

• A baby should not co-sleep on sofas, water beds, or with other children.

• Never leave your baby unattended in or on top of an adult bed.

Studies have shown that the majority of babies in South East Asian families sleep with their parents at night. Some researchers believe that this factor may be linked to the low incidence of SIDS (sudden infant death syndrome) in South East Asian populations.

• **No overheated rooms.** Rooms should be between 16 and 20ºC (61 and 68ºF). Don't guess, check with a thermometer.

• **Don't cover your baby with a duvet;** use a blanket and make sure it comes no higher than your baby's shoulders.

• **No duvets, soft toys, pillows, or sheepskins** should be near the baby. A baby should never sleep on a pillow or a sheepskin.

• **Mattresses must be firm** – babies shouldn't sleep on soft ones. Make sure there is no gap between the headboard and the mattress or between the mattress and the wall.

• **Babies shouldn't sleep between two people** and don't allow siblings in the bed if your baby is less than a year old.

• **Never co-sleep with your baby if anyone** in the house smokes (or you smoked in pregnancy) or there's any reason your vigilance could be impaired. This means no alcohol – not even one glass of wine; no drugs (illegal or legal); no medication to aid sleep; and no exhaustion on your part. Even with all these safety measures in place, if you are still too anxious about the risk of SIDS, place your baby in a cot by the side of your bed. Always seek medical advice if your baby is having trouble breathing, is pale, has a rash, is not responding to you normally, is hot and sweaty or unwell.

The protective factors and benefits of co-sleeping

The media repeatedly communicates the risks of co-sleeping, while withholding information about the evidence-based protective factors. So parents are presented with neither a balanced nor scientifically informed view. There are risks in babies co-sleeping if safety factors are not followed, but there are also risks in babies sleeping alone. It is unhelpful when the advice is simply "Don't sleep with your baby". You have a right to know about the protective factors, not just the risks of co-sleeping, and then to make up your own mind.

Extensive medical research has shown that co-sleeping, particularly with skin-to-skin contact, can do the following:

• **Regulate a baby's heart rate,** digestive system, breathing and temperature.[12]

- **Dramatically lower a baby's stress** (bad stress) chemicals, and release oxytocin and opioids in the baby's brain.[13]
- **Support the development of a baby's stress response** systems, sleep patterns, bodily functions, and maturation of the higher brain, which enhances cognitive functions. One study found that these effects still showed up years later.[14]
- **Enhance a baby's immune system,** so he is less likely to have a serious illness in his first six months.[15]
- **Result in babies spending more time in lighter sleep.** This can protect against SIDS, as a baby is more able to wake up to stop non-breathing episodes. If alone, babies tend to enter a deep sleep that is far more difficult to arouse from.[16]
- **Improve your sleep.** If your child stirs and you are next to him, he can be quickly comforted (because of the opioids triggered by your soothing voice and your cuddles). Research shows that if you are awake for less than 15 seconds you can usually quickly drop off to sleep again. You will definitely be awake if you have to get out of bed to attend to your baby.[17]

Observations in a sleep laboratory

Sleep laboratories have revealed that when co-sleeping both babies and mothers sleep more, not less.[18] Babies breastfeed two to four times more frequently and for longer, so receive more of their mother's antibodies, potentially reducing child illness.[19] Conversely, if babies are on their own, breastfeeding may be disrupted (even when a baby is in a cot next to mum's bed). Co-sleeping babies hardly ever cry (unless in pain or discomfort). Mothers were very responsive and attentive to their babies. They kept checking them, making sure they were in a safe position, touching, soothing, stroking (all within the 15-second soothing time, above). Amazingly, in the morning most were unaware that they had been doing this all night.

If a baby sleeps alone

Isolation and sensory deprivation in early life has been linked to mental illness in later life.[20] If a baby sleeps alone, his body

> **"** In some cultures, co-sleeping is pretty much problem-free for parents; in others, it is not. **"**

ANIMAL INSIGHTS

Other primates don't share our human dilemmas about whether to co-sleep or not. They follow their instincts (the same instincts we have, unless we over-ride them). Many infant apes and chimpanzees sleep with their parents until about the age of eight, although they will leave the parental bed earlier if another baby comes along.

temperature may be sub-normal, and there can be erratic fluctuations in heart and breathing rates. When a baby is placed next to the mother's body again, these stabilize. If a baby is separated from his mother for six hours, his stress hormone level will be twice as high as that of a baby whose mother is close by. As soon as the baby is placed next to his mother, stress hormones drop to safe levels.[21]

Co-sleeping and sleep problems

If you can't get the sleep you need with a child in your bed, the secure bedtimes and safe sleep training ideas in this chapter may be better suited to you. Your sleep is vital if you are to be an effective emotion regulator for your child during the day. If you are tired, your brain is far more likely to activate a negative brain chemistry, which will do your child no good. By co-sleeping, you are helping him to regulate his emotional and physiological systems during the night, but you are likely to fail him during the day if loss of sleep has made you irritable, agitated, and lacking in interest.

When do you stop co-sleeping?

There are no rights and wrongs about when to stop. If you are considering getting your child to sleep in his own bed, you should ask yourself whether you want to do this, or has someone suggested it? If you and your child get enough sleep, and you and your partner have enough physical intimacy, there's no reason to give up. Moreover, you may cause a lot of stress by pressurizing yourself to meet a fictitious norm.

Studies show that most preschoolers need an adult next to them until they fall asleep, and many come to their parents' beds for comfort.[22] Such is the power of the lower brain's FEAR and PANIC/GRIEF systems in early childhood. Parents who are emotionally responsive accept this natural stage of infant brain development and don't try to over-ride genetic programming.

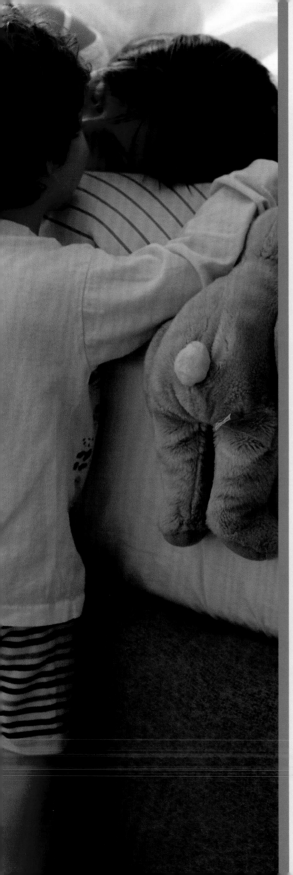

If I let my toddler co-sleep, will he ever settle in his own bed?

When parents worry about their children being dependent, clingy, and in their bed for ever, they should take comfort from the fact that the PANIC/GRIEF system in a child's brain becomes far less sensitive over time. This is largely because the child's rapidly developing higher brain naturally starts to inhibit this system. Also, as your child moves towards puberty, increasing levels of testosterone (in boys) and testosterone and oestrogen (in girls) have a further inhibiting effect. Neuroscientists don't really know why this happens. Some think it is because we are genetically programmed in adolescence to move away from parents to relationships with peers. As your child gets older, separation from you at night will not trigger the emotional pain that affected him when younger.

What about our needs as parents? We want some privacy.

You need to weigh up your needs as adults with all the psychological and physiological benefits co-sleeping can have for your child. Of course, there are costs if you choose co-sleeping, but many parents take a creative attitude. They have sex at other times, or start off the children in their own beds and then allow them to come into the parental bed in the middle of the night for that vital emotional and bodily regulation. If you are at the end of your tether and desperate for time away from your children, then these feelings must also be considered when you make decisions about sleeping arrangements.

All about sleep training

Some children go to sleep happily in their own beds, without ever having been trained to sleep or left to cry. They have built up a very strong association between bedtime and feeling completely safe in the world. But for many children, bedtime activates primitive alarm systems in the brain and body and they need gentle help to calm down.

Babies are programmed to be highly dependent, and they need us to regulate their distress states. A child left alone to cry for hours will eventually go to sleep, but only from exhaustion, or because he's given up crying for help.

Beginning sleep training

Most parents begin sleep training because they and their child are in need of better sleep. A child of one to three years of age needs 12–14 hours sleep a night; from three to five years, he needs 11–13 hours, while children from five to twelve years old need 10–11 hours. Sleep is vital for physical growth (the growth hormone is released only during sleep). The effects of sleep deprivation can include poor performance at school, lack of attention, and hyperactivity.[23]

If you do decide to sleep train, make sure that you don't use a method that involves prolonged crying, even for a few nights (see below). As the higher brain develops, children grow out of PANIC/GRIEF responses, but until they do, it's vital that you meet their frightened or distressed states with reassurance and comfort. See it from their point of view; the thought of being parted from you at night and being put in a dark room on their own can provoke extreme anxiety.

Some experts advocate leaving a child to "cry it out"

The theory is that after a few nights of fruitless crying, a child will go to sleep without fuss. Often, however, this entails prolonged periods of crying of an hour or more, and for many nights, not just a few. The technique is effective from the parents' point of view, but it can never be considered as a worthwhile achievement. And what is the cost for the child?

Babies cannot calm themselves down

A baby is not capable of settling himself to a state of inner peace and well-being. What he can do, however, is eventually give up in the absence of response and go to sleep after endless exhausted, unanswered cries for help. And going to sleep stressed from all that desperate calling means he may wake up frequently in the middle of the night, just as adults would if they had gone to sleep in a very stressed state. This cannot be counted as successful sleep training; it's simply what happens with any mammal (human or otherwise) whose cries are ignored by its parent. The most determined infants with the strongest wills will cry the longest.

A baby who is trained out of his instinct to cry on being separated from a parent should never be mistaken for being in a state of calm. His stress levels will have gone up, not down. Studies show that after being left to cry, babies move into a primitive defence mode. This results in an irregularity in breathing and heart rate, both of which can fluctuate wildly, and high levels of cortisol. Infants who have been trained not to cry can often be seen staring into space with a fixed stare. Allan Schore, a neuropsychoanalyst, calls it "the black spot in going-on-being" or "conservation-withdrawal". [24] In attachment theory, when a child starts to bottle up his feelings rather than express them, the process is known as Protest–Despair–Detachment.

Without your help, your baby cannot bring his stress hormone levels down to base rate, or adjust his bodily arousal states, or change his brain chemistry so that relaxing oxytocin and opioids flood in. To make these things happen, your baby needs you next to him, soothing him and regulating his immature brain and body systems.

Kind sleep training

Of course, not all sleep training is bad for the brain. Here are some safe no-cry options that you can try for young children, and older babies where appropriate. First, if you

BRAIN STORY

Children can be highly sensitive to separation at bedtime. If a child feels anxious about being alone, the pituitary gland in his brain sends the hormone ACTH to his adrenal glands, which respond by producing high levels of the stress hormone cortisol (se page 41). Studies of other infant mammals showed that the longer an infant was left for, the greater the increase in the cortisol level. [25] Even when crying and restlessness decreased, cortisol stayed high or increased.

The possible long-term effect of repeated separation anxiety is an extreme sensitivity to stress. Adults with this hypersensitivity find it difficult to calm themselves down.

A child who receives reassurance and calming touch at bedtime, however, is likely to have oxytocin and opioids washing over his brain, helping him to sleep peacefully.

The systems involved in stress response

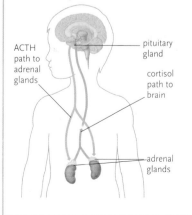

ACTH path to adrenal glands

pituitary gland

cortisol path to brain

adrenal glands

Bedtime has become a battle with my toddler – why?

Sadly, scenes at bedtime are all too often mistaken for a battle of wills rather than the activation of pain and panic in a child's brain. When children cry for their parents not to leave them at night, they are acting as other infant mammals are genetically programmed to do when left on their own. It is not about control; that's an adult interpretation of events. It's the effect of a powerful hormonal system in the lower mammalian part of the brain.

My child is desperately clingy at bedtime. What should I do?

If your child needs to cling to you to get to sleep, then let him. Children cling if they feel very unsafe. They also cling to you to change their negative brain chemistry (high levels of stress chemicals) to a positive one. Body contact with you can activate opioids and oxytocin in the brain, naturally lowering levels of stress chemicals. Sometimes a child's anxiety is increased because something has made his little world feel insecure. One way to help him is for you to tell him the story of his day, which will help him process all the emotional ups and downs he went through. As adults we can't get to sleep when worries and concerns keep swirling round our minds, because no one has helped us to manage them. It's just the same with children.

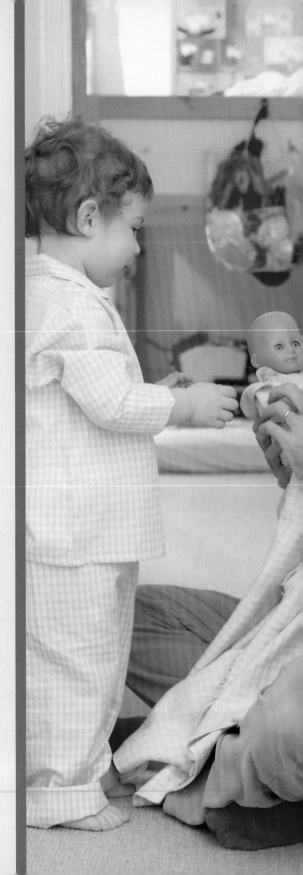

have done everything to settle your child in his own bed, but he follows you out of the room, turn round immediately and put him back into bed. Reassure him that he is safe and that you will see him in the morning. Don't leave him to cry, and don't just plonk him in his bed like a sack of potatoes and walk away. If you do, you are giving him an experience of rupture, which can activate his lower brain PANIC/GRIEF system. Tell him again that he is safe and loved and give him a cuddle. Keep doing this every time he gets out of bed.

If he gets distressed, this is not the right technique for him right now (bearing in mind those so vulnerable immature brain systems). Instead, you can sit by his bed until he feels safe enough to fall asleep.

Avoid sleep training that is based on a deal to leave the door open

This is the technique where you tell your child that if he gets out of bed to follow you, you will close the door – but if he stays in bed, you will leave the door open. This method works because it activates the FEAR system in the child's lower brain. The fear of the door being shut (and completely cutting off access to you) is so awful that the child stays in bed. But in using this method, we are back to those worrying levels of cortisol (see pages 40–41). For centuries, people have got children to behave by activating the brain's FEAR system. But studies show that repeated activation of this system in childhood can lead to anxiety disorders in later life.[26]

When it's time for your child to sleep on his own, use science to inform your methods

Studies with other mammals show that the acoustic presence of the mother (in other words, the sound of her voice) can effectively bring down stress chemical levels in a baby separated from its mother.[27] Give your child a recording of you saying something like, "Hi, little one, you are really safe. I love you very much." You could also make a recording of you

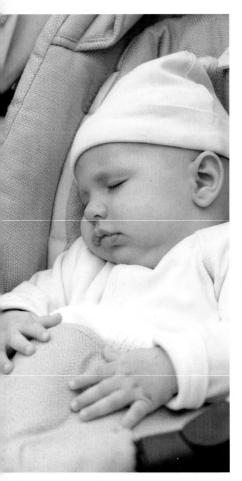

Daytime naps are important for babies and very young children, but it can also be very tempting to go on putting a child down for a sleep simply for your own benefit. There is no point in insisting your child has a nap if he has long outgrown the need. Children will catch up on sleep anywhere – on the sofa, in a pushchair, or in a car seat – if they are really tired.

telling one of his favourite stories. Then, if he gets into a state of painful opioid withdrawal in the night, he can just switch on the player by his bed.[28]

Give him something that smells of you

Your smell can also trigger powerful positive feelings in your child's brain. Give him something to hold in the night that smells of you – for example, a piece of your clothing. With a baby, placing a soft piece of cloth with the smell of your breast milk near him (but out of reach) can be highly effective in settling him down. This is because the olfactory bulb in the brain, which registers scent, is right next to the amygdala, the part of the brain that triggers strong emotional associations.

Create a cosy room space

We know that opioids can be activated in the brain when someone enters a familiar, cosy place. So make your child's bedroom a really special sanctuary where he loves to be. If your child is older, he can help you design it, choose the bedding, pillows, posters for the walls, and so on.

Massage, cuddly toys, and rewards are also effective

Research shows that preschool children who received massage before bed experienced less difficulty falling asleep and better sleep patterns.[29] Encourage your older child to have a cuddly toy. This may also activate comforting brain chemicals. Try a reward system: each time your child sleeps in his own bed the whole night through, he gets a sticker. Agree with him that a certain number of stickers means a little present or special treat.

Key points

- Most babies are terrible sleepers. Your parenting is not inadequate just because your baby won't settle at night.

- Co-sleeping is the norm in many parts of the world; fears about the level of risk appear to be unfounded, provided parents follow all the safety rules.

- Skin-to-skin contact and close physical proximity during the night can play a key role in maintaining the mental and physical health of your child, regulating his immature body and brain systems.

- Leaving a child to cry himself to sleep is putting him at risk of adverse changes to his immature brain systems.

- Sleep training doesn't have to involve tears. The gentle approach will work without having damaging long-term effects.

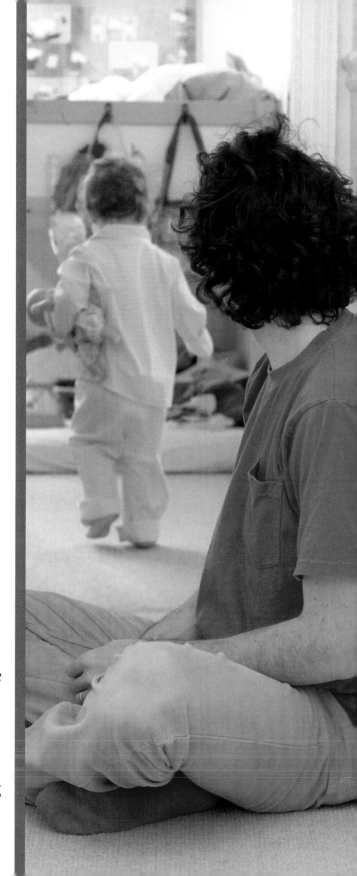

chemistry of
love & joy

This chapter shows you how to enable your child to grow up with a wonderful capacity for joy, and the ability to love in peace and not in torment. It looks at love, from the early love between parent and child to loving relationships in adult life. When we love deeply, we are also intensely alive. The reverse is true, too. If we cannot fully love, we cannot fully live. This section also explores the power of playful parenting and how you can help your child to develop a capacity for fun, humour, and spontaneity, as well as foster her ability to "fly" with others in life.

Powerful brain chemicals

Hormones and neurotransmitters are powerful chemicals produced in the body and brain that can make us feel wonderful or awful. We tend to think of hormones only in relation to our sexuality, but there are many different types that affect us in all manner of ways – influencing our feelings, perception, and behaviour.

CONSIDER THIS...

Touching base is when little kids run about happily then, all of a sudden, sit on Mum or Dad's lap or lean on them or touch them in some way. This can last a matter of seconds or minutes. Then off they go to run about happily again. This is called "emotional re-fuelling"[2] and it serves to create a lovely chemical balance in their brains. If your child is doing this with you, it's a real compliment – she is experiencing you as a source of natural brain opioids.

Hormonal heaven

Neuroscientist Candice Pert says, "Each of us has his or her own… finest drugstore available at the cheapest cost – to produce all the drugs we ever need to run our body and mind."[1] The natural hormones and neurochemicals that we have in our bodies and brains can not only make us feel just great, but also enable us to thrive. The problem is that because of too much relational stress in childhood, some people may never gain access to the finest chemicals in the "drugstore" of their minds.

When opioids and oxytocin are in dominance in the brain, the world feels like a warm, inviting place When they are strongly activated in combination, these neurochemicals can bring us the deepest sense of calm and contentment, with the capacity to take life's stresses in our stride. If you provide your child with lots of early experiences of loving calm, she will repeatedly experience oxytocin and opioids being in dominance in her brain. This will make her feel very calm, safe, and warm inside. She is likely to be better able to enjoy:

• the capacity to savour
• the capacity to linger in the moment
• the capacity to drift and let go.

Through experiencing these neurochemical states on a regular basis, your child will start to greet the world with interest and wonder, rather than with a sense of fear and threat. What's more, she will also be building up resilience to deal well with painful and stressful times in life, which no human being can avoid.[3]

Hormonal hell

If a child repeatedly feels fear and rage in childhood, say from a strict parenting style that regularly involves shouting at her, or lots of commands, criticisms, and angry facial expressions, it can block the release of opioids and oxytocin in her brain. Unrelieved by calmness, comfort, and warm physical affection, her body and brain can then become accustomed to high levels of the chemicals cortisol, adrenaline, and noradrenaline, which are pumped out by the adrenal glands in times of stress. This can make her feel threatened and unsafe at all times.[4]

When the hormone cortisol is activated in the brain and body at high levels for too long, the world can feel like a hostile, attacking place

High levels of cortisol can make us feel overwhelmed, fearful, and miserable, colouring our thoughts, feelings, and perceptions with a sense of threat or dread as if everything we need to do is far too hard.

Adrenaline and noradrenaline can also strongly affect our mood, both telling the heart to pump faster and harder, the liver to release glucose, the fat stores to release fat, and the muscles to mobilize energy stores. With optimal levels of these hormones, we can feel alert with clear thinking, but when strongly activated, just like cortisol, they can make us feel anxious or angry or both. We become intensely focused on a feeling of threat (real or imagined) and our bodies move into a state of hyperarousal, activating all manner of lower brain "fight" (aggression) or "flight or freeze" impulses (withdrawal and avoidance). Research shows that a child's early experiences of parenting are extremely influential in determining whether stress chemicals are strongly activated

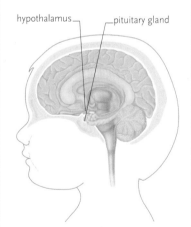

ANIMAL INSIGHTS

Research with other mammals has shown that:

• The more physical contact the mothers gave to their babies, the less fearful and more courageous their babies grew up to be, and this effect lasted a lifetime. Baby mammals who experienced lower levels of touch from their mothers showed more fearfulness in adulthood.

• The more physically demonstrative the mother, the more mentally healthy the infant in later life. In adulthood they became confident, attentive mothers with calmer infants.

• Babies who experienced more physical contact also aged better, with fewer degenerative changes in their brain; and they were less anxious when placed in a new environment, explored more, and coped well with stress.[9]

on a regular basis in later life.[6] If they are, they can leave her in a sort of hell on earth, in a persistent state of hyperarousal. She may feel threatened for much of the time. Tragically, this sense of being fundamentally unsafe in the world can eventually become her way of knowing herself and other people. As a result, your child may move into living her life in a chronic state of mistrust and take one of two fundamental positions: either "shrinking from life or doing battle with it".[7]

Warm physical contact

The problem is that you can't just inject children or adults with oxytocin, as it doesn't travel to the brain. And you can't give it orally as it just gets digested. These chemicals can only be highly activated in the human brain through warm human connection! In short, if we want children to grow up able to feel calm and safe in the world, and at ease with themselves and other people, we need to ensure that safe physical contact and physical comforting of distress is integral to their lives.[8]

Any form of warm physical contact between parent and child can have a positive effect

Cuddles and hugs, affectionate little squeezes, carrying your baby in a sling, baby massage (see page 47), and falling asleep in your arms can all have a wonderful effect on your child. All these "one-to-one" moments with a loving parent will activate opioids and oxytocin in your child's brain. When she is lying next to your calm body, your child is likely to have oxytocin and opioids cascading all over her brain. This will feel delicious and satisfying for both of you. For this to happen, it is important that you are in a calm state, as this is when opioids and oxytocin are in dominance in your brain. Monitor your mood, because lying next to your child when you are anxious or tense will release stress chemicals in her brain.

Don't forget to cuddle your over-fives as well as your little ones

The amazing brain effects of touch are just as powerful with older children. The oxytocin your child gets from the cuddles will keep the opioid bond with your child alive for far longer.[10] What's more, if you keep lots of lovely cuddles going right through childhood into adolescence (as long as the young person still wants them, of course), it can mean there is far less tension in your relationship when your children become teenagers (see also page 99).

" These wonderful emotion chemicals are nature's gifts to us. "
Professor Jaak Panksepp

" Please pick me up "

Only body-to-body contact releases wonderful stress-relieving chemicals. It is such a common sight to see a baby in a pushchair screaming in spite of all attempts at rocking and jiggling to soothe her. Once picked up, she often becomes quiet within seconds.

All about love

Each one of us has a genetically ingrained system in the brain that gives us the capacity to love – the CARE (attachment) system. But this system is "experience dependent", which means that how it will be expressed (or not) depends on the types of experiences we have, and, in particular, those we have in childhood.

CONSIDER THIS...

The ability to form loving relationships is often established very early in life. Your children will learn about love and kindness with others through your consistent example. In this picture, Camilla, aged four, is so tender towards her baby brother because her parents have loved her with tenderness.

There are two types of love

We can love in peace or in torment. Loving in peace means that you associate love with deep states of well-being. Loved ones bring security, comfort, and meaning to your life. You see your loved ones realistically and have a basic trust in them. Loving in torment can means peaks of excitement marred with jealousy, destructive rage, and fears of both dependency and abandonment. You can have a basic mistrust, which may lead to an impossible need for reassurance as well as clinging behaviour. Or you may destroy love or run away from it. Whether your child will love in peace or love in torment will be profoundly influenced by the way you love her now, and the brain chemistries and systems activated as a result.

In this chapter, I'll be looking at the science of love between parent and child and how it impacts on a child's ability to form rewarding relationships in later life. In the UK, almost two out of three marriages end in divorce and half of all couples who live together (unmarried) split up before a child's fifth birthday.[11] Half of all children will see their parents split by the time they are 16 years old.[12] This means millions of people know what it is like to love in torment and/ or suffer emotional starvation in their primary relationship. This chapter aims to help you ensure that your child does not suffer like this in her adult life. Her first experiences with you will have a dramatic influence on how the genetically ingrained systems for love and human warmth unfold.

The science and psychology of loving in peace

Whether it's a child with her parent, or a pair of adult partners, loving in peace means that for most of the time the other person gives you a profound sense of feeling safe in the world, a deep level of comfort, and real meaning and purpose. You trust that the person you love will not frighten or disrespect you, and when they hurt you or make you angry (as they inevitably will at times of misconnection), you know they will listen to your point of view, and be motivated to find a way to make up. When we love deeply we are also intensely alive. So what is happening in the brain that supports this fortunate way of being in the world, and what has parenting got to do with it?

Activation of the CARE (attachment) system

When parenting enables a child to love in peace it means that the CARE (attachment) system deep in the lower brain has been repeatedly and consistently activated. In addition, when the child has felt rage, fear, or distress her parents have helped her cope with these feelings; they have soothed, calmed and listened to her, not taken a "just get over it" attitude. The child then carries her parent around in her mind as a "secure base" and knows that whenever she is hurting, frightened, or unhappy, her parent will respond to her in a sensitive, attuned way. In addition, securely attached children trust that when they feel joyous, excited, or proud, their parents will always meet them in these high-energy states with appropriate words, energy, and tone of voice. In short, secure attachment is known as "meeting the child in pain and meeting the child in joy".[13]

Loving in peace activates cascades of exquisite well-being chemicals in the brain including opioids (see page 87). As I have described, it's when these cascades are triggered again and again that we feel warm, expansive, potent, and that all is

CONSIDER THIS...

If your child grows up able to love in peace, in later life she will be able to:

• choose partners well, by walking towards the people who are good for her and away from those who are not
• develop and sustain long-term, fulfilling intimate relationships
• have the vital resources for tenderness, kindness, compassion, and passion
• listen, soothe, and comfort and support the other emotionally
• spontaneously give of herself in the moment to the person she loves
• be loving and sexual at the same time
• feed an intimate relationship with compliments, appreciation, lovely surprises, and being generous in sharing her inner world of thoughts and feelings, even when this feels difficult.

"Loving in peace means that your moment-to-moment stream of consciousness, your thoughts and feelings, take you to a warm world inside your head."

well. This feeling is intensified if we are physically affectionate with our loved ones; touch in this context triggers oxytocin (see page 88), which sensitizes the opioid system. Oxytocin and opioids are anti-aggression, anti-anxiety chemicals, so when they are triggered, we do not feel anxious or worried and we do not feel angry. What's more, when they are activated in your child she'll also be building up resilience and the ability to deal with the inevitable painful and stressful times in her life.[14]

The chemistry of secure attachment enriches quality of life

Secure attachment can give your child:

• **A capacity for awe and wonder, and to savour and linger in the moment** Through experiencing neurochemical well-being states on a regular basis, your child will greet the world with interest and wonder, rather than with a sense of worry or threat. Activation of the CARE system within the context of the parent–child relationship enables us to enjoy states of awe and wonder, feel at ease and relaxed, and so re-fuel.

• **A capacity for tenderness and compassion** When the CARE system works in a well-coordinated way with the higher brain, we experience feelings of compassion and empathy, and carry out acts of generosity. With warm secure upbringings, some primates, like us, prioritize helping other animals in distress. Neuroscientist Jean Decety, for example, found that a carefree rat chose to prioritize releasing a trapped rat over eating a piece of chocolate (a favourite rat treat!). And even after the rat had helped his trapped mate to freedom, he shared the chocolate with him.[15]

• **Psychological strength** Scientists have found that psychological strength is opioid-mediated, too. Children who are securely attached benefit from resilience, which means that after a bad news shock for example, they can calm themselves down and think well (after the initial dysregulation, which derails anybody). Secure attachment

A capacity for awe is vital if we are to experience being transported from the ordinary and everyday into the exquisite and wondrous. It is also key to experiencing beauty in people, in music, in nature, in breath-taking human creations. Awe shows us what is possible... and so is the antidote to feelings of defeat or hopelessness.

"I love being with you"

How you love your child now, the emotional energies and qualities of that love, are directly transferable to your child's relationships with others. If you love in a spontaneously affectionate way, you will be empowering your child to be the same with others. If you delight in your child, and express that openly, she in turn will be able to delight in others. If you express your warmth through fun and play, she will be building up a vital life resource to be fun in her own relationships.

The strong loving-in-peace bond a child develops with her parent is directly related to having enough moments together that trigger the opioids, oxytocin, and prolactin in her brain. A parent who scoops up her child in loving arms when she cries and when she is joyful, throws her up in the air, and showers her with lovely tickles and "raspberries" on her tummy sets the scene for the formation of a deeply loving bond. These simple responses can strongly activate the bonding chemicals.

ANIMAL INSIGHTS

It doesn't matter if you are an otter, squirrel, big cat, or a human. As mammals we all have this wonderful brain opioid system. So we all have the capacity for a profound sense of well-being and contentment. There has been some ground-breaking research about the brain chemistries that trigger bonding behaviours. The research compared mammals who had little oxytocin activity in their brains with those who had a lot. The animals with weak firings of oxytocin in their brains didn't form close relationships and chose to live in isolation. After having sex, they left their mates.

The other mammals, who had a far stronger activation of oxytocin in their brains, had strong preferences for one partner. They also found social contact very rewarding and were far less aggressive. When oxytocin was pumped into the brains of the aggressive, isolated animals, there was a dramatic decrease in aggression.[19]

also means they have the capacity to seek help from another person, instead of turning to drugs, drink, food, cigarettes, or self-harm to calm themselves down.

• **Popularity and social confidence** Research shows that humans and animals prefer to spend more time in the presence of those with a strong activation of well-being chemicals. People who activate opioids in our own brains make us feel safe and warm – they make the sun shine.[16]

• **Better physical health** Your child is more likely to enjoy far better health as her immune system benefits too.[17]

The science and psychology of loving in torment

Loving in "torment" by contrast, whether in a parent–child or an adult relationship, is marred by fear and psychological pain. The systems triggered in this instance are: RAGE, FEAR, and PANIC/GRIEF (see page 29). As a result, you or your child may destroy the love you have, or run away from it. Neither you nor your child, or both, will have the skills or motivation to repair relationships and re-connect after the inevitable misconnections and hurt arising in any intimate relationship. Loving in torment means threats to leave, or leaving, and brings repeated stress-hormone-driven self states that lead to ill-health, unhappiness, and a shorter life.[18]

When a relationship with a parent leaves the child loving in torment, she is very vulnerable to loving in torment in her adult relationships, too. Your child may:

• **Only be able to sustain short-term** intimate relationships that break down after the honeymoon period.

• **Have a "love-and-run" approach** to relationships – she becomes close to someone quickly, and then quickly withdraws.

• **Be so needy and desperate for love** that it drives people away, including her own children.

• **Muddle love with issues of power and control**, or submission and dominance.

• **Find that her love can trigger fear** in another person, or she may stay in destructive relationships.
• **Not be able to love at all.**

Your parenting can affect how your child loves

How you love your child will dramatically influence whether she loves in peace or loves in torment in adulthood. Parent–child interactions have a long-term impact on the genetically ingrained systems in the lower brain: CARE (attachment), SEEKING, PLAY (loving in peace); or RAGE, FEAR, and PANIC/GRIEF (loving in torment). Of course, a child's love for a parent is not automatic – no parent can command love from their child.

" There are biological mechanisms behind the most sublime human behaviour. **"**
Antonio Damasio

BRAIN STORY

The CARE (attachment) system extends throughout the lower brain. The structures include:
• anterior cingulate gyrus
• parts of the hypothalamus
• ventral tegmental area (VTA).
Key chemicals in this system include opioids, released from many parts of the brain including the anterior cingulate, and prolactin and oxytocin, which are released from the pituitary gland.

When we feel passionate love, the VTA releases dopamine, stimulating a network of pathways in the lower brain and in the frontal lobes, and producing an effect like cocaine. Scientists think the VTA may activate the drive to express caring behaviour.

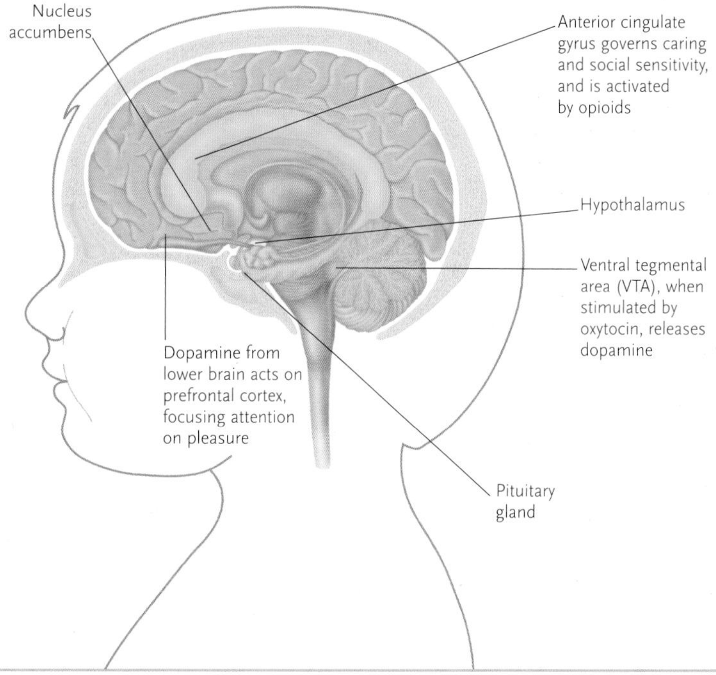

Nucleus accumbens

Anterior cingulate gyrus governs caring and social sensitivity, and is activated by opioids

Hypothalamus

Ventral tegmental area (VTA), when stimulated by oxytocin, releases dopamine

Dopamine from lower brain acts on prefrontal cortex, focusing attention on pleasure

Pituitary gland

Parenting for love in peace

So, how do you ensure your child loves in peace not torment? Some parents mistakenly think that to enable a child to become securely attached, you just need to love them. This isn't the case. Secure attachment means that the child feels secure in the adult's ability to provide attuned emotional responsiveness whenever they have an emotional need.

An affectionate relationship with a parent or carer, involving lots of cuddles and play, will strengthen the emotional bond between parent and child. The warm physical contact causes the release of oxytocin in the brain. This sensitizes the brain's opioid system, making the child feel calm and securely loved.

The science of attuned emotional responsiveness

Also known as maternal synchrony, attuned emotional responsiveness happens when parents read their baby's or child's signals accurately and empathically – they are "in tune" with them. Research shows that parent and infants influence one another with face-to-face interaction at intervals as small as a third of a second![20] A child experiences this as a deep enlivening connection with her parent.

In order to offer attuned emotional responsiveness you need to be self-aware and to always be thinking about how you come over to your child – remembering that she needs empathy. Are you being too rough, too intrusive, or too anxious? Is your voice too harsh, too irritated, or low-key in response to a child's moment of pride? Think about these factors whatever you are doing, for example when you change her nappy, dress her, or play with her. With an older child, think about how you discipline her, praise her, and help her with friendship problems. In those early years when a child has need after need after need, it's important to see this as attachment seeking (which requires emotional regulation) not attention seeking (which is sometimes punished).

The importance of relationship repair

Hearing all this can make parents feel guilty as it sounds a bit like they have to be superhuman in terms of sensitive awareness and empathy and doesn't take into account all the pressures of being a modern-day parent. So now the reassuring bit! American developmental psychologist Ed Tronick did some vital research asking a group of parents with securely attached children the key question: how often do they have to be attuned to their baby or child to have a securely attached child? He found that a third of the time these parents were beautifully attuned and a third of the time they were not attuned, but they repaired this by realizing they were mis-attuned (known as "interactive repair", see page 159). For the rest of the time they weren't tuning in well. However, the two-thirds was enough for the child to become securely attached and so to flourish in life in all the ways I have described.[21]

What's happening in the brains of parents who enable their children to be securely attached?

Research shows that if parents are able to offer secure attachment, reward systems are activated in the parts of their brain called the nucleus accumbens and the ventral tegmental area (see page 95). The child then picks up on how much she is delighting her parent and reward chemicals trigger in the same parts of her brain, too,[22] and so it becomes a mutually rewarding cycle.

Parents who enable their children to become securely attached are also able for much of the time to release optimal levels of the calming well-being chemicals, which in turn calms and regulates their children. The is also activation of the parts of their own brains associated with theory of mind, emotional regulation, and empathy (prefrontal cortex). In other words, we have the science to show that the parents are holding in mind the mind of their child.[23] In contrast, parents who frequently misattune have stress hormones in dominance when they are with their children.[24] This is particularly so with parents with too high levels of arousal (intrusive parents) or too low arousal (a depressed mother).

CONSIDER THIS...

A father and his son Eric, aged three, sat at a table in a restaurant. Eric merrily drives his toy train into his plate of spaghetti. His father raises his voice and speaks a little too sharply to say "no" to Eric. This frightens Eric, but he is securely attached, so he rushes round the table to his dad to seek comfort. Daddy apologizes and says, "I am sorry. I wanted you to stop putting your toy in your food, but I should not have told you in a voice that frightened you." Eric stops crying and sits down happily.

❝The theory of mind is the ability to attribute mental states —beliefs, intents, desires, pretending, knowledge – to oneself and others, and to understand that other people have different beliefs, desires, intentions, and perspectives to yours.❞

The role of playful parenting

There are some people on this earth who are just lovely to be around. Their vitality, expansiveness, and warmth are infectious and people light up in their presence. In comparison, others are somewhat squashed and contracted, living, for a lot of the time, within a narrow band of safe emotions. They can be very likeable, but you can never really go "flying" with them. You cannot experience shared moments of intense joy with them, moments that make you feel incredibly alive.

CONSIDER THIS...

Some parents fall in love with their baby as soon as she is born. For others, it takes a little longer, often because they don't believe a baby is all that interesting until she begins to talk. What they fail to realize is that young babies are capable of the most wonderful conversations (see page 110). And because parents aren't aware of this, their baby loses out on some wonderful early brain-sculpting opportunities.

The first love affair

It's a wonderful gift when you fall in love with your infant and even more amazing if she falls in love with you. In this section I look at how you can have the best chance of forming a deeply fulfilling relationship with your child. In the penultimate chapter, The best relationship with your child (see pages 242–59), I will show you activities that help you build and maintain your relationship through play. It is important, too, to know what to do if the emotionally attuned dance goes wrong; for this turn to pages 114–17.

Beginning at around two and a half months, when infants begin to engage strongly with their eyes, you may spend long periods locked in a mutual gaze with your new baby. Infants do not do this when looking at other objects; they love to look at faces. The delighted expression on your face "tells" your baby just how delightful she is.

These one-to-one times are also the very foundation stones for a child's self-esteem

Children lucky enough to have such beautiful intimate moments with a parent repeatedly in early life are rich indeed. The ability to "light you up" is the very basis of your baby's sense of herself as lovely and loveable, as fun to be with, and as capable of bringing joy to another. Children who miss out on these early intense, loving one-to-one times are likely to struggle far more with self-esteem in later life.

Falling in love with a parent is very important as this love is so often transferred to a love of life

Take four-year-old Emma, for example – she is, quite simply, in love with her Daddy. He has just put some new little pots of jam on the table for breakfast. Emma says with a genuine sense of exhilaration, "Wow, these are the best little pots of jam I have ever seen!". This response shows that Emma has already started transferring her love for her father to a love of life.

Keeping physical affection alive into middle childhood and through the teenage years

Any form of warm physical contact between a parent and child can strengthen the bond between them. Any "one-to-one" moments with a loving parent will activate well-being chemicals (see pages 86–89). Skin-to-skin contact is the most powerful bonding touch (see page 46).

In some families, unfortunately, there is a steep drop of cuddles and physical play after babyhood, and then another steep drop when children reach adolescence. Telling your child, for example, that she is "too big for cuddles now" is a grave mistake. Some children with this experience start to drift away from their parents, and the emotional bond weakens. Many such children reach a very defensive point, and on the few occasions that cuddles are offered by their parents, they are rejected – it's too little, too late. What's more, from touch-starved childhoods people can grow up with "troubled bodies". Self-harm, smoking, drinking, drug abuse, and bodily neglect can all be testimony to the lack of comforting through touch and physical parent–child play.[26]

Research shows that societies and families rich in warm physical affection have far fewer problems with anger and aggression, yet in some families there is a steep drop in cuddles and physically playful times after babyhood. This is followed by another steep drop after age five, and then another one when their children reach adolescence. There is a natural moving away from parents in adolescence, but this can start much earlier in parent–child relationships starved of physical affection.[25]

As we have explained, you can't just prescribe oxytocin. For children to grow up feeling calm and safe, and at ease with themselves and their bodies, parents need to ensure safe physical contact and physical comforting for every child.[27]

High-intensity moments

These are moments of real meeting between you and your child, and are key to your child feeling loved and loveable. High-intensity relational moments are times of very strong emotional connection without distraction, and without focusing on some third object, such as a TV or a computer game. For example, your child suddenly flings her arms around you and says "I love you, Mummy." You then pick her up in response, turn her upside down, and give her a delicious cuddle. She laughs and laughs with glee.

High-intensity moments involve lingering in the sheer intimacy of the moment. They involve reaching out to each other spontaneously. They are moments through which your child feels deeply met in her joy or in her pain. Such moments can become treasured memories in adulthood.

Children are great teachers of high-intensity relational moments, if we are open to learning

Children can teach us all about emotional connection or re-teach us about it if we have forgotten. Babies who have been on the receiving end of enough high-intensity relational moments soon become experts. Many babies are superb at intense gazing. They can have real "meetings" with strangers. For example, if you are in a café, a baby will often catch your eye and then you are both caught in a delicious intimate meeting across a crowded room. However, if your capacity for intimacy has been blighted or never properly developed in your own childhood, then babies cannot use you in this vital brain-sculpting way.

Some families are fertile grounds for positive high-intensity relational moments, others are not. Some families just get out

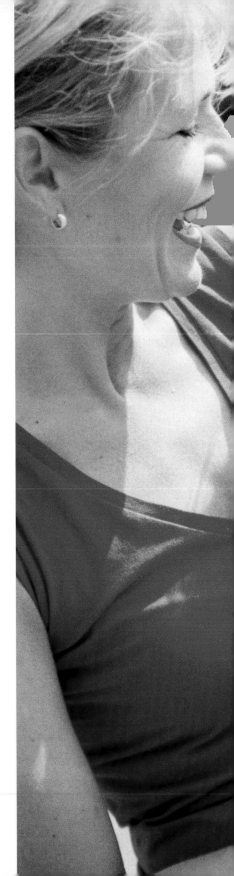

How many high-intensity positive relational moments are you having with your child?

You can monitor yourself by doing this assessment. Think of a day recently when you were with your child for several hours. Did any of the following occur?

• You spontaneously gave your child a cuddle, or some other physically affectionate gesture. She spontaneously gave you a cuddle or kiss and you met this with grace.

• You spontaneously told your child that she was good at something.

• You engaged in rough-and-tumble or gentle-and-tumble play (see page 106).

• Your eyes met for a while, with feelings of love or warmth, or you engaged in shared laughter.

• You shared moments of calm (for example, snuggled up together on the sofa, reading together).

• Your hellos and goodbyes were lovely moments of connection, rather than rushed non-events.

• Your child wanted to tell you something important, or simply wanted to chat to you, and you responded with really good, full-attention listening.

If some or most of the above are common occurrences, congratulate yourself. Your way of being with your child will be developing her capacity to love in peace. If they are not common occurrences, don't beat yourself up. See Looking after you (pages 260–85) for ways forward.

BRAIN STORY

High-intensity relational moments are likely to activate opioids in your child's brain. They may also activate dopamine, due to the novelty value of these events. Studies have found a link between psychological strength and the activation of brain opioids, while optimal levels of dopamine are vital for a child to feel intensely alive. What a combination: warmth, well-being, and life force!

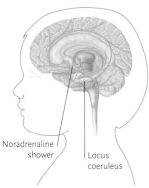

Noradrenaline shower | Locus coeruleus

The locus coeruleus (meaning "blue spot") is a structure deep in the brain stem that is strongly activated when something of significance is happening – a high-intensity relational moment. It then showers the brain with noradrenaline. When this happens, events, thoughts, and impressions are more likely to become fixed in the memory. These delightful memories will be important to your child. She will build a strong sense that she is fun to be with and that shared lovely moments with other people make her feel great.

of the habit of coming together to make something lovely happen. This can particularly be the case as children get older and the family home becomes simply a place of solo activities in different rooms. Sometimes it takes very little to change the culture for the better. When it feels stuck, try a period of parent–child counselling or family therapy.

Parent–child physical play is key to learning to love in peace

There is a PLAY system deep in the lower brain, and it's a great system! It's very powerful and plays a key role in your child's social and emotional intelligence and general mental health (see page 29). The brain's PLAY system is key for social joy. There are people who you can really "fly" with, experiencing precious shared moments of intense joy when you feel incredibly alive. By and large, the "flyer" is likely to have been parented in ways that have repeatedly activated his brain's PLAY system.

This system is not activated when playing with toys, but when a person is engaged in physical play with people – rough-and-tumble or gentle-and-tumble play – body against body (see page 106). The more you activate your child's PLAY system through joyous physical play interactions, the more her brain and bodily arousal system will be set up to bear intense states of social joy and excitement in later life. It doesn't happen automatically.

How the brain's PLAY system unfolds depends on the relationship experiences we have, particularly those in childhood. Many people can feel pleasure and enjoyment, but not intense joy or exhilaration because their PLAY system was not sufficiently activated in their adult–child relationships.

Activating joy

Joy is a bodily state. If we feel joy, this means that, alongside the activation of the brain's joy juice (opioids are some of the key chemicals, see pages 86–87), the autonomic nervous system, ANS (the body's arousal system, see page 44), has activated optimal levels of adrenaline, which surges around the body. This gives rise to that feeling you have when you laugh from the very pit of your stomach in states of shared fun or delight. We can feel this adrenaline boost as our heart rate goes up, we breathe faster, and our appetite is suppressed.

Dopamine and opioids in combination have to be activated at optimum levels in the brain if we are to feel joy. The repeated activation of these brain chemicals in childhood can enable your child to access many other wonderful human gifts – namely, to be spontaneous, to have the drive and hope to follow a dream, and to feel awe, wonder, and sheer delight in response to the beautiful and amazing things in the world. This particular brain chemistry also promotes resilience in the face of stress, which makes minor stressors feel manageable. This solid foundation is likely to make a child far more able throughout life to maintain, or quickly regain, a sense of hope, optimism, and a "yes-I-can" attitude to life.

There are good stress hormones, too

Interestingly, there are stress hormones triggered in the PLAY system, too, but not ones that cause cell death and other harmful activies (see pages 31–32). The "stress" of joy occurs because it is a high-arousal state, so a child needs parents who meet her in joy, in order to emotionally regulate her in that state. It's called "excitement regulation". The opioids of the PLAY system trigger dopamine (a reward chemical) so we feel intensely alive, wide-awake, and have masses of energy. Dopamine fuels curiosity, drive, and will, too (see Chemistry of drive & will, pages 126–43).

Think for a moment of people who have met you in joyous relational moments when you were a child. Think of those happy moments when for example your parents played games with you and laughed with you. These are all high-intensity moments of being deeply met in joy.

CONSIDER THIS...

Hellos and goodbyes can be high-intensity relational moments or weak or failed connections. They can speak so loudly to a child about how much he is loved. Was he missed? Are you delighted to see him? A key neuroscientist speaks at length about the possible adverse effect on brain and body systems of poor parental responsiveness during these reunion experiences.[28]

Do you have enough generosity of spirit, love, and spontaneity that next time you greet your child you can say hello with open arms and perhaps scoop him up in your arms, showing warmth and delight in your face?

Rough-and-tumble and other physical play, such as chasing and blowing raspberries, is appealing to children of all ages.

What is physical–social play?

This is play that involves rough-and-tumble or gentle-and-tumble. Physical–social play will influence your child's brain as it promotes bonding, happiness, and laughter, and many scientists say it also reduces depression.[29] For centuries people have known that play is essential for a child, but now we have some astounding brain science to back this up. Physical–social play:

• **Brings about brain growth and maturation** in the frontal lobes of the higher brain (involved in cognitive functioning, social intelligence, concentration, attention, and the ability to manage stress well).[30]

• **Allows us to stop, look, listen,** and feel the more subtle social pulse around us.

• **Activates anti-stress, health-promoting** mechanisms in the brain and body (the PLAY system).

• **Decreases impulsivity, overactivity** and attention deficit hyperactivity disorder (ADHD) type behaviour and increases the capacity for well-focused, goal-directed behaviour that may last a lifetime.

• **Develops brain capacities for emotional regulation** and natural, inhibition of primitive aggressive impulses (for example wanting to "hit" someone with words or fists).[31] Play-enriched animals show less aggression in adulthood than play-impoverished ones.

• **Reduces feelings of psychological pain** because of opioid release. If your child is missing someone or you have to work away for a while (which triggers painful opioid withdrawal in her brain), physical–social play can reduce the pain.

• **Helps the brain's PLAY system work** in a beautifully coordinated way with the frontal lobes.

Parent–child physical play even promotes growth factors in the higher human brain

We know from research with animals that physical play triggers brain-derived neurotrophic growth factor (BDNF), a brain "fertilizer", to be expressed in areas of the brain's frontal

"We have fantastic times together!"

Joy is the result of human connection. With high levels of bodily arousal, optimal levels of adrenaline rushing through the body, and optimal levels of dopamine and opioids cascading over the brain, we feel intensely alive, wide awake, and with masses of energy to do what we want to do. "When lots of dopamine synapses are firing, a person feels as if he or she can do anything."[32]

The difference between people who can let themselves experience excitement and those who seem to defend against it is a direct result of parenting. Parenting affects whether a child's brain and bodily arousal system will be set up to bear intense states of joy and excitement in later life.

BRAIN STORY

Physical interactive play increases the activation of a very important "fertilizer" in the higher brain (frontal lobes) called brain-derived neurotrophic factor (BDNF). This helps to programme the regions in the frontal lobes that are involved in emotional behaviour. Research shows that there is increased gene expression of BDNF in the frontal lobes after play.[33]

If you have lots of physical playtimes with your child, it's highly likely that you are enhancing the development of her higher human brain, with all its amazing functions, including better management of emotions and stress.

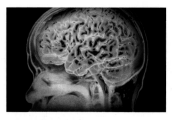

The emotion-regulating areas in the brain's frontal lobes (on the left in this scan) are stimulated by physical play.

lobes. BDNF is a protein that "fertilizes" the synapses (structures that permit a neuron, or nerve cell, to pass an electrical or chemical signal to another neuron), protects brain cells, and – in certain areas of the brain – regenerates brain cells, so aiding neuronal development.[34] BDNF also enhances the development of the noradrenaline and dopamine systems in the child's brain (systems vital for a child to be able to focus on learning). These systems are underdeveloped in many children diagnosed with attention deficit hyperactivity disorder (ADHD). Because of this, relational, or physical–social, play has been shown to be as effective for some children as low doses of the drug methylphenidate (brand name Ritalin), that may be prescribed for this condition[35] (see also pages 111–12).

Relational play can even bring about new brain growth in the hippocampus (see page 19). This part of the brain often shows signs of damage from stress in children who've had a hard life.[36] Longitudinal studies, carried out over a long period of time, with humans show that repeated positive feeling states are directly related to resilience to depression and anxiety in later life and lead to an increase in overall physical health and a decrease in mortality from all causes.[37] Relational play also has natural anti-stress effects, and because it strongly releases opioids it promotes powerful positive emotional states. Interactive play can enhance the emotion-regulating functions in the frontal lobes, helping children to manage their feelings better. Children in orphanages have been seen to make dramatic developmental progress after programmes of relational play.

Physical relational play can take the form of rough-and-tumble between an adult and child. It is boisterous play that can transport children into states of joy and often results in a child bursting into squeals of laughter or delight. You are engaging in this form of social play with your child when you spin her round or tickle her, for example. Face-to-face play that includes touching is also this sort of play, as are spontaneous, unpredictable, humorous moments with your baby, for example when you say, "Oops, I may have to eat your foot!" and then pretend to do it. Or you might pretend to be a postman and say to the child, "Ah, a parcel has arrived!" and then scoop her up and plonk her into another adult's lap.

Does child-to-child physical play have the same effect as adult to child?

All the above can happen with child-to-child physical play, but I would argue it's all the more powerful in the context of an attachment relationship with an emotionally regulating adult. Child-to-child rough-and-tumble or gentle-and-tumble play involves all manner of delightful rolling around on the floor, toppling over each other, and play-fighting. It is so physically free that it can sometimes tip into hurting if an adult is not there to keep watch. So physical play with you is arguably far preferable because your adult responses, with your more advanced frontal lobe functions, will be more attuning than those of a child. Also, the play will be sustained for longer without interruption.

"Can a fully social brain emerge without play or will it remain socially stunted for life?"
Professor Jaak Panksepp

"I am having so much fun!"

Rolling around on the floor laughing together can transport your child into incredible states of joy that she may remember when she is an adult.

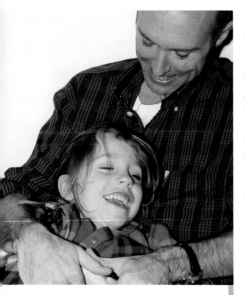

CONSIDER THIS...

Intense feelings of joy produce lovely chemicals in the brain but also high levels of bodily arousal and the activation of stress chemicals. So an essential parenting function is to help your child to handle "the stress of joy", so that she does not feel overwhelmed by it. You will be doing this every time you meet your child's joyful energy with your own joyful energy. So if your child runs up to you in a state of true delight with a picture she has drawn, or when she is exhilarated when on the trampoline, try to match her delight with your own facial expression, tone of voice, posture, and movement. If you are engaged in joyful play with your child and then have to stop abruptly to answer the phone, her joy levels may plummet. Her level of bodily arousal may be just too intense for her to cope with alone, which can lead to tears and upset.[14]

Physical relational play with you is key to your child's self-esteem

Just as with babies, the ability to share frequent joyful times with you ensures your child's sense of herself as a loveable, endearing, and capable of bringing joy. The playful times between the two of you are moments of real meeting – they are moments of intense energetic charge. You reach out to each other, spontaneously, freely, and with love and delight.

When your two-year-old little girl suddenly flings her arms around you and says "Come play, Mummy", you might rugby tackle her on the sofa while she laughs and laughs in response. These moments will form very important memories that convey vital psychological meanings about self. Your reactions tell her that she is fun to be with; someone who is delighted in; and deeply loved.

What's more, the locus coeruleus in the brain stem is activated when something of significance happens to a child, and showers the brain with noradrenaline (see page 102). The fact that strong activation of noradrenaline means new memories are likely to be laid down, is probably why such memories are held so dear by so many adults who have been fortunate to experience them.

What happens if children don't get enough rough-and-tumble play?

We ignore play at our peril. Research shows that if children don't get enough socially interactive play, they will make up for lost time and play harder, often at all the wrong times[38] – their play impulse comes out inappropriately. This happens with some children labelled as having ADHD (see page 111). One study found that children deprived of playtime at school developed ADHD symptoms and could not sit still and focus in class.[39]

How often does your child need physical play?

Brain scientists studying play estimate that infants need about an hour a day of relational play with you or another

"This is good for my brain!"

It seems hard to believe, but tumbling on the grass with a friend is essential for healthy brain development. Not only is this type of play an outlet for primitive motoric impulses, such as the urge to run and climb, but it also enhances higher brain development. In later life, these boys may be better able to manage their emotions and cope with stress as a result.

child or adult. This can be broken up into several sessions that make up an hour of course, perhaps one before breakfast, one at nursery or school pick-up time, some in the evening, and maybe one before bed.[40]

It would be so good to have more nurseries that actively support relational play, providing rough-and-tumble and gentle-and-tumble play sessions as well as toys to play with. Another good idea would be play sanctuaries in the community. Parents who never experienced relational play with their own parents could also sit and watch other parents in relational play with their infants.

"Children deprived of playtime at school developed ADHD symptoms."

> **"** The first six months can be one of the most sociable times of a child's life. **"**

"Joy juice" for babies

Some people are of the opinion that babies can't enter into any real dialogue until they can walk and talk, yet the first six months can be one of the most sociable times of a child's life.[41] During these early months, babies are usually far more interested in faces than toys and you can have a fabulous conversation with your baby from about three months onwards, using sounds, words, and a variety of facial expressions and movements.

Sadly, some parents miss out on these vital face-to-face communication times in the first year of their child's life. As a result, the child misses out on early vital brain development time and the regular activation of "joy juice".[42] So the next time you and your baby are enjoying time with an adult

" I love talking to you! **"**

John holds three-month-old Mabel a short distance from his face and starts a one-to-one conversation. Babies are wired to respond to familiar faces from day one.

Babies respond to communication much more slowly than an adult or child, so John is patient while Mabel works up her response.

It may be a smile, a copycat expression, a wave, or a little whoop of delight. Then Mabel pauses and waits for John to reply to her.

The joy juices in Mabel's brain are fully activated and vital brain connections are being forged. This is baby play at its finest.

friend, remember to talk to your young baby, too! Your baby will enjoy "joining in" with the laughter and conversation.

One-to-one conversations with a baby have a pattern that is somewhat different to adult conversations. Pick a time when your baby is wide awake and not hungry. Make eye contact, and give her time to respond (see opposite). Be sensitive to her cues. She will find the communication very stimulating, and will need lots of breaks. All babies need to look away from time to time, and when she is ready, she will look back.

Infant researcher Beatrice Beebe found that some parents did not read these "let's have a break" cues and tried to keep their baby looking at them and engaging with them. The babies began to "chase and dodge", moving their heads from side to side and finally breaking contact by becoming still and staring into space. This not only switches off the positive chemicals that have been activated in their brain, but also switches on high levels of stress chemicals.[43]

Moments of physical–social play in the evening after school can be a special time for both of you. They not only strengthen the bond between you, but they also provide amazing feelings of intense energetic charge.

Hyperactivity – or not enough play?

Children with attention deficit hyperactivity disorder (ADHD) have symptoms of hyperactivity, impulsiveness, and poor attention. They find it hard to concentrate, to keep their minds on tasks, to follow instructions, to organize anything, and to listen. They often run about and climb on things inappropriately as if driven by a motor. They are easily bored, and become extremely frustrated if they can't manage a learning task. They frequently fidget and squirm about, and may lash out impulsively at other children. A child with ADHD can talk excessively at you, and find it very hard to wait her turn – interrupting, intruding, and being disruptive.

In ADHD, one major problem is that the frontal lobes are not yet fully "on-line". As we have seen, interactive play can develop a child's frontal lobes, which helps an ADHD child to naturally inhibit her primitive "motoric impulses" and better manage stressful situations.[44]

Why drugs may not be the answer

Some people, unaware that interactive play can develop the regulating functions in the frontal lobes, think that the only answer to ADHD is drug treatment with methylphenidate (brand name Ritalin), which is an amphetamine, like cocaine. Methylphenidate has common side effects including headache, nausea, insomnia, and loss of appetite. Parents often report that children on Ritalin seem to lose their fun, sparkle, and ability to play. The result of stopping the drug can be a "rebound effect", which includes agitation, depression, and exhaustion. What's more, research shows that when this drug was given to pre-pubescent mammals, they had life-long reductions in dopamine activity because the drug puts a great deal of strain on the brain's dopamine system. Parkinson's disease results from a reduction in the brain's dopamine levels, although we do not yet know whether pre-pubescent children taking methylphenidate are at particlar risk of Parkinson's disease. [45]

Research with mammals shows that interactive play can be as effective as mild doses of methylphenidate.[46] Many children also stop being hyperactive if they take fish oil rather than drugs. Fish oil can increase serotonin levels, which naturally inhibits impulsiveness.

Play well and live life well

The activation of the brain's PLAY system is key to living life well. When this system is optimally activated in childhood, it is likely to set vital foundations for the ability in later life to bring fun and a sense of play into relationships. The "play urge" can be channelled into vital social capacities.

In adulthood, when the PLAY system works in combination with the higher verbal brain it is likely to result in new forms of play, such as humour and the play of ideas, a kind of "playground in the mind". Humour is a vital capacity for mental health in the face of adversity.

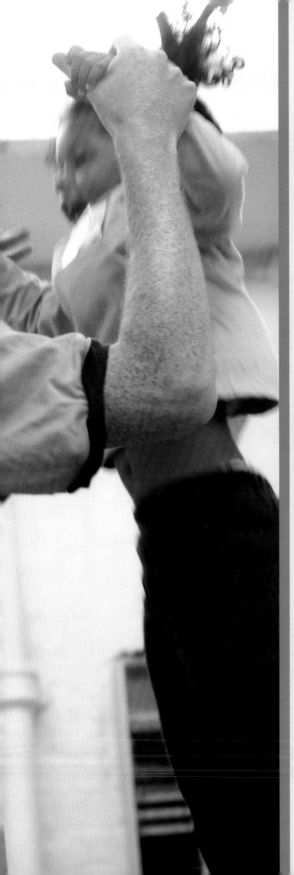

Q But I've never been very good at play – how do I start?

If you find it difficult to play with your child, the first thing is to stop giving yourself a hard time – it doesn't come naturally to everyone. One possible reason is that in your own childhood you may never have been on the receiving end of high-quality one-to-one parent–child play.

Here are some ideas for playing with a child under five. Sit on the floor opposite your child. If you feel uncomfortable, get some props to help you. For example, start by blowing bubbles, or taking turns to throw a bag of feathers in the air to see who can catch them before they fall. Have a mutual face-painting session. It's vital to keep your voice light and fun. If it all gets too serious, your child is not going to want to play with you. (See also The best relationship with your child, pages 242–59.)

Although play is a genetically ingrained impulse, it requires the right environment for expression, which means your child has to feel psychologically very safe with you. Once you have managed to activate the PLAY system in your child's brain, her squeals of delight will soon be so reinforcing that you will both want more playtimes like this.

If play remains awkward for you, make sure there are some people in your child's life (including other children) who can give her social play for about an hour a day.

When you are not in tune

What happens when the emotionally attuned dance you strive for goes wrong? From the start, it's important to say that there is no such thing as a mother or father who is perfectly attuned at all times. As already discussed, research by American psychiatrist Ed Tronick and, child psychoanalyst, Donald Winnicott has also confimed that "There is no such thing as a perfect parent".

CONSIDER THIS...

Children love toys and gadgets with lots of functions. If you press this button, it makes a noise. They particularly like to turn up the volume. If your child is able to make you shout and scream, you become the perfect toy! But if you give your child a positive relational moment instead, the activation of opioids in her brain will outweigh the quick adrenaline fix she gets from winding you up.

Life can get in the way

The reality of life is that parents, or parents-to-be, can sometimes be confronted by dreadful, shocking life events, and it is totally understandable that if this happens it can adversely affect any sense of joyful parenting for a while. If your life circumstances are truly awful it is likely that the FEAR and PANIC/GRIEF systems in your lower brain will keep triggering. This means high levels of stress hormones block the opioid-mediated feelings towards your child (from your CARE and PLAY brain systems). So on many occasions with your child, you just don't feel warm, loving, empathic, or playful. What's more, if you are suffering from shock, you are likely to be desperately trying to regulate your own intense states of anxiety, anger, and grief with the result that you just can't be there consistently in an emotionally attuned way for your child. All your efforts are going towards trying to emotionally regulate yourself. It is nobody's fault. It's just how it is. When you are suffering from pre- or postnatal depression all of the above applies, too. It's a brain biochemical reality. You can't just "pull yourself together": you need help.

How you were parented can affect the "dance"

At other times, the dance goes wrong because the way you were parented gets in the way of your parenting now. Often parents are determined not to repeat the ways they were parented, but this can mean swinging to an opposite extreme.

If your parent was too strict, you may end up being too lenient, and vice versa – if your parent was too lenient you may be too controlling. At other times, it is so easy to follow what your parents did and when the dance goes wrong, this often means being too emotionally distant or too intrusive.

So what can you do?

First, acknowledge that you might not be "in tune" for any of the reasons suggested that are not your fault. Ask yourself:
• **Do I feel like withdrawing** when my child is in distress rather than comforting her?
• **Do I feel that the time I spend** with my child is increasingly stressful and unrewarding for me, so I withdraw or do the opposite – get irritated or angry too often?
• **Do I try desperately** to get my baby/child to relate to me, but she doesn't seem to want to?
• **Does my baby/child actively avoid** eye contact?
• **Does my child never bring me** her worries or problems?
• **Would my child rather relate** to another member of the family than me? Does she actively avoid me – does she prefer her computer or tablet to time with me?

The intrusive dance and how to recognize it

Intrusive parenting often means not reading a child's emotional cues and imposing your needs on her instead. With babies this can be seen in such things as over-wiping (at mealtimes) or over-cleaning her or picking her up just when she has settled. It can also mean over-directing your baby or child using lots of commands such as: "do this", "sit here", "play with this", "no don't play with that", and so on. This is often referred to as "forceful guidance". Intrusive parenting can also mean lecturing a child more than listening to her. Sometimes parents do not have the space in their minds to realize when they're being too anxious, intrusive, needy, or bossy with their child, or to be able to feel and think about what their child is feeling or needing. Some parents "need"

Some parents are great at doing exciting activities with their children, vital for developing the brain's SEEKING system (see Chemistry of drive and will, pages 126–43), but they are not so great at helping them with their painful feelings. Interesting activities activate dopamine, not opioids, in the brain, and science points to the fact that dopamine is not key to social bonding. So being good at activities as a parent, but without the ability to be emotionally responsive to your child's painful feelings is unlikely to strengthen the love bond between you.

" Brain oxytocin, opoiods, and prolactic systems appear to be the key partcipants in the subtle feelings that we humans call acceptance, nurturance, love, and warmth. "

Professor Jaak Panksepp

their child to respond to them instead of the other way round, as a result of unmet emotional needs in their own childhoods.
• **How does intrusive parenting affect parents' and children's brains?** There's a greater activation of the parent's amygdala leading to over-arousal, which can trigger anxiety in relating to their child. The child can pick up on this and withdraw. Stress systems are activated in both the parent's and the infant's brains when they are together. There's an increase of cortisol in infants and children. High levels of cortisol levels in a baby can lead to more intrusive interactions from the mother. Without infant face cues, dopamine and oxytocin levels in the parent's brain decrease, which can cause a baby to avoid eye contact.[47]

The depressed or emotionally withdrawn dance

With this type of parenting there are few positive interactions between parent and child. The voices of mildly depressed mothers tend to be flat. Parents talk less with their infants, and are less playful and nurturing.[48] Babies are lethargic with signs of distress and self-comforting behaviour. Depressed parents can be more hostile, punishing, and intrusive when interacting with their infants and don't respond to their cues.[49]

When babies and children are not able to connect with their parent in a meaningful way, they can just give up trying. For some children, this starts a long slow journey of "self-help", which can continue right into the teenage years.
• **What happens in the parent's brain** Brain scans of depressed mothers show a relatively unresponsive prefrontal cortex when their baby cries. When they see positive images of their baby there is reduced amygdala activation – so less emotional arousal at seeing their baby.[50] Poor stress-regulating systems in the brain show that affected parents find it difficult to manage their own stress, so they over- or under-react when their baby is distressed.[51] Mothers suffering from post-traumatic stress have an aroused FEAR system so they tend to withdraw from a distressed baby, so becoming less "available".[52]

• **What's happening in the child's brain** Babies are acutely aware of their mother's distress and stress, particularly in her voice and face, and pick up on atmospheres in milliseconds. Changes in the child's physiology, heart rate, vagal tone (see page 45), and cortisol levels adversely affect her sleep, eating, toileting and even her immune system.[53] The part of the infant's brain responsible for approach emotions (the desire to make contact and move towards another person) is not activated in 11–17-month-old children in playful interactions with their depressed mothers, so they are less likely to seek out their attention. Researchers found that when mothers were asked to look blankly at infants, the children were disturbed by the expressionless face and their stress levels rocketed.[54] A child's brain can still show higher cortisol levels at age four to seven, which can result in a greater risk of mental health problems later.[55] The lack of emotionally engaged interactions with a mother in particular in the early months of life can still show up as high levels of cortisol in teenagers. In some instances, this contributes to lower social competence and more mental health problems. Children of postnatally depressed mothers are also far more likely to suffer from depression.[56]

How to correct the "dance"

It's never too late to change your negative biochemical systems through good therapy or counselling because an adult's frontal lobes and stress regulatory systems have the ability to change just like a child's. Counselling is a gift for your child, and you will have someone who can attune to you and emotionally regulate you and can help you process and work through painful experiences. Research shows that when parents get help, and improve within three months, the outcome is so good for their children.[57] In the meantime another family member can provide secure attachment. As long as your child has a person in her life with whom she can have a secure attachment she can be emotionally well. This person needs to be someone your child sees very regularly.

CONSIDER THIS...

My child loves his nanny more than he loves me. Opioid activation in the brain dictates the strength of an emotional bond between a parent and child. An emotionally inhibited parent cannot compete with a very warm, physically affectionate nanny who consistently scoops up the child in her loving arms when he cries (so deeply meeting him when in pain) and throws him in the air, spinning him round and round, showering him with lovely tickles (in shared joy states). But if you have a nanny like this, what a gift for your child in terms of engendering his future emotional health and repeatedly activating the CARE and PLAY system in his brain.

Dealing with broken hearts

What happens when a child suffers pain because of a family break-up or bereavement, or feels he has lost a parent to depression, to drugs or drink, to long-term illness, or to a new baby? This section is about meeting a child's grief or pain in love, and helping to restore well-being.

CONSIDER THIS...

Professor Jaak Panksepp compares the grief of losing a person, or someone's love, to the pain of coming off heroin (which taps into the brain's opioid system artificially).

Coming off heroin
- Psychic pain
- Crying
- Loss of appetite
- Despondency
- Sleeplessness
- Aggressiveness

Coming off a person
- Loneliness
- Crying
- Loss of appetite
- Depression
- Sleeplessness
- Irritability

As we have seen in previous chapters, the opioids that are triggered by being with people we love can make us feel that everything is well with our world. And when we lose that love, or feel that our love is threatened in some way, that feeling of well-being is completely gone.

So let's look at what is happening in a grieving child's brain

Grief can result in the withdrawal of opioids in key parts of the brain, along with reduced levels of other bonding chemicals – oxytocin and prolactin. This causes a marked increase in negative feelings as well as a reduction in positive feelings.[58] When these bonding chemicals are being optimally activated in the brain, they can naturally diminish our anxieties, fear, and stress responses. But when opioids are withdrawn, fear and stress are no longer regulated in the same way and can return with a vengeance.

In a child with a broken heart, the PANIC/GRIEF system in the lower, or mammalian, brain is strongly activated (see page 31). This is a system of separation, distress, desolation, and loneliness, which activates pain centres in the brain. Key to the PANIC/GRIEF system is a chemical called glutamate, which plays a vital role in our capacity to form thoughts. Grief can activate overly high levels of glutamate. This can both dramatically increase crying and block you from feeling any of the comforting effects of things such as music and the company of friends.[59]

We know about the pain of broken hearts in childhood from observations of orphaned primates such as chimpanzees, who can die from grief just weeks after losing their mother.[60] They are perfectly capable of physical survival, but their grief is too awful to bear. After the genocide in Rwanda, many children who had seen their parents killed also gave up and died.[61]

Love can be made angry

We often hear in the news about "love made angry", and when we look closer at the brain chemistry of broken hearts, this is not at all surprising. We have already seen that grief leads

> " Grief can result in the withdrawal of opioids in key parts of the brain. "

> " My world is broken "

A child does not have to experience the loss of a parent through death or divorce to suffer pain. A parent who is physically present but unable to show enough love can break a child's heart, too. On–off parental love (loving one minute, emotionally distant the next) means a rollercoaster for the child in terms of activation of opioids in his brain. He can be locked into a cycle of strong opioid activation followed by extremely painful opioid withdrawal. This cycle awakens an intensity of yearning in a child and often sets up an addiction to that parent. This can lead to loving in torment in later life.[62]

"It is all too easy for society to start to hate children who are locked in anger from a broken heart."

to opioid withdrawal. As opioid systems are involved in the regulation of emotional states, opioid withdrawal means we can feel angry and anxious without being able to regulate our feelings properly. Opioids and oxytocin are also powerful anti-aggression molecules, so their withdrawal can lead to even more anger. In addition, pain in love activates:

• **CRF (corticotrophin-releasing factor)** High levels of this stress chemical can block the release of positive arousal chemicals – dopamine, serotonin, and noradrenaline. A reduction in levels of these chemicals can trigger impulsive outbursts of irritation, anger, or rage.

• **Acetylcholine** When opioids are withdrawn, what are known as "opponent forces" are released in the brain. These forces involve the release of high levels of a chemical called acetylcholine. Acetylcholine at optimal levels helps us concentrate and feel alert, but at high levels it makes people angry, hostile, or frequently irritated.

"I want my Dad back"

When a compassionate teacher takes the time to listen and to help a grieving child, it can make all the difference between him thriving and failing to thrive. Sometimes it is easier for a child to talk to a teacher or counsellor than to a parent, because of fears that "it will only upset Mummy if I talk about Daddy leaving".

Many children with broken hearts behave in angry, aggressive ways because of their changed brain chemistry

Tragically, it's all too easy for society to start to hate children who are locked in anger from a broken heart, and want to exclude them – from schools or from the wider world in general. Such children need help, not punishment. Hopefully, increasing public knowledge of the dramatic changes in the brain that result from the loss of a beloved parent, or from the loss of their love, will help to improve levels of compassion in society. It may also help to motivate governmental bodies to offer far more counselling and therapy resources for children and young people.

Children with broken hearts don't need to grow up into angry or violent adults

If a grieving child has someone in her life who can recognize her pain (even when she's very skilled at disguising it) and offer her comfort, she has every chance of becoming an emotionally stable adult. The awful brain chemistry that can set a child on the road to hostility or real violence in later life doesn't need to happen. The physical comforting of grief will release opioids and oxytocin, deactivating the toxic chemistry in the brain that causes the damage.

This is why it is vital for children who are suffering from the pain of loss (even if on the surface they look just fine) to receive loving attention. Schools, in particular, need to be aware of children who have lost a parent or who they think may be loving in torment at home. Help at the right time for such children can often stop years of misery.

If a child moves into "love made angry" or gets stuck in grief, there can be serious consequences in terms of long-term behaviour problems and learning difficulties. More than 75 percent of people in prison have suffered the pain of broken relationships in childhood.

Sibling arrival

To watch an older child with a new baby can be to witness that child's agony at seeing what was once given to her now going to her sibling. The pain of the arrival of a sibling, with all its accompanying confusions, should never be underestimated. That feeling of well-being can be completely lost, fuelled by the insidious belief that "I'm not as lovable to my Mummy as my little sister".

CONSIDER THIS...

When the excitement and novelty of a new brother or sister begin to fade, painful emotions may begin to surface in the older child, such as:

- Feeling that she is on the outside of a couple (mother and new baby)
- feeling that she is the unfavoured one
- Feeling unworthy of her mother's love in direct comparison with her rival
- Feeling invisible
- Feeling that there is not enough love to go round
- Feeling that "my place in my mother's mind feels all too precarious. My connection with her is far too fragile."

Sibling arrival can encompass a multitude of feelings in a child, not least the pain of watching the love-duet of her mother with a rival who has equal claim on her affection. Weininger, a psychotherapist, describes the very essence of this pain in love: "There are two people who have what I want and they are giving it to each other and not to me".[63] Brain scans confirm that feeling on the "outside" can activate pain centres in the brain.[64] The aggressive behaviour and impulsivity that comes from sibling pain in love is often due to opioid withdrawal in the brain from this perceived outsider status, the blocking of vital mood-stabilizing systems, and increases in other brain chemicals (see pages 118–19). Hence the occurrence of all sorts of problem behaviour in an older sibling after the birth of a new baby. This can range from regression, renewed bedwetting, anxiety problems, and aggression to failing to thrive in school with friendships or with learning.

Helping your older child

Your child is not going to walk up to you and say, "I think you prefer my brother to me, and that is making me feel so hurt inside." Instead, children's language of feeling is their behaviour.[65] So a child may show you her pain by hurting her sibling or being defiant or moody.

To help your child, watch her carefully and be acutely vigilant to the times when she is watching you have a

"Why does he hate me?**"**

It is vital that parents take sibling rivalry seriously. Potential risks to the development of a twin's or sibling's brain are very real if he has to cope with unexplained hatred whenever his parents' backs are turned. The human brain is designed to be highly adaptive to the environment, particularly in the first years of life, when rapid moulding is going on. The brain of a frequently attacked sibling can all too easily start to adapt itself to survive in a bullying world (see page 165).

delightful encounter with your other child. If the pain of sibling arrival is expressed as fighting, talk to your child. If she finds this difficult, you might like to have a family of puppets at home to help with "describing" difficult feelings.

Here's an example of a mother finding a way to talk to her child about her sibling pain. This mother used hand puppets to stop Laura from being horrid to her baby brother, Georgie. She asked Laura if she would like to do a puppet game and to choose a puppet. Laura chose a seal for herself and a brown bear for her Mum. Mum asked her to do a "thumbs up" if the seal got what Laura was feeling right and "thumbs down" if it was wrong. Mum had a puppet on each hand and conducted the conversation. She used the seal to say, "Hey, Brown Bear, it was so much better before baby Georgie came along. I had

" Be vigilant when one child is watching you have a delightful encounter with your other child. **"**

you all to myself. Now Georgie is here, it's like I've got this pain in my heart." Laura put a thumb up in a very definite way. The Brown Bear spoke back, "I am so sorry to hear that you have so much pain in your heart, Little Seal. How brave you are to let me know all this. But you are my very special seal and baby Georgie can never take the special place in my heart that is just for you. I love you so very much, and am so sorry if I forget sometimes to show you that I do." The bear gave the seal a big cuddle and kissed her on the nose.

Empathy like this is likely to activate opioids in a child's brain, making her feel deeply secure. As a result, Laura no longer has that impulse to be aggressive towards her brother.

It's never too late to fall in love with your child

It is a myth that parents love their children equally. They love each of them with different intensities and in different ways. If you find you give more love to one child, actively do things to reconnect to the other child in a special way. Timetable in quality one-to-one times with each one each week, such as lovely child-led play or a visit to the park or to the zoo.

Sometimes it's hard to love a child. You may be in a negative lock – meeting in anger or seeing your child as the enemy. Perhaps you were the unfavoured child in your family, and so you are unconsciously repeating this with one of your children now. If this is the case, you need compassion, not criticism. If those bonding brain chemicals are not strongly activated when you are with your child, you won't feel loving towards her. The first step is to understand what might be blocking the CARE (attachment) system in your lower brain. If you think your childhood is affecting your ability to love, consider seeking parent–child therapy and/or counselling for yourself (see also Looking after you, pages 260–85, for ways forward). Remember, you can fall in love with your child at any time, even if you've had a rocky start.

Key points

• To love in peace throughout life, children need to feel safe in their parents' unconditional love.

• If children love in torment, it can have enduring effects on their ability to have lasting relationships.

• One-to-ones and high-intensity moments with you are the foundation stones of your child's self-esteem.

• Learn to recognize when emotional attunement goes wrong, and needs to be repaired – know when to say sorry.

• Taking time to understand your child's painful feelings will deepen the emotional bond between you and your child.

• Children with broken hearts need compassion and understanding to restore their positive brain chemistry.

chemistry
of drive
& will

This chapter focuses on the SEEKING system in your child's lower, or mammalian, brain. This is the system responsible for your child's urge to go enthusiastically into the world, both now and in the future. Again, as a parent, you can have a vital impact on this system. The SEEKING system needs to be optimally activated in your child's brain if he is to find the drive and will in later life to do what he wants to do, and to know long-term, profound satisfaction in his work, life, and the interests he is passionate about.

The SEEKING system

The lower, or mammalian, brain contains a SEEKING system, one of the seven genetically ingrained systems, which, when working well, is a super-efficient "get-up-and-go-get-it system".[1] It can activate the energy to explore the new, and an eagerness to seek out what the world has to offer. It stimulates curiosity, intense interest in something, and the sustained motivation to achieve our goals.

Your child's interest and curiosity about the world will come from you. Encouraging him to explore and experiment from an early age will serve him well into adulthood. The SEEKING system "coaxes animals and humans to move energetically from where they are presently situated to the places where they can find and consume the fruits of the world".[2]

If your child is going to make his dreams and ambitions come true and find the fortitude and staying power to fulfil his goals he needs these vital skills. It is no surprise that top of the Harvard Business Review's list of vital qualities for business success is "a high level of drive and energy".

People have the capacity to be breathtakingly creative

All mammals have a SEEKING system, and if they are emotionally healthy, they can enjoy an energized engagement in life, explorative urges, curiosity, and the desire to venture into the world. Humans differ from other mammals in that the frontal lobes of our higher brain, when working in a beautifully coordinated way with the SEEKING system, enable us to find the drive to be incredibly creative and enjoy truly meaningful long-term satisfactions. It's this creative union between the lower and higher human brain that is responsible for many activities; from a child's desire to build a magnificent sandcastle, to an adult turning a seed of an idea discussed in a restaurant into a successful business that touches many people's lives.

Optimally activated in childhood, the SEEKING system dramatically increases an adult's chances of being able to:

• **Follow through his dreams** and seeds of ideas so they become a reality.

- **Pursue a goal** in the service of something far greater than merely gain for himself.
- **Feel deeply satisfied** from using his talents and abilities well and knowing he's made a truly positive impact on the world.
- **Produce ideas,** and have the drive and motivation to go after them. If these ideas involve others, he'll have the social skills for successful joint creative ventures.

"Everyone looks for that sparkle" in friends and lovers to "make things happen". Most of all, everybody is looking for energy within themselves: the motivation and energy to do something, and the endurance, stamina, and resolve to carry it through.[3]

Dopamine is the big "light-switch"

There are many chemicals involved in the SEEKING system, but dopamine (see page 95) is the one that turns things on. It cascades from the nucleus accumbens all over the frontal lobes, quite literally fuelling exciting ideas, curiosity, drive, and will. As a result, the SEEKING system is especially effective in arousing cognitive areas of the frontal lobes, which is why we can have inspired thoughts about what is possible and what we want to do in the moment and in the future. It's the very opposite of depression!

Dopamine pathways are key to the SEEKING system

As Professor Jaak Panksepp says, "When lots of dopamine synapses are firing, a person feels as if he or she can do anything".[4] Dopamine not only enables your child to have a great idea, but also to have the directed purpose to see it through to completion. If your child's SEEKING system is optimally activated in the context of your relationship, his brain is likely to habituate to optimal levels of dopamine in combination with the other key chemicals in the SEEKING system – opioids and the anti-anxiety anti-aggression chemicals (see pages 86–89).

TRY THIS...

Talking to your child about new and interesting things can also be a brilliant way to activate her SEEKING system. This is because your interest, curiosity, and your own strongly activated SEEKING system will activate optimal levels of dopamine in your child's brain. On outings or in the garden, take the time to talk to your child about what you see. Tell her about your hobbies and interests; you will be amazed at how much she will absorb.

❝ When we work towards something and achieve it – it's the SEEKING system that energizes our behaviours. **❞**

Professor Jaak Panksepp [5]

Supporting the SEEKING system

The SEEKING system is like a muscle. The more you activate it, particularly in childhood, the stronger it gets and the more it becomes part of a child's personality. This section will look at how you as a parent can optimally activate your child's SEEKING system! But first I want to explain what happens if it's not "exercised".

A child's SEEKING system is very vulnerable. Criticism, irritated reactions to his natural explorative urges and curiosity, or the shame of being told off can all trigger the FEAR system in a child's brain. This blocks the natural creativity of the SEEKING system, which if not addressed in the short term can affect his ability to achieve his life's goals in the long term.

Why do some children have an under-exercised seeking system?

If children loll about in front of the TV for hours on end, their brains' SEEKING systems become underactive. Research shows that on average a child in the UK watches 28 hours of TV each week. The resulting low levels of dopamine can lead to procrastination, uncreative thinking, and lethargy. So much so that in the UK in 2015, there were more than 900,000 young people aged 16 to 24 not in education, employment, or training (so-called NEETs).[6] It's shocking that so many have not had sufficient support for their SEEKING systems to enable them to follow through with their dreams and plans, or perhaps even to have had dreams in the first place.

How does it happen?

So what has happened to these disaffected young people? Sadly some parents unintentionally block their child's SEEKING system not realizing just how sensitive it is; it's a system that needs to be treated with the utmost respect.

If a parent is critical or a perfectionist, the child's FEAR system will block his SEEKING system. The squashers or discouragers in a child's life – at home or at school – have an awful power. It's not just parents or teachers, it can be siblings and relatives, too. A child's SEEKING system is very vulnerable to an adult's criticism or irritated reactions to natural explorative urges. Here are some examples:

• **Commands:** "Don't do that!"

• **Negative teaching:** "You have drawn the octopus wrong. See, you have missed out a leg. Now do it again correctly."

• **Too many "No's":** "No, stop that at once, the paint is going all over the floor!"

• **Criticism:** "Now stop being so messy with the paint, try to be tidy with it."

The shame of being told off triggers the brain's FEAR system. When this happens, all that dopamine is withdrawn and replaced with stress hormones. So instead of "No, you can't do that!" try re-direction. For example, "You can't do that, but what you CAN do is…". Or to look at it another way, "You can't make your dolly's cake here on the carpet, but you can do it in the kitchen and I will go and get you a bowl and spoon to stir the ingredients with."

What does low dopamine feel like?

An adult or child with low dopamine can feel depressed, have a "can't be bothered" attitude to life, lack motivation, and is more likely to procrastinate. He may be unable to focus, lack the will to carry something through to its conclusion, not have a clear vision of what he wants, and often start something then give up. Since they can't get excited about anything naturally, people with low dopamine are more vulnerable to extreme ways of trying to feel aroused, such as drug addiction and high-risk behaviour. Teenagers take psycho-stimulants to give them a sense of "vigorously pursuing courses of action that they would get from a healthy SEEKING circuit"; cocaine produces "a highly energized state of psychic power and engagement with the world".[7]

Parents with low dopamine, particularly those whose own FEAR, RAGE, or PANIC/GRIEF systems are blocking their SEEKING system, can also unintentionally block their child's SEEKING system, too. And these parents are often just too

CASE STUDY

Life passing by

Howard follows the same routine day after day. He works each day and returns home to his family in the evening. He watches television and then the whole thing starts again the next day. Each year, Howard goes on holiday to the same place.

Howard is not satisfied in his job, but doesn't really know what else to do. When asked about his job, he often replies, "Well, it brings in the money." Once Howard started a novel, but now it sits in a drawer. He never seems to find the energy to get on and finish it. Mid-life, Howard asks himself, "Isn't there more to life than this?"

Howard's life isn't bigger than it is because he doesn't have enough drive and energy to make it into a bigger life. Howard's SEEKING system is not activated strongly enough. In many ways, therefore, Howard is no longer developing as a human being.

Howard's childhood was very quiet. He spent a lot of his out-of-school-time watching television or doing homework. These activities failed to strongly activate his SEEKING system, and this legacy has stayed with Howard for life.

" As you walk into a primary school you can often feel a natural urge for knowledge that is totally lacking in the classrooms of secondary schools. **"**

stressed or depressed to be able to enter into accompanied play with the child.

Can the SEEKING system be activated later?

For many people, it is hard to activate the drive for life in adulthood if it was not truly awakened in childhood. However, if a person faces a crisis or shock in life, such as a period of serious illness or the loss of a "secure" job, or even if he or she meets a vibrant new person, it can act like a wake-up call and the person can start to use the "muscle" of the SEEKING system, often for the first time. For many adults, however, this doesn't happen and they never use their SEEKING system well.

How do computer games and television affect my child's brain?

The results of over 4,000 studies suggest a connection in children between high rates of viewing violence on TV and aggressive and violent behaviour, lower academic performance, and stereotyped behaviours in matters of sex, race, and age. While watching violent television, the motor programming parts of a child's brain are often activated, which means that the child is rehearsing the violence he is watching. Parts of the brain that detect threat can also be activated, and the memory of a disturbing film can be laid down in the brain in the same way as the memory of a traumatic event in real life[8] (see pages 160–63). As far as we know, playing solitary computer games does not result in the highly positive brain events activated by play, fun, and laughter with another human being.

Parenting can activate your child's SEEKING system

In order for the SEEKING system to be optimally activated in childhood the aim is to provide the richest relational as well as environmental conditions possible (see also pages 138–43). In the past, many parents were unaware of how important it is to work consciously to strengthen a child's SEEKING system, and those that were aware believed it was okay to leave all that to schools. But schools, especially at secondary level, support the learning of subjects and are often not able to provide the optimal conditions for relational experiences or the one-to-one activities needed for drive, passion, and the ability to follow through.

Optimal activation of the SEEKING system is about attunement on a one-to-one basis – parents commenting, matching positive emotions, and praising – which enables a child to stay in energized engagement with a play task, or in the "flow" (see overleaf). Many parents never play like this with their children and, as a result, too many children grow up leading ordinary lives, but not just the extraordinary ones that they may be capable of.

Help your child "ride" the SEEKING systems of key adults

Your child's interest and curiosity about the world around him will come from you. Encourage him to explore and experiment from an early age. Point out the wonders of the world; keep saying, "Wow, look at that!". Chat to him when you are out in the park, at the shops, or at home playing.

However, some parents are not great at raising their child's dopamine levels due to their own childhood experiences (too little support for their own creativity or too much shaming or discouragement). If this is the case for you, find another key adult in your child's life who is a good dopamine activator and who can have regular explorative playtime with your child.

CASE STUDY

Getting started at the beach

When Ted takes his son, Jake, to the beach, he gets out his newspaper and tells Jake to amuse himself. Jake sifts the sand through his hands, picks up a few rocks and hits them together, then stands in the sea. After 15 minutes, he tells his father he wants to go home. Without a few ideas from Dad on how to use a beach well, the SEEKING system in Jake's brain is poorly activated. He needs help to get started.

Another time, Sally, a friend of the family, comes to the beach, too. Sally makes sure she takes a bucket and spade. She shows Jake how to make sandcastles and how to dig a large crater and make a sand car to sit in. She has also brought a few little lorries. Jake picks them up eagerly and drives them on a track around his sandcastles. When Jake is really engrossed in his play, Sally can relax and read her newspaper for a while.

Children with strongly activated SEEKING systems will find opportunities for play wherever they look! Parents, carers, and teachers can inspire this by providing an "enriched environment" with space, toys, equipment, and, most of all, ideas.

The importance of a "let's" attitude

"Let's" times are about intense together activities born out of true spontaneity. While playing together, you are modelling the capacity for a "together-in-fun" relationship. "Let's" time can be any number of activities:

• Let's make a sandcastle or cake!
• Let's make a den with the bedding and have tea in it!

Help to keep your child in the flow

A "flow" state is characterized by an almost effortless, yet highly focused, state of consciousness. It happens when a person becomes so deeply engrossed in a task and pursues it with such passion that all else disappears, including a sense of time and/or the worry of failure. The person experiences an almost euphoric state of joy and pleasure in which the task is performed, doing so without strain or effort.[9]

If you see your child in a state of flow, support him to stay there. One of the most powerful ways of doing this is to accompany his explorative flow with commenting on the activity, praising him, and making suggestions. If, for example, he is making a magic potion with flour and water on the kitchen floor, don't say, "Look you are making a mess on the floor, now just clear that up right now!". Instead, spread out some newspaper and support his flow by giving him props such as jugs, bowls, and spoons and/or more rice, water, or cereal to add to his potion.

"But why does my child need me? He seems to play perfectly well on his own."

Of course, solitary play is very important for some of the time. It gives your child time to disengage, to withdraw from all that relating, to get "sensorally" involved in things in his own time at his own pace, to develop his own ideas, and to know that he can do certain tasks. It is not an "either/or" situation. Children need both solitary play and adult-accompanied play. The point about accompanied play is attention span, which in brain chemical terms is about keeping up the dopamine flow in his brain so that "states" of absorption, creativity, and imagination become "traits". The attention span of a two year old in solitary play is usually anything from 15 seconds to two minutes. Many younger children can't get started on an activity or sustain full engagement over a period of time without you suggesting, modelling, commenting, and attuning with them – in other words, children need to ride your dopamine system. Put a two-year-old in front of an amazing array of sand tools by a sand pit, for example, and he will probably just sit there. But get in the sandpit with him and show him how to use the sand tools and he will be off.

Consider the three-year-old whose delighted parent observes him in "small world" play on his own for the very first time. The little boy acts out a conversation between a toothbrush, a banana, and his pet frog. Delightful! However, it will probably

"Let's build a dam together"

Children of all ages enjoy the space and sense of freedom they get from being outdoors. Show them how to explore and search for fun in their environment.

They may need suggestions to get them started, such as "Can you climb that mound?", or "That bush looks like a little house". Once inspired, they can be occupied happily for hours.

For over an hour these two boys have been building a dam in a stream to make their own rock pool. Totally absorbed in their project, they no longer need adult help.

> **"**You can do a great deal for your child by providing lots of stimuli to trigger his imagination.**"**

only last for about a minute. If you listen to him and develop his ideas through observing, commenting, and entering into the role-play with the greatest respect for, and interest in, his ideas, he will get to know that amazing feeling of having truly entered into a fantastical world because you've "travelled" with him. What a boost for his self-esteem! Verbal attention-focused behaviour used in this way has also been shown to develop a child's attention, and his exploratory, language, and social skills.[10]

In those early years, to fully exercise their imagination, children need to ride your dopamine, borrowing your sophisticated frontal lobes to develop their ideas, and help them sustain attention, engagement, and absorption over time. So adult-accompanied play can take a child into a far deeper level of imagination, creativity, and development of their play themes. Conversely, research also shows that isolation can block the SEEKING system.[11] Benefits gained from "enriched play environments" (see pages 138–42) are dependent on this type of play not being a solitary activity.

"I can do this myself now**"**

Good teachers can encourage children to try new skills for themselves, and foster a sense of independence and achievement. Schools that focus too closely on a curriculum may fail to inspire children with a love of knowledge and learning.

The importance of "Commenting"

Instead of walking past a young child who is engaged in something (thinking, "phew, at last he is occupying himself!"), support what he is doing with a key communicative strategy called commenting (see pages 248–49). This means describing what the child is doing. "Ah, so you are feeling the water on your hand, splish, splash!" (echo his sounds or movements). Or, "What a lovely stone pile you have made." Don't ask questions ("What are you making? What are you drawing?") as they interrupt flow. The child has to interrupt his flow to respond to you. As the child's frontal lobe functioning is still underdeveloped, he is not being rude in not answering your question. He simply can't switch attention as quickly as adults. Commenting also helps sustain a child's interest and is vital for developing his self-esteem.

Parents should be a bit crazy, funny, exciting

If your child is set on conflict, simply diffuse it with play, humour, and by being a bit surreal – use your creative flow. It's called "crossing the transaction". For example, if your child says, "I'm not going to bed!", respond with, "Would you like to go up to bed on my back with a space ship/dinosaur/banana-boat ride?" Don't punish explorative behaviour that is causing mess or conflict, just give some gentle re-direction into some other activity.

Is it too late for my teenager?

It is never too late to awaken the SEEKING system in a disaffected teenager, but he is going to have to meet adults whose own SEEKING systems are working very well and so can inspire him to re-engage with life and all it can offer. Research shows that teenagers who have had the benefit of inspirational adults in and out of school hours by the time they are 30 are less likely to have no qualifications or to be depressed, single, separated or divorced, in social housing, on a low income, or an offender.[12]

Commenting on your child's activity helps sustain her interest in what she is doing. It helps her feel as if she can make interesting things happen in the world. It makes her feel important and that what she is doing is worth continuing.

"Creative people... don't want the world as it is today, but want to make another world. In order to be able to do that, they have to sail right off the surface of the earth, to imagine, to fantasize and even to be crazy or nutty..."
Abraham Maslow[13]

The best environment

There is a particular body of brain science research called "enriched environment studies" that looks into the effects of such environments on the brain. Studies have found that specific situations that engage a child in many different ways (see below) not only optimally activate the child's SEEKING system, but bring about incredibly positive brain changes into the bargain.

Playing with foam can really engage a child. Here the child is moving, thinking, and clearly enjoying herself – all her senses are engaged. Use a children's bath foam such as Crazy Foam, or a cheaper option is unscented shaving foam.

What is an enriched environment?

An enriched environment is one that fully engages a child in all of the following four ways:
- **Cognitively** (the child is thinking).
- **Physically** (the child is moving).
- **Socially** (the child is relating to you and/or others).
- **Sensorially** (all the child's senses are aroused – touch, vision, hearing, smell, and taste).

Activities such as adult-accompanied messy play or where you create "mini" worlds for him, in which you are supporting your child by commenting on and copying what he is doing in order to keep him in "flow", all qualify as enriched environments. With your support in these activities all four essential elements will be in place.

What happens to the brain?

Research found that attempts to isolate one or more of the four critical factors listed above failed to bring about positive brain changes. Enriched environments have an amazing effect on the brain. They were seen to:
- **Lower levels of stress chemicals.**
- **Cause anxious children to become less anxious** (and stop the continuing adverse effects of past stress such as pre- or postnatal stress).[14]
- **Result in new brain cell growth** (neurogenesis).[15] In one fascinating study, rats were given an enriched environment

"We're going to the moon"

Encourage children in creative play by starting them off with a few ideas and providing objects with creative potential to play with. Show them how to fly to the moon on a broom, look for elves, or build a castle. They will soon be captivated. Simple "toys" such as pots and pans, a bowl of water, or a tray of sand are usually all children need to get started. There is no need to provide an array of expensive, manufactured toys. Children enjoy finding their own way to play once the game is underway.

BRAIN STORY

Just as fertilizers make plants grow better, so brain fertilizers make the human brain function better. Brain fertilizers enhance brain development and are critical to your child's physical and mental health.[16] Two of these brain fertilizers are BDNF (brain-derived neurotrophic factor) and IGF-1 (insulin-like growth factor 1).

BDNF and IGF-1 promote brain growth in the frontal lobes, positively affecting your child's higher brain functions. Research with eight- and nine-year-old children revealed a clear association of higher levels of IGF-1 in the frontal lobes of children with a higher IQ.[17]

Increased brain connections The scan on the left was taken before a mammal had experienced an enriched environment. After exposure, the number of connections is significantly higher (right).[18]

with "climbing tubes and running wheels, novel food, and lots of social interaction". Two months later they had an extra 50,000 brain cells in each side of the hippocampus.[19]

• **Trigger amazing brain growth fertilizers** (see left).

Long-term benefits

The hippocampus is a key system in your child's brain associated with memory (see page 19). It's vital for your child's ability to learn. We know from animal research that the hippocampus will also show higher levels of brain fertilizer activation after enriched environment play and the development of new synaptic connections.[20]

Research has shown that deprived, at-risk children who experienced an enriched-environment nursery intervention between the ages of three and five, did far better socially, emotionally, and academically as adults than children who had not experienced an enriched environment. At the age of 11 they were given EEG tests (to measure brain wave patterns) and skin-conductance tests (measuring bodily arousal levels) and were found to have far better attention, concentration, and a calmer physiology – key for good decision making, emotion processing, and socializing.[21]

Creating an enriched environment for children

To qualify as an enriched environment an activity or toy must feel new to the child. If you supply the same toys day after day they cease to provide the benefits described above. We know this from research on chimpanzees: give them a banana and the dopamine systems will trigger. Then give them another banana and another – eventually there will be very weak firings of dopamine in their brains, so much so that they walk away from any bananas! You will have noticed the same phenomenon with your child's toys. You excitedly bring home a new toy and your child is eager to play with it. Two days later, it's discarded and you feel resentful. All that effort and money you put in to that thoughtful present seems no longer to be of any value to your child.

However, providing new activities does not mean you have to keep running to the toyshop. There are some wonderful ways of creating new stimulating messy play and small worlds with little expense. Simply invest in a large plastic black base tray. Then using miniature toy animals and "found objects" – you can use wood, stones, leaves, or even food substances – set up a different "world" each week. There is no need to go to great expense. Children love playing with water, or try a food world with cooked rice coloured with food colouring or even coloured spaghetti – or both. Here are some more ideas:

- Snow scene (use fake snow – or even artifical foam)
- Farm scene (use shredded wheat cereal for hay or straw)
- Beach scene with sand and animals
- Dinosaur's world with cornflakes
- Crazy Foam or a jelly bath world with some objects (such as bugs, toys, or plastic animals) in it.

❝ The true sign of intelligence is not knowledge but imagination. **❞**
Albert Einstein

❝ My family are going for a walk! **❞**

Children love exploring mini worlds. Choose toys that grip a child's imagination and facilitate free play. Create a "world" on a little tray on a table or buy a larger freestanding tray on legs so several children can play around it together.

CONSIDER THIS...

Treasure boxes are perfect for babies from six to 18 months. Child psychologist Elinor Goldschmeid coined the term "heuristic" play, to describe offering a baby natural "objects" to play with. She felt that plastic objects do not stimulate an infant's senses as well as natural ones do.

So set up a special treasure box for your young child. Use interesting shapes made from cardboard, wood, rubber, fur, cotton, and place them in a basket. Add pegs, kitchen utensils, bean bags, shells, ribbons, wool, pine cones, brushes, door stops – but ban all plastic objects. Sit beside your baby in a calm, attuning, commenting way. Watch him pick up toys and comment and praise as he does so.

If as a parent you are feeling overwhelmed – "Don't ask me to do another thing"– it's possible to buy ready-made treasure boxes.

Can't children just play with other children?

Some four- and five-year-olds (particularly those who have benefited from lots of adult-accompanied play) can sometimes happily sustain "small world" play together for over 20 minutes before one of them attacks the other, they have a toy war, or one of them loses interest. Child-to-child small-world or messy play is great for the development of social skills such as give and take and listening to the ideas of the other child. Over-fives can do even better in child-to-child imaginative play. They can sustain flow together and develop a narrative in their play for a considerable length of time without needing you (all the more so if you have put in lots of accompanied play in the early years). But even when children are able to play well together with imagination, absorption, and creativity, accompanied parent–child play adds a different and vital dimension for development of drive, will, and creativity.

Other children quite simply don't have the sophisticated frontal lobe development of an adult. Accompanied play with a socially intelligent adult provides children with fine attunement (use of voice, words, tone, movement), sensitive commenting, affirmation of their ideas, and play narratives moment by moment. In this sense, parents are also natural play therapists. An important study looked at 93 different play therapy research studies in terms of successful outcomes. The best outcomes of all didn't come from the studies where a therapist played with a child in a therapy room, but those where parents were taught to do child-led play in the home environment with their child (commenting, joining in, following the child's lead, role playing, praising as appropriate and so keeping the child's energized engagement in the task).[22] In other words, parents were giving the very best support to their child's SEEKING system.

In addition, by joining in during those early years from birth to five, you are supporting the development of your child's imagination as a vital life skill.

Key points

• In the early years, provide your child with lots of imaginative explorative activities in the context of adult-accompanied play, to develop the SEEKING system in his brain. When this system is working well, your child will have an appetite for life, curiosity, and the drive and motivation to make his creative ideas into a reality.

• As parents we can easily crush a child's will and blight his explorative urge by discouragement, too many commands and "no's", or by using frightening or shaming discipline.

• Far better than running to the toy shop, create new enriched environments every week — messy play or small world play with natural objects and "small world" animals and people. This will stimulate your child cognitively, physically, socially, and sensorially.

your socially intelligent child

The ability to form meaningful human relationships is fundamental to happiness and mental health. It's the quality of contact we have with other people that is arguably the most important determining factor in quality of life. We can also only develop ourselves through relationships with others. This chapter offers the science and psychology for ensuring your child grows up to be able to sustain loving relationships over time and doesn't end up living in a destructive or painful relationship.

Developing social intelligence

Getting along well with people requires social intelligence – it is nothing whatsoever to do with cleverness. There are many very clever people who have poor social intelligence, and as a result they can find it difficult to sustain profoundly satisfying, intimate, long-term relationships.

CONSIDER THIS...

Responding to the emotional cues of others is key to social intelligence. Studies show that eleven-year-olds who responded well to another child's feelings were significantly more likely to have had a good response to their own feelings from their parents.[1]

In addition, some people relate to others in a flat, dull way, devoid of humour, which lacks any curiosity about the person they are talking to; they talk at them rather than listen to them. These people may be successful in terms of making money, but often they are unable to function well in their personal lives. What's more, research in the business world shows that the most successful leaders are not the most pushy or determined people, but are those who are the most socially aware of the feelings and needs of others. There is no social intelligence gene. To become a socially developed human being, your child needs help from you.

Many people don't get the support they need

You need all sorts of relationship skills and social intelligence to be able to sustain, nurture, and develop loving intimate relationships over time. Millions of people can't do it. In other words, what they have learnt in childhood from their parents in terms of social intelligence and key relational skills has not supported them. As a result, two out of three marriages ends in divorce in the UK alone[2] and 50 percent of co-habiting couples split before their child is five.[3] A quarter of all children experience stress due to family breakdown[4] and the same number watch parents screaming and shouting at each other.[5] Moreover research shows that poor-quality intimate relationships are very bad for your health.[6] But then living on your own isn't the answer either, as loneliness is so bad for the immune system that it's as big a killer as obesity, and as dangerous to your health as smoking 15 cigarettes a day.[7]

Children need their parents' help

If children are to develop key relational skills, we as parents need to "model" them to each child. This means not only how you relate to your child, but also how you help her relate to both you, her siblings, and others. You need to demonstrate to your child that you have following skills:
- **You can be moved** by another's distress
- **You can reflect rather than react** when you are feeling really angry with someone
- **You can repair relationship ruptures**
- **You can express hurt and anger** in a way that leaves the other person feeling respected, not shamed or criticized
- **You can really listen to another person** in an interested, curious way
- **You have the capacity to comfort** and emotionally regulate a distressed person.

Some avenues to social intelligence can be opened up to children by teaching them specific skills, but many can't. This is because the "social dance" is very subtle and highly complex. You can teach a child simple social skills, such as how to ask someone to be her friend, how to talk about her feelings, how to say no, and how to ask for something in a clear and polite way. But social intelligence is far more than this. You can't teach a child how to be moved by another's distress – she either is or she isn't. You can't teach a child how to be emotionally warm – she either is or she isn't. You can't teach a child how to be naturally curious about another person, and to voice that curiosity in such a way that the other person feels valued and interesting. You can't teach a child the capacity to soothe and comfort a person who is in distress. All these wonderful higher human functions will only be possible if she has developed the necessary brain

CASE STUDY
Recovering from hurt
When Sarah was a child, she was constantly shouted at by her depressed mother. Her father was unable to relate well to children, so he had very little quality contact time with Sarah. Most of his exchanges with his daughter were to "bring her into line". Neither parent had the ability to respond sensitively to Sarah's feelings, because their parents had not responded sensitively to their feelings.

From all this, Sarah learnt that relationships are all about power and feelings of hurt and rejection. When Sarah met lovely people in her life, she always drove them away because she tried to control them. She just didn't know another way of being with people. After Sarah was sacked from a good job for bullying her colleagues in the workplace, she realized she needed counselling. With her counsellor, she was able to mourn the fact that she had felt so alone as a child. Sarah was able, over time, to develop warmer, gentler ways of relating. She is now happily married and her children feel very safe and loved by her.

"Being a good team player means giving and taking rather than having your own way.**"**

These boys are only four years old, yet they are already skilled in the art of relating to each other. They can listen to each other well and time their responses. They have a sense of ease in each other's company.

pathways and complex chemical cascades in her brain, along with a truly embodied response. This development can only take place through particular relationship experiences, and parents are her starting point. It is sometimes the case that adults who have never been on the receiving end of enriching and emotionally responsive "one-to-ones" in childhood can stay developmentally arrested and have the social intelligence of a young child.

The science of social intelligence

Social intelligence involves higher and lower brain pathways working together in a beautifully coordinated way. You, as a parent, will have a powerful influence over whether these vital networking systems develop well in your child's brain. If, for example, a child has experienced mainly superficial emotional connections in the family home, she is likely to grow up simply not knowing how to develop more meaningful ways of relating to people. If parent–child interactions have frequently been frightening, shaming, or hurtful, a child can grow up deeply mistrustful of people and so push away overtures offering friendship, kindness, or concern. They may feel too dangerous. If a child repeatedly witnesses her parents arguing, she may believe relationships are all about power and control, or only know how to relate with power and control when people are hurt or angry.

The sensitive brain and social intelligence

There are several parts of your child's brain that are key to social intelligence: the frontal lobes, the cerebellum, the corpus callosum, and the anterior cingulate. With relationally aware parenting a mass of new brain pathways will develop in these areas of your child's brain.

The important frontal lobes

There are several areas in this part of the brain: one of the key ones is the orbitofrontal region (see page 150). The setting

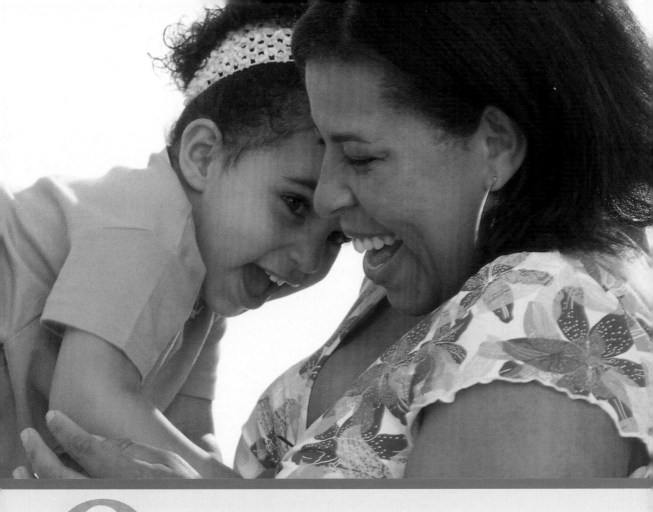

How does parenting have such an impact on a child's social brain?

In adulthood, powerful relationship experiences can still result in the development of the social brain (it's not only something that happens in childhood). But we have to be open to change. The problem is that negative ways of relating established in childhood can so easily become fixed. Children who experience mainly superficial emotional connections at home may grow up closed to deeper connections with others as they have not learned how to relate to people when they were younger. A child will be more likely to be open to offers of friendship, kindness, or concern if her interactions with her parents are always met with empathy; if they are not she can grow up mistrustful. What's more, a diet of angry parent–child or parent-to-parent exchanges in childhood can mean a child has a lifelong ingrained belief that all relationships are about power and control.

BRAIN STORY

One key frontal lobe area important to social intelligence is the orbitofrontal region, which is located just above the orbit of the eye; hence its name. Brain pathways established here help us to respond well to other people.

Another important area of the higher brain is the ventromedial part. Pathways laid down here will be key to your child developing self-awareness and the capacities to negotiate, make decisions, resolve conflict, and be a great team-player. Strong connections from the ventromedial area to the lower brain can also calm strong feelings and enable you to think about them instead of discharging them in outbursts of rage, agitation, or anxiety.[8]

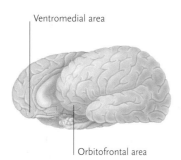

Ventromedial area

Orbitofrontal area

The orbitofrontal and ventromedial areas are regions of the frontal lobes involved in our social intelligence.

down of new brain pathways in this area will, over time, enable your child to read accurately, and respond sensitively to, a person's social and emotional cues. Interestingly, this part of the brain is less active in adults and children who are depressed, so it's harder for them to be socially sensitive. New pathways connecting the orbitofrontal area to the lower, mammalian, brain can enable your child to calm her primitive impulses of fear and anger and regulate her bodily high arousal states. Known as "top-down brain pathways"[9] these connections are also vital for the ability to repair relationships that go wrong.

The role of the cerebellum

This structure is situated behind the brain stem, at the lowest part of the brain (see page 19). Good parenting can also lay down pathways between the frontal lobes, above, and the cerebellum. These pathways enable your child to learn to time her response accurately, to what another person is saying, and give it appropriate rhythm and emotional expression. They can also help your child become skilled at shifting her attention from one aspect of a conversation to another. Scientists have realized only recently that the cerebellum is involved in social behaviour. Research on children with autism almost always shows malformations in this part of the brain.[10]

The corpus callosum connects the right and left brain

This is the structure that enables communication between the right and left sides of the higher brain (see page 18). The left brain houses our verbal centres for understanding and forming speech, but the right brain needs to register feelings in the first place. The corpus callosum, when working well, helps us find words for feelings, hence emotional literacy. While the left brain has weak links with the lower emotional brain and weak links with feedback about bodily arousal, the right is a deeply feeling brain with strong links to emotion systems and "gut" feelings. It picks up emotional atmospheres very quickly. In infants and young children this structure is still developing so there is poor communication between the two sides of the brain, which is why they can completely "lose it" as they react to rather than reflect on stressful life events.

• **You can help to develop communication between the two sides of her brain.** It is all too easy to assume that children can put words to feelings well, but by and large they can't because corpus callosum is underdeveloped. Instead, they tend to "behave" their feelings, because they remain at a sensation level rather than a "thought about" level. If you help a child put words to feelings, you will be helping her to develop her corpus callosum. When adults haven't had help like this in their childhood they will still react not reflect under stress.

Parent–child communication experts Adele Faber and Elaine Mazlish suggest giving the child words to express their

> **"** Children who have not been met with empathy themselves cannot register the distress of another child. **"**

" Let's make up **"**

It's a real art for a parent to help children resolve painful clashes when so many primitive lower brain feelings have been activated.

Here a thoughtful Daddy is helping these two-year-olds by speaking to them about how painful it has been for both of them to share the toy car.

What a gift for a parent to show children that the most painful conflicts can be resolved.

BRAIN STORY

The corpus callosum is an amazing network of fibres enabling communication between the right and left side of the higher brain. The corpus callosum plays a vital role in social intelligence, as it passes information about what we are experiencing in milliseconds from one side of our higher brain to the other. So it helps someone to think and feel clearly about all the things that happen to them.

corpus callosum

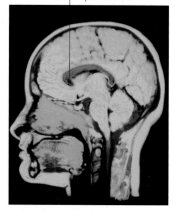

An MRI scan through the head clearly shows the corpus callosum (blue). This band of tissue is composed of nerve fibres (some 300 million in a fully developed adult brain) and functions as an information highway between the two halves of the brain.

anger with siblings rather than punishing the anger.[11] On this principle if, for example, four-year-old Toby lashes out at his younger brother Joey because he's picked up his brother's new yellow lorry, your reaction might be to say to Toby, "That's a bad thing. Stop that right now. Your brother was only looking at it". Instead, however, give Toby words to help him by saying, "Stop Toby. It's never okay to hurt someone's body. Tell your brother how angry you are – you could say something like, 'Hey Joey, I don't like it when you play with my yellow lorry. I want you to ask first.'" Then suggest that you and Toby talk to Joey together, which helps Toby.

• **Where there is conflict,** if you help your child to put words to feelings you are again supporting the development of her ability to reflect not react. When we put words to feelings, the alarm systems in our brains calm, lowering heart rate and stress hormone levels.[12] The same is true of sulking, which of course is a wordless state. So help a child to make it "worded". If we just ignore sulking or criticize it, we are missing a key opportunity for social intelligence development. If a child is sulking, try saying, "Do you want to carry on sulking or do you need a hug?" If there is no response, say, "Okay, I am assuming that no response means you want to carry on sulking. I'll come back in a while and ask again." Or, I have found it very effective to ask a child, "Would you finish the sentence: I feel angry because… I feel sad because…". Repeat each one slowly to give her time to think.

The anterior cingulate is key for empathy and compassion

This structure (see page 95) is part of the brain's limbic system. When activated in the face of another person's distress it enables you to feel pain because of their pain, so much so that you are moved to act.[13] If we parent with empathy our children will have the capacity to empathize this way (see also pages 154–59). Interestingly, the anterior cingulate does not activate in bullies, who instead of wanting to help the vulnerable or defenseless (distress averse) are "distress excited" and want to hurt them. What lights up in their brain is the nucleus accumbens, triggering reward chemicals.

The parietal lobes are important, too

The parietal lobes are involved in sensation of movement and navigation of space. Emotionally responsive parenting may also help to set down important new pathways between a child's parietal lobes and her frontal lobes. These pathways (particularly on the right side of the brain) are responsible for gauging the correct interpersonal space when with another person. This means the ability not to invade someone's private space or appear too distant from them!

Low levels of serotonin can spoil relationships

The brain chemical serotonin is a major factor in social and emotional intelligence. Optimal levels can stabilize mood, reduce aggression, and so play a key role in promoting good relationships. Research studies have shown that monkeys who were highly respected in their group and at the top of their social hierarchy, had optimal levels of serotonin.[14] Low levels of serotonin in the brain are associated with impulsive behaviour. If you are unable to inhibit primitive impulses, frequent angry or anxious outbursts may spoil your relationships. You are also more likely to suffer from bad moods. Children and adults with low levels of serotonin can find it hard to express negative feelings calmly.

Serotonin levels are dramatically influenced by human relationships, for better or worse. Research shows that stress in early life can adversely affect the serotonin system in an infant's developing brain, whereas lovely one-to-ones with you can have a positive effect on serotonin levels in your child's ventromedial cortex. By sharing lots of good times with you, your child can be accustomed to optimal levels of serotonin in her brain and this can then become part of who she is – her core personality.

ANIMAL INSIGHTS

Low levels of serotonin in both animals and humans are associated with impulsive behaviour. The person's or animal's emotional responses are not moderated by serotonin, which is a mood-stabilizing chemical. When they get angry it's big, blow-up anger, rather than mild irritation or annoyance. We know that monkeys who have low serotonin are impulsive and aggressive. "Given the opportunity, they will make dangerous leaps from tree to tree that other monkeys won't attempt. They get into frequent fights."[15]

Parenting with empathy

Children who are parented in a way where empathy is offered at times of high emotion do far better socially, emotionally, and academically in middle childhood and the teenage years than children who have not received empathic responses.[16] They also have a far calmer physiology so can handle stress well.

It is all too easy to tell a child who is experiencing a negative emotion that she should just "get over it" or that whatever she's feeling "is not that bad" – known as "emotion dismissing". Empathic parenting is exactly the opposite – acknowledge the child's feelings, especially the pain of what she is feeling, then help her with it. Likewise, if you respond empathically to a child's anger as opposed to telling her to stop just being angry, she'll do so much better.

Studies show that children who have been parented empathetically had higher academic marks at ages eight and 15 because of good stress regulation – their ability to think was not derailed by emotions. These children also experienced less negative play with their best friends, fewer behaviour problems, and were physically healthier.[17]

So what is the best approach?

Empathic parenting means activating the key structures of the brain involved with social intelligence. Help your child put words to feelings (developing the corpus callosum); empathize with her so that she will do the same for others (activating up the anterior cingulate); and help her learn to be able to reflect on life's knocks, not just react to them (improving frontal lobe functions).

It is all about changing your appoach

Here is an example of non-empathic factual responses to a child's emotional pain (no positive brain or mind change

CONSIDER THIS...

There are some very sensitive babies for whom face-to-face conversations have to be just right. If a sensitive baby finds communication with you worrying in any way whatsoever, he may cut off and withdraw. This may make you pursue him more for a response. As a result, he may then withdraw even more. Both of you can end up feeling hopeless and awful, so make sure that you follow your child's cues.

here) and how to alter it to an empathic response. Two-year-old Annie is screaming about not wanting to leave playgroup – she is enjoying herself and does not want to go home. Dad, using a factual response, might start saying, "Annie, you have to calm down." Her response is to scream even louder. Her dad, now shouting and moving into facts, responds with, "Stop this behaviour right now. You know we can't stay here, we have to go home." The empathy response would be to say, "I understand that you love the playgroup. You want to stay here, not go home." When she screams more loudly, repeat this saying, "Daddy knows. Annie wants to stay here and not go home." She will quieten, let you pick her up, and cuddle you.

Empathic approach to a toy war

Sophie screams because during a play date, her friend Emma has taken her new toy pig. Instead of saying, "Now come on, Sophie, you need to learn to share. Sharing is a good thing

> **"** When parents experience their child's negative emotional states with him, these states get smaller. When parents experience their child's positive emotional states with him, these states get larger. **"**
> Dan Hughes

" I am really sorry **"**

After Grandma lost her temper when six-year-old Clare took the last three chocolate biscuits she apologized. "I was angry when you left no biscuits for the rest of us, but I am sorry, I shouldn't have shouted. I should have found another way of letting you know that was not okay." This is known as interactive repair, and it's vital for healthy relationships and helps children to learn to reflect, not react.

As your child grows up, keep listening well to what he is telling you. Some parents are great at talking "at" their child, but they are not good at listening to them. Bend down to his level when he is talking to you, so he can have eye contact with you as he is telling you this most important thing. Give him time to say it, and respond in age-appropriate language. Use lots of colour in your voice because infants find this delightfully stimulating, whereas flat voices turn them off conversation.

and then you can both be friends," try this: "Sometimes it's hard to share something that you really care about so much. Let's put this toy away for the moment and show Emma the toys you are okay taking turns with."

Empathizing can develop brain connections

Five-year-old Timmy's little sister has drawn all over the beautiful card he has just made for his grandmother, so Timmy screams, shouts, and throws himself on the floor. Instead of responding with, "Now come on, Timmy, that's enough. Stop that behaviour right now. She didn't mean it. She's only a baby," try the empathy version. "I can see why you feel so mad and so miserable. You made the card so beautifully. Of course you are hurting now it's spoilt". Your empathetic response will help your child make sense of his painful experiences and develop the new neuronal networks in his brain helping him to reflect, not react.

Dealing with conflict and anger

Conflicts are inevitable in parent–child relationships. We don't want to stop conflict, but if we want our children to become socially intelligent we need to use these moments to model how to handle conflict well. The shocking statistics in terms of how many adult intimate relationships fail are proof enough of just how many adults can't handle conflict. That said, couple therapist Ellyn Bader suggests that "Marriage vows are ridiculously hard, unless you marry late in life and have done a lot of personal therapy."[18]

Relationship expert John Gottman has studied the dynamics between more couples than anyone in the world. He found that couples' ability to handle anger well is key to whether they are happy or not, or stay together or not, and many break up because they don't handle conflicts well. Conflicts are most acute when one or both partners is stonewalling or turning away, is critical of the other, or is defensive, and/or full of contempt towards the other. In contrast, happily married couples handle their conflicts in gentle, positive ways, are able to repair negative interactions during an argument, and can process negative emotions fully.[19]

The same is true of parent–child relationships. If children are going to grow up socially intelligent, parents need to handle conflicts with their children in gentle, positive ways and repair the relationship after an argument.

How to handle conflicts in gentle, positive ways

A child is not going to grow up socially intelligent if her parents treat her anger as something to be punished rather than acknowledged. It is common for parents to be good with a child's sadness or fear, but critical or punishing when the child is angry. We need our anger – it's part of the human condition and lets us know what is good or bad for us. If a child learns that she mustn't feel anger because it meets with such parental disapproval, she's likely to reach adulthood handicapped on the social stage. She may not be able to find her passionate "No", so people may walk all over her, or she

There are many studies in which infants as young as 18 months have been observed showing concern and a desire to help people in need. However, a child's capacity for empathy is dependent on it being modelled consistently by her primary carers. Sadly with parenting that lacks empathy, research shows that children respond to the distress of others with no emotion – as if they were looking at a piece of furniture.[20]

"I understand your pain"

By acknowledging the child's feelings – especially the pain of what he is feeling – and then helping him to work through them you are emotionally regulating him. Children whose parents empathize with all their feelings, including anger, are also physically healthier than those whose parents do not empathize.

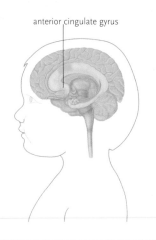

may repeatedly fail to lay down firm boundaries in exploitative situations. The ability to be angry at appropriate moments is a key component of a child's social intelligence. If a child inhibits emotions such as anger, her relationships in her adult life are likely to lack full authenticity. If she feels she can never fully be herself with that parent, she can take that feeling of "fear of being myself in case I am too much", into her adulthood, too.

Don't discipline with anger

Anger is just as present in the best parent–child relationships as it is in those that are struggling. So when your child is angry, don't put her in Time Out because she is disrespecting you and saying she hates you (see also page 234), or punish her for having the feeling she is having. Instead regulate her anger by acknowledging it. One proviso of course – no swearing at you!

• **Empathize with your child when she is furious with you for putting down a boundary,** rather than criticizing her for it.[22] For example, five-year-old Sally says a really mean thing to her little sister. So her mum says that due to her meanness Sally won't be able to watch her new DVD today. Sally is then furious with her mum. But Mum hears her anger and says, " I understand you are furious with me for not letting you watch the DVD and you are really hurting about that now and so disappointed, but I need you to learn that mean words hurt people." Your child is more likely to understand if you have acknowledged her anger in this way.

• **If your child attacks you personally,** acknowledge that whatever she is feeling towards you is real for her. Start your sentence – "So you are experiencing me as...", "So you are seeing me as...", or "So it feels like...". That way you are not saying, "I am x or y", but acknowledging her perception.

• **Know how to express anger with your child.** Keep it short. Start the sentence "I feel angry with you because...". But no shouting or shaming voice. Remember the research that shows that shouting or shaming leads to toxic levels of stress hormones in the child's brain.

• **Repair the relationship as soon as possible**. But to do this you need to be able to emotionally regulate yourself so you have enough frontal-lobe functioning to think about how you are coming across to your child. Check that you're elevating, not shaming, your child's dignity. If you feel overwhelmed and your RAGE system is in the driving seat say, "I feel very angry about this, so I am going to leave the room and spend a short time getting my thinking back" then leave the room, breathe, and return when you feel more regulated.

• **Try an empathy drawing.** Because young children often do not have words for their feelings, there are other ways of helping by modelling how to express feelings. Tell your child you are going to draw or write what you imagine might be reasons why she is angry. Take a felt pen and a piece of paper and draw a big empathy drawing – this can be phrases or images (squiggles and stick people are fine) showing possibilities for the emotional pain fuelling her behaviour. Then ask her to colour in or cross out any of the things you have drawn that feel wrong and tick any that feel right for her. If she rings one, thank her for being brave and letting you know what's wrong.

The importance of relationship repair

Relationship repair (learning how to say sorry) and modelling it in your relationship with your child is a gift for her. She will develop the skill and can then take it into her adult relationships. So many couples split up because after an argument there is a disconnnect and they don't know how to repair it – their parents did not "show them". After a disconnect with your child you might say, "I am so sorry I shouted at you. I wanted you to stop what you were doing, but I should have found another way of helping you stop". Or, "Sorry I used such a stern voice. I have had a hard day at work and my stress came out at you. I apologize".

ANIMAL INSIGHTS

Some animals are incapable of compassion and concern towards others who are vulnerable, defenceless, or in distress, because they haven't the brain chemistry and brain anatomical systems required to feel these emotions. Reptiles don't have a developed CARE system in their brains. Many of them produce their young and leave them to fend for themselves.

The female sea turtle, for example, digs a hole in the sand to bury her eggs. A chemical called vasotocin (the reptilian version of our oxytocin) is activated in her brain. Once she has covered her eggs, this "caring" chemical in her brain drops dramatically, so she just wanders off. This means that when her baby turtles are born, their mother is nowhere to be seen. It's just a matter of chance whether the little turtles get to the sea before they are eaten.[23]

Modern technology

Let's get real here. There are very few parents who don't use TV, a DVD, or a games console or tablet as a babysitter from time to time. Technology in some form can help provide a solution to sibling conflicts, and TV in particular can be great for downtime and disengagement time for everyone.

Here we aim to give you the key facts abut technology so you can make informed decisions about how much screen time per day is acceptable and what sort of TV programmes, films, and electronic games – whether on a games console, computer, tablet, or smart phone – to allow.

The facts about screen time

Is screen time a good or a bad thing overall? The researchers' current recommendation is for no more than two hours a day for children, but what happens if they exceed that? A study in Glasgow looked at the habits of 11,000 five-year-olds[28] and found that by the age of seven there was a less than two percent increase in behaviour problems with the children who had watched TV for more than three hours a day, compared with those watching for less than an hour. There was no increase in emotional symptoms, hyperactivity/inattention, or relationship problems with peers. Alison Parkes, one of the authors of the study, said, "Our work suggests that limiting the amount of time children spend in front of the TV is unlikely to improve psychosocial adjustment".[29] However, there have been other findings:

• **Risk of obesity.** Children who watched just one hour of television a day were up to 60 percent more likely to be overweight and 73 percent more likely to be obese in Reception or Year One compared to those who watched less.[30] Lack of physical activity increased the risk by 50 percent.

• **Increased likelihood of being bullied** at school for children

DID YOU KNOW...

It is recommended that children from the age of two upwards should have no more than than two hours screen time (TV and electronic games) per day.[24] Most five-year-olds spend around 14 hours a week (that's two hours a day) in front of a screen.[25] In contrast, children usually spend only 38 minutes a day with a parent[26] and they are spending 10 times more time watching TV than playing outside.[27]

who watch a lot of TV from the age of two, probably because it cuts down on family relational time.[31]
• **Reduced concentration levels** in children under four in homes where the TV is on in the background. It also adversely affected the quality and quantity of parent–child interaction.[31]

There are benefits of film together time

Although excess solitary TV watching has some very worrying features, in contrast, sitting down and watching a film together with your child can improve your child's social intelligence. Research shows that when parents explain character's motives and feelings to their child as they watch a film they actually help the child think psychologically, which develops sophisticated social and theory of mind skills. This activates parts of the child's brain to do with higher social intelligence.[32] The same research observed that the brain networks used to listen to stories or watch films together were the same as those we use for skilfully managing our interactions with people. Television watching does not have the same effect. This is probably because programmes are shorter, interrupted by commercials, there's less in-depth development of a story or characters, and because parents are more likely to leave children watching TV on their own.[33]

What about educational DVDs for babies?

There are lots of DVDs on the market for children aged one or younger and many claim to improve a baby's cognitive development. In fact, research has shown that watching these videos can adversely affect a baby's language development. One research study found that with every hour per day spent watching baby DVDs, infants learned six to eight fewer new words than babies who never watched the videos.[34] This is because the major contributor to good speech, vocabulary, and comprehension is the amount of time a parent or carer spends reading and talking to a child. After a group of nine-month-old babies interacted with a Mandarin speaker, they

Children love computer games and these can enhance development of the frontal lobes and can even help a child discharge stress and anger instead of bottling it up. Research shows that more and more children have access to tablets: they are used by one in five three- to four-year-olds, a quarter of all five- to seven-year-olds, a third of eight- to 11-year-olds, and nearly half of 12- to 15-year-olds.[35]

Although there are apps and games that can help a child learn to read, research shows that children who read in print score significantly higher on reading comprehension tests than those who read on a screen. Text in print has more visual and tactile cues, and the paper provides physical, tactile, spatio-temporal cues, too.[36]

showed an enhanced ability to discriminate speech sounds in Mandarin compared to a control group. The experiment was repeated with another group, but this time the Mandarin speaker was on TV; these babies were no more likely than the control group to discriminate Mandarin speech sounds.[37]

Are tablet apps or computer games good or bad?
The bright, fun, and appealing images can be good for getting children's attention and motivating them. They often provide lots of lovely quick feedback, verbal praise, and cheering when the child gets an answer right, which reinforces and encourages repeated practice. One of the key arguments some people make against games is that they are so appealing they could make everyday life and the slower-paced information at school seem boring. However, the latest research using tablets for early literacy in primary schools with three- to five-year-olds found none of this to be true. These games can enhance development of frontal lobe functions, and improve literacy and numeracy, hand–eye coordination, visual spatial skills, speed of processing, and the ability to make fine discriminations with colour and contrast sensitivity. That said, these skills are not necessarily centrally useful in the school learning environment, where the approach is to build up information more slowly.

Letting a three-year-old play with a tablet on a boring car journey or that visit to a café for a lengthy family meal can actually be a good idea. Remember, boredom in young children triggers high levels of stress hormones and states of bodily hyperarousal, which they are otherwise likely to discharge by climbing on the table, hitting their sibling, or spilling the sugar (see page 251). So, download age-appropriate apps that are about colouring in, sorting, counting, spelling, or practising writing skills and let them "play". Don't make the mistake of putting films on the tablet, though, as children are more likely to go for the films (passive) and ignore the apps (interactive).

Does violence in games or films impact on a child's brain and mind?

It's often hard to find a film without violence; even children's movies and cartoons marked suitable for any audience have plenty. By the time a child is 18 years old, she will have seen 16,000 murders on the screen.[38] Some teenagers have actually developed post-traumatic stress from exposure to violent or fearful scenes on TV as the memory of a disturbing film can be laid down in the brain in the same way as that of a traumatic event in real life, and this often shows as troubled behaviour.[39] With as little as three months' high exposure to violent video games, school-aged children in one study showed increased aggressive feelings and actions towards other children, manifesting as punching or kicking, getting into fights, arguments with teachers, and poor performance in schools.[40] The violent actions in the games trigger reward chemicals in the brain at levels similar to that when taking amphetamines. This adrenaline rush is potentially addictive.[41]

So what is the best approach overall?

Interactive screen time is good and bad for the developing brain. The message as ever is moderation. Keep to the limits of no more than two hours screen time a day (consoles, tablets, and TV/DVDs combined). That said, don't get over-anxious about it. Screen time is just one influence in a child's life. When choosing how long and what game, think about what else your child is doing each day, and in particular how much quality together time she has had with you.

Time spent on screen steals time from all the bonding and brain developing activities and together times described in this book. So an important consideration is the ratio of screen time to all the other imaginative, physical, and relational play time in the child's life that is so key for brain development and bonding. Finally, try out a computer game first to check if it's good and not too hard, too boring, or violent. That way you can also help your child if she gets stuck or frustrated.

CONSIDER THIS...

Research has found that excessive gaming can have the following effects:

• **It disrupts a child's daily routines**. For example, children were seen to be sleeping during the day and gaming at night, eating irregular meals, and had poor hygiene. The children were irritable, aggressive, and violent when family members asked them to stop playing.

• **Anxiety, social phobia, and school performance worsened** in teenagers who became game addicts (those who are gaming for more than four hours a day). If they stopped gaming, depression, anxiety, and social phobia decreased and school performance improved.[42]

• **There's evidence of adverse** brain changes. Teenagers who were playing on average 10 hours of on-line video games per day for nearly three years showed chronic social, emotional, and cognitive dysfunction. Their frontal lobes showed structural abnormalities and a reduction in grey matter.[43]

" For some teenagers... video games feel like a better world to be in than the... story line that is the player's real life. **"**

Professor Susan Greenfield

The impact of bullying

There are those who argue that bullying is not in the same league as child abuse. But when you look at the long-term effects of severe psychological stress, be it the misuse of power by one child against another or an adult bullying a child in the name of discipline, it is clear they are much the same.

CONSIDER THIS...

If you suspect your child is being bullied, watch out for an obsession with war, fighting, and bombing in his play, to the exclusion of all else. Many boys enjoy these activities, but it is the intensity of the fighting and its repetition throughout the day that can be a concern. When a child has a consuming obsession with fighting and war play, it can indicate an attempt at defence against unmanageable feelings of fear and living in a world that has failed him in terms of "making the bullying stop".

Your child may move into being a bully himself. This is a kind of last-ditch defence. It's a defence of "if you can't beat them, join them".

Long-term consequences

The problem is that in the early years of life, the human brain moulds itself to adapt to its environment. So, amazingly and tragically, the brain of the bullied child can start to actually alter itself to be more suited to living in a bullying world (see also pages 166–67). This can result in hypervigilance (always being on guard), reptilian brain fight-or-flight defence mechanisms, and overactive RAGE or FEAR systems in the lower, or mammalian, brain.

In some children, it results in emotional coldness and underactive social-emotion systems in the lower brain. As with other forms of distress, such as prolonged crying in childhood (see pages 34–63), frequent childhood experiences of high stress levels, and stressful relationships, where the child is not comforted to regain a state of calm, can bring about a permanent over-reactivity in key stress response systems in the child's brain. Moreover, living with intense fear from being bullied at home and/or at school over a prolonged period can start to show itself in actual alterations to key structures in the brain, such as the amygdala (see page 19). After bullying, this part of the brain can become oversensitive and so over-react to minor stressors, treating them as if they are big threats. It's called "fear kindling", which means that fear can become an ingrained part of the child's personality. Other studies with bullied children have shown lack of activation in the amygdala, resulting in lack of response to another's fear.[44]

Bullying can seriously affect a child's social confidence and result in brain changes

We have known for a long time that there are likely to be psychological scars from being bullied, but there has usually been hope for recovery – the belief that, with help and support, a bullied child can quickly recover. But now the advancement of brain scans shows a far bleaker picture. They reveal actual structural and enduring biochemical changes in the brain of the child who has suffered the intense relational stress of psychological abuse. In short, there can be a real cost to the brain itself. In the UK, around 46 percent of children and young people have been bullied, and in 2013 almost 45,000 children called the Childline helpline to talk about it.[45] Clearly, as a society, we are aware and concerned, but arguably when we look at the scans that reveal how being bullied can change a child's brain, we are not worried enough.

"Fear can become an ingrained part of the child's personality."

"I hate what they do"

When bullying is subtle, it may pass unnoticed. Whispering and name-calling, ostracizing and isolating can cause just as much distress and long-term damage to a child's brain as physical assaults. So parents and teachers need to be watchful for signs (see page 168). School days are long, and no child should have to spend her waking hours in a state of fear.

The brain legacy of bullying

For many children who have been bullied, you can see both "fight" and "flight" responses in their day-to-day behaviour. A child may develop a dislike of school, or start bedwetting or having other physical symptoms. Scientists have also found a number of worrying changes in the brains of bullied children.

• **Cell death and/or a reduced activation in the anterior cingulate gyrus.** This area helps moderate the fear response in the brain. It is key to our capacity for empathy.[46]

• **Long-term alterations in brain circuits and systems** that are to do with managing stress well. A child can develop an over-reactive stress response system in the brain, resulting in her being impulsive, aggressive, and/or anxious frequently.

• **Long-term changes to the adrenaline systems** in the brain. Too much noradrenaline and adrenaline washing over the brain can make you feel anxious and unable to think clearly.

• **Decrease in blood flow and impairment** in the "cerebellar vermis" in the brain stem. This area controls some of the production and release of noradrenaline and dopamine. Abnormalities here have been associated with ADHD (see page 111), depression, and impaired attention. This area also helps regulate electrical activity in the brain, so when it's not functioning well, more aggression and irritability can result.

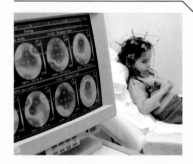

The effects of bullying can be seen in EEG irregularities in the frontal and temporal brain regions. These regions are vital for the management of stress and the regulation of intense feelings.

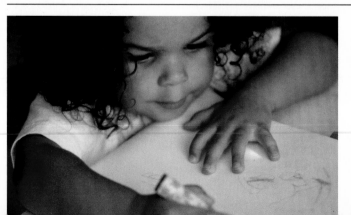

Prolonged stress can cause a reduction in the size of the hippocampus and the amygdala. The hippocampus is very important in memory function, and maltreated people score lower on verbal memory tests. A reduction in the left amygdala is associated with depression, irritability, or hostility.

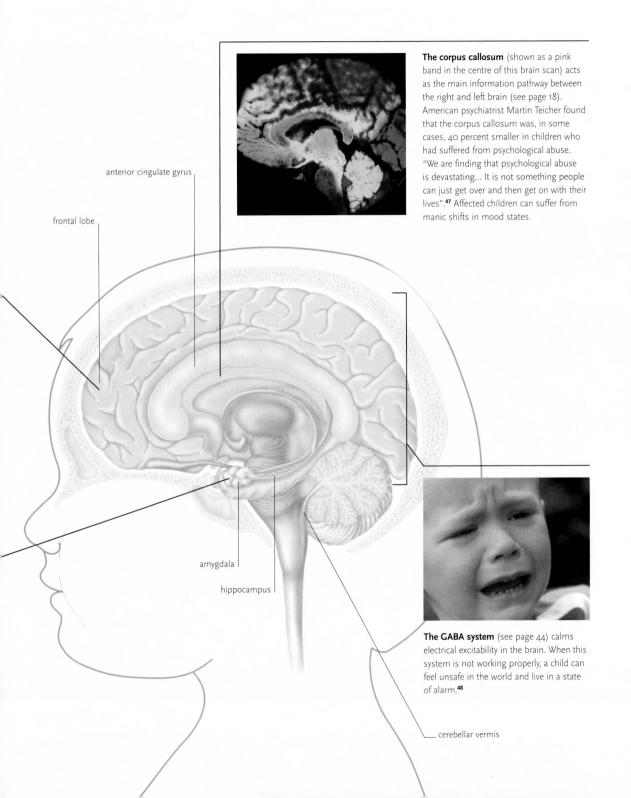

The corpus callosum (shown as a pink band in the centre of this brain scan) acts as the main information pathway between the right and left brain (see page 18). American psychiatrist Martin Teicher found that the corpus callosum was, in some cases, 40 percent smaller in children who had suffered from psychological abuse. "We are finding that psychological abuse is devastating... It is not something people can just get over and then get on with their lives".[47] Affected children can suffer from manic shifts in mood states.

anterior cingulate gyrus

frontal lobe

amygdala

hippocampus

The GABA system (see page 44) calms electrical excitability in the brain. When this system is not working properly, a child can feel unsafe in the world and live in a state of alarm.[48]

cerebellar vermis

Bully-proof your child

Both in school and at home, there are measures that can help protect children from being bullied or becoming bullies. As parents, you can boost your child's self-defences by helping her to develop emotional strength, a lively personality that responds warmly to others, and friendship skills that will last her for life.

Some children who have been bullied suffer from post-traumatic stress disorder. The core arousal system in the brain stem is grossly affected. Children can have problems with sleeping, eating, and breathing, and suffer from headaches and other symptoms. Children like this do not feel safe enough to learn, and school work is often badly affected. Therapy and counselling can help enormously.

What schools can do

When it comes to looking for a suitable school, although you cannot eliminate all risks of bullying there are certain things that can guide your choice. If the headteacher is a very warm person, this is a good indicator. There should also be a watertight and highly effective bullying policy. Many people in the UK like to think we are pretty hot on child-protection issues. I would argue that where bullying in schools is concerned we are failing very badly.

Some schools say that they can't properly police the playground or that they don't have the staff

If all schools knew the true effects of bullying on the brain of a child, I think there might be a shift in concern both at school and at government level. I would put CCTV cameras in every school playground (where most bullying occurs). Some would argue this is an infringement of children's rights, yet surely we have a duty to protect every child from the brain damage and often life-long psychological scars that can result from bullying, with all its unbearable feelings of impotence, aloneness, and often terror.

Some schools do appreciate the urgency of putting into place effective bullying policies with an absolute zero tolerance. If every school is to ensure against damaging the brains they are supposed to be developing, bullying at school has to stop, whatever the costs to the government in terms of extra staffing. Be especially wary of relatives, teachers, or

I've found out that my child is being bullied regularly. What can I do?

If your child has suffered bullying that is persistent rather than being stopped promptly, consider getting him counselling or therapy. (For organizations that provide it, see Useful addresses, page 297.) Children are good at acting as if they are just fine, while hiding feelings of fear and impotence. Many adults still reel from the hurt of being bullied years ago. Research shows that the effects of bullying, such as changes in the corpus callosum (the nerve fibres connecting the two halves of the brain), can be partly repaired by such activities as learning the piano, which helps to integrate right and left brain processing.[49]

friends who fail children by minimizing bullying, saying something like "they're only teasing" or "boys will be boys".

What you can do at home

Some forms of discipline, such as shouting, shaming, and smacking (see page 222), are bullying by other names. Keep an eye on your own methods of dealing with difficult behaviour, and confront your partner and relatives if you think their treatment of your child comes close to bullying.

Hold back criticism and give lots of praise

If parents keep criticizing their child and giving no praise, she will become acclimatized to living in a bullying world. If, in other words, they keep "hitting" their child with words, and that child is then bullied at school, she can all too easily move into thinking, "I deserve this. I'm rubbish", or, "This is normal; the world is so harsh." A child who has known a warm, kind world at home can move far more effectively into asking for help. This child is far more likely to have an attitude of, "This is not okay; I am a valued and special person. I deserve to be treated well." You can do a lot to help a child realize that she has a right to feel safe and empower her to assert her rights.

Take sibling fighting very seriously

The contribution of sibling fighting to bullying in schools is vastly under-rated.[50] When a young child is hurt by her sibling, she hasn't yet developed the frontal lobe capacities to reflect on her emotional experiences. She may simply cut off from her pain and move into fight-or-flight impulses. This can result in her hurting another child at school, and so a bully is made. Parenting has a great deal of influence on the development of this type of personality. Helping siblings to talk to each other about conflicts, modelling how to do this, being there while they talk, offering empathy for both points of view, and helping them negotiate, can be crucial, as it won't come naturally to your children.

Key points

• The capacity for meaningful relationships deepened over time is key for physical and mental health and long-term happiness.

• Good parenting can develop your child's social intelligence, including the ability to relate to others and have a capacity for compassion and empathy.

• Limit the amount of screen time your child has and balance it with times for imaginative and physical play and together times that develop social intelligence.

• Bullying and sibling abuse can have long-term damaging effects on the brain and must be taken very seriously by parents, teachers, and carers.

• Help your child to avoid bullying (as bully or victim) by building her confidence and social skills. If it happens act immediately.

behaving badly

All parents experience challenging behaviour from their children at some time. This chapter is all about empowering parents with the scientific and psychological explanations for bad behaviour. It also focuses on temper tantrums – a time when most parents feel that they could do with practical help. Some child behaviour specialists advise ignoring a tantrum, but this is not always the best advice. In this chapter, I will explain why looking only at a child's behaviour, rather than at his distress levels and his needs, can fail a child.

Why children behave badly

When your child is being horrid, he is not just a bundle of naughtiness – although it may feel like this at times. He is a little person with highly complex emotional reactions, and psychological and physiological needs. What's more, if we reduce everything to a matter of behaviour, we can all too easily forget to think about what's causing the behaviour.

"Children can be horrid when they are hungry because hunger disrupts their hormones."

Parents can do a great deal to prevent their children from behaving badly. This chapter aims to empower parents by explaining what is going on inside a child's head when he is being naughty and how parents can help to avoid or resolve troublesome episodes. It shows how, when addressing challenging behaviour, we need to hold in mind a child's feelings and relationship issues as well as just the behaviour. Whenever your child is behaving badly it is due to one or more of the following six reasons, and knowing what they are will help you to respond to your child appropriately.

"Sorry, I'm just fed up"

When a child is being naughty, it can be difficult to think about why. Children are highly complex beings, yet they do not have the maturity to communicate these feelings effectively. This can lead to outbursts of bad behaviour. If you take time to talk to your child about her behaviour, in an attempt to understand the underlying causes, her real feelings often come out, and you can find a creative way to resolve the situation.

Reason one: tiredness and hunger

Children often behave badly when they have an unmet physical need for sleep or food. Consuming certain foods or drink may also play havoc with their brains and bodies.

Research shows that sleep deprivation is associated with imbalances in the autonomic nervous system (see page 44), which regulates bodily arousal. When this system is balanced, natural calming mechanisms come into play to help stabilize mood. When we are short of sleep, these mechanisms may no longer function well and the arousal branch of the system is left in the driving seat, often tipping the child into states of over-arousal.[1]

Sleep loss also intensifies negative emotions when we are under stress. In addition, it can cause imbalances in blood sugar levels, with consequent effects on mood – including aggression, anxiety, and depression.[2]

But you can't blame tiredness for everything

Because it's easier to look for a physical cause for bad behaviour than it is to reflect on the complexities of emotional and relationship needs, many parents too easily blame tiredness when their child is being horrid. If the child is not tired and is feeling awful for another reason, this incorrect labelling means a painful experience of misunderstanding for the child and the missing of an opportunity for real resolution of the problem.

The hunger monster plays havoc with the brain

Children can be horrid when they are hungry because hunger disrupts their hormones. If your child's blood sugar level falls too low, his body will respond by releasing stress hormones from the adrenal glands. These hormones include cortisol and adrenaline, which are designed to raise blood sugar levels. However, the strong activation of adrenaline and cortisol means that your child may then suffer from any of the following: anxiety, agitation, aggression, feelings of panic,

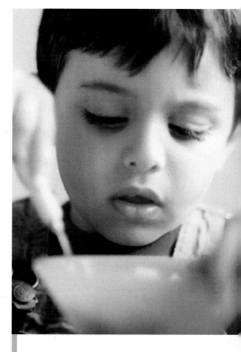

CONSIDER THIS...

Research shows that missing breakfast can result in hyperactive behaviour. A proper breakfast improves a child's academic performance, psychological well-being, and behaviour. When children who didn't eat breakfast started eating it, they had a far more stable mood for the rest of the day.[3]

"Chocolate and sweets eaten on an empty stomach send a child's sugar levels sky high."

CONSIDER THIS...

Research on infants shows that DHA (one of the omega 3 fatty acids) from fish oil is essential for normal brain development, thinking, and concentration. It also boosts serotonin levels. One study shows that low levels of DHA were associated with more:
- temper tantrums
- sleep problems
- behaviour problems
- learning problems.[5]

and confusion. These painful feelings may be discharged in a temper tantrum.

Low blood sugar (technically known as hypoglycaemia) also deprives the brain of glucose, which can lead to out-of-control behaviour, similar to the way people behave under the influence of alcohol.

Sugar and sweets may cause bad behaviour

Chocolate and sweets eaten on an empty stomach, instead of with a proper meal (or eaten without the presence of adequate protein), send a child's sugar levels sky high. The child gets an energy boost within 10–15 minutes, but then, because blood sugar levels rise too high, insulin kicks in to drop the blood sugar back to safe levels. After about 30 minutes, the child experiences a dramatic drop in blood sugar that is lower than before he ate the sweets. This can lead to hypoglycaemia, which in turn leads to aggression, anxiety, and hyperactive behaviour such as rushing about and climbing up things.[4]

This same child can play very well for some time if he eats a proper meal, which boosts levels of the mood-stabilizing chemical serotonin in his brain. If you do give snacks, a piece of toast with honey or a banana is better than chocolate. These foods will not cause a dramatic drop in blood sugar, and they also raise levels of serotonin.

Food additives can impact on the brain

Children are particularly vulnerable to food additives because their bodies and brains are so immature. Some additives reduce levels of dopamine and noradrenaline in the brain, resulting in hyperactive behaviour in some children. So, if your child has just had an ice-cream or fizzy drink, and starts being hyperactive, you'll know why. Watch out for:
- **E110,** which is used in some biscuits. It is carcinogenic when fed to animals.
- **E122,** found in some jams. It is also carcinogenic when fed to animals.

"I'm being hyperactive!"

Food additives in processed foods such as biscuits, sweets, and soft drinks can have mood-altering effects on a child's brain and are common triggers of bad behaviour. Sometimes this is the reason why children's parties end with at least one overexcited child in tears. Try to choose appealing, healthy alternatives that are low in additives, colouring, and sugar.

- **E127** is used in some sweets. It is also a dopamine and noradrenaline inhibitor, and can lead to loss of concentration and behaviour such as ADHD (see page 111).
- **E150** is added to some soft drinks and crisps.
- **E210–E219** is used in some soft drinks, jam, and salad cream, and is linked to asthma and childhood hyperactivity.
- **E220–227** is in some desserts, biscuits, and fruit juices.
- **E249–252** is added to some cured meats and some cheeses. It causes headaches and is linked to cancer in human studies.
- **Sweeteners** are added to some soft drinks and sweet foods. They can reduce levels of tryptophan, which is vital for the brain to make the mood-stabilizing chemical serotonin. Low tryptophan levels are linked to both hyperactive and aggressive behaviour.[6]

"Children are particularly vulnerable to food additives because their bodies and brains are so immature."

Reason two: an undeveloped emotional brain

" Young children can't naturally inhibit their primitive impulses to run about and climb up things. **"**

Children are sometimes criticized for bad behaviour that they simply can't be held responsible for, because their emotional brains are too immature for them to behave better. In young children, the higher brain is still underdeveloped, so they can't naturally inhibit their primitive impulses to lash out, or run about and climb up things all the time.

There is much unfair punishment due to lack of understanding about immature brains. In a 2012 survey in the UK by the NSPCC:

• **More than 40 percent of parents** admitted to physically punshing or smacking a child in the past year; around 67 percent had threatened smacking.

• **Around 77 percent of parents** shouted at their children.[7]

" I feel really angry **"**

There are many reasons why a child may behave badly at school or nursery. Tiredness and hunger may play a part, but there may be emotional reasons, too. Difficulties at home can have a dramatic influence on a child's relationships with her peer group and with carers and teachers.

Some people hit a baby or lash out in anger at a toddler, because they think the child is being deliberately naughty. In other words, they read intention into what the child is doing. Many previous generations of parents have subscribed to the view that to "give in" to a crying baby will "spoil" him or that children can have their parents "wrapped around their little finger". However, we now know that a baby's or young child's brain isn't developed enough to have clearly defined thoughts about manipulating adults (see box, right).

Reason three: psychological hungers

The three psychological hungers – for stimulation, recognition, and structure – were originally defined by a psychologist called Eric Berne. He found that, over time, if one or more of these hungers remains unsatisfied, people can become emotionally unwell and even, in the long term, be affected by mental and physical ill health.[8]

Understimulation is a pain in the brain

The brain registers understimulation as stress. To change this painful state, people will do something to increase their arousal state and to change the chemical state in the brain. Adults, for example, may turn on the radio or light a cigarette; infants may start head-banging; children might start running around screaming. Because children have fewer resources than adults, the stimulation they choose is often aggressive, noisy, or destructive – such as hitting a sibling or pouring juice all over the table. Part of stimulation hunger is incident hunger. Again, if a child is not experiencing enough incidents, he will make his own, perhaps by fighting his brother or throwing a temper tantrum (see pages 182–83).

Recognition hunger makes a child seek attention

Recognition hunger is the genetically programmed human need for attention, which means having an impact on

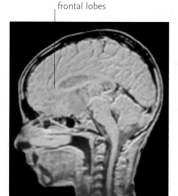

"Children need lots of attention for healthy brain development."

CONSIDER THIS...

We are all attention-seeking, but children especially need lots of attention for the healthy development of their brains, and they are generally far more overt about their recognition needs than many adults. Children don't know about the psychology of recognition hunger, but they soon discover that bad behaviour guarantees getting attention.

someone in a way that makes them respond. We all have a fundamental psychological need to feel that we can have an impact on the world, because, "If I have an impact, I know that I exist."[9] If a child feels that good behaviour does not impact on his parent, he resorts to bad behaviour instead.

Bad behaviour that stems from recognition hunger comes from an inner scream of "Please don't ignore me". If your child thinks the only way to get your attention is to be naughty or to scream or cry, then this is what he will do. Of course, for all children lovely attention is better than angry attention, but if angry attention is all that is available then this is what children will seek.

Structure hunger can lead to bad behaviour

We all have a psychological need for structure. Lack of structure can make adults feel depressed, anxious, or angry or lose focus and meaning. A society without structure is an extremely fertile ground for bad behaviour. Without the structure of rules and the law, we would have a breakdown in civilization. It's just the same with children. They need the structure of clear house rules and clear routines.

Think of the structureless time for a child of waiting in a queue or following you around a shop. Your child suddenly becomes horrid. But when you do some structured activity with him, you have a great child!

Reason four: needing help with a big feeling

Sometimes children behave badly because they are discharging tension from a very painful emotion. They may be angry or frustrated with someone; they may be being bullied at school or jealous of attention being paid to a sibling; they may be struggling with some event, such as the loss of a relative, a friend, or a pet. A big painful feeling activates stress chemicals in a child's brain and body, so ear-piercing outbursts are often a child's way of relieving tension. A child does not have the words to express his emotions, so he vents his feelings in a scream or a shout. Some parents immediately punish their child for this rather than treating it as a cry for help. If we help children with their painful feelings (disappointment, jealousy, loss, frustration) rather than criticizing them for their lower brain-triggered emotional outbursts, we can help their higher brain to develop the nerve pathways essential for naturally regulating such feelings.[10]

Reason five: picking up on your stress

A child's behaviour is often a barometer of parental stress, depression, anger, or grief. Persistent screaming and raging in a child can be a way of discharging his parents' emotions.

Parenting is one of the most stressful jobs there is, and the more stressed you are, the more likely your children are to behave badly. Why? The right prefrontal part of a child's brain can pick up emotional atmospheres in milliseconds. Just as some dogs are susceptible to the emotions of their owners, so children are deeply affected on a bodily and emotional level by stress or unhappiness in their family. If you are relaxed, the chances are your child will be calm. If the atmosphere at home is tense, your child can be horrid.[11]

Reason six: you activate the wrong part of your child's brain

Your way of relating to your child may be activating the wrong part of his brain. For example, if you shout and issue endless commands – "Do this, don't do that" – you could be unwittingly activating the primitive RAGE and FEAR systems deep in the lower, or mammalian, part of his brain (see page 19). In contrast, lots of play, laughter, and cuddles are likely to activate the brain's PLAY system and CARE system. These systems trigger the release of lovely calming opioids. So hey presto, you have a calm, contented child.[11]

"You're being horrid"

One of the main reasons why children behave badly is because the way a parent is relating to a child is activating the wrong part of a child's brain. You will have a horrid time with your child if your parenting activates her lower brain RAGE, FEAR, or PANIC/GRIEF systems (see page 31). You can have a delightful time if you activate her lower brain CARE (attachment), PLAY, or SEEKING systems (see page 30).

Temper tantrums

Intense storms of feeling, temper tantrums usually happen because a child's higher brain is not sufficiently developed to deal with powerful feelings in more socially acceptable ways. As we shall see, many tantrums are the result of genuine emotional pain, which should be taken seriously: the pain of impotence, deep frustration, loss, disappointment, and feeling misunderstood. Only some tantrums are primarily motivated by a wish to have control over a parent.

" There are two types of tantrums and each needs a specific response. "

Because of their intensity, temper tantrums are often not only frightening to the child himself, but also leave the parent feeling lacking in skills, helpless, overwhelmed, or ready to explode. This is particularly true when parents' own intense feelings were not handled well in their childhood. It can be a real art for a parent to manage their own feelings during a child's tantrum. It's vital that the whole thing doesn't turn into a matter of winners and losers, but instead involves a parent staying calm and thinking of rational or creative ways to manage the child's feelings.

Conflict with parents over food and eating accounts for around 17 percent of toddler tantrums. The reasons are often complex (see page 205).

Being strapped in a car seat or high chair can activate the lower brain's RAGE system, and accounts for more than 11 percent of tantrums.

Getting dressed restricts a child's movements in much the same way as being put in a pushchair, and accounts for about 11 percent of tantrums.

Why tantrums are important

Temper tantrums are key times for brain sculpting. This is because the emotional regulation of a child's feelings during storms of feeling enable him to establish essential brain pathways for managing stress and being assertive in later life.

The too-good child who does not have tantrums may have learned early on that when he expressed big feelings, he elicited a frightening parental response, and that the price of parental love and approval is total compliance. The too-good child misses out on the vital brain sculpting that he gets from his parents when he expresses big, dramatic feelings. This means that when he faces frustration in later life, he may respond with angry outbursts or struggle to be assertive.

Not all tantrums are battles for power

Many tantrums are about genuine emotional pain. It is a mistake to think that rage is always just about control. There can be terrible pain in some rage, as, for example, in the rage of failing to get your beloved parent to understand something that is deeply important to you.

When faced with a potential conflict, ask yourself if this is worth fighting over

Imagine you are two years old and the people in your life have control over everything you do. Wouldn't it make you mad? Work out what is worth fighting about (for example, behaviour that is dangerous) and areas where you can give your child some slack.

There are two different types of tantrum

I call the first type a "distress" tantrum and the second a "Little Nero" tantrum (see page 190). It's important to know what's happening to your child's brain during each type, because they require specific responses. You need to move away from a child having a Little Nero tantrum, but move towards a child having a distress one to provide comfort and solace.

"It's not fair!"

One of the two types of tantrum is the "distress" tantrum. It can be triggered by strong feelings such as disappointment, loss, or frustration and can make the child feel hugely upset. This type of tantrum needs sensitive handling, and an understanding that the child cannot handle these big feelings without your help.

Distress tantrums

A distress tantrum means that one or more of the three alarm systems in your child's lower brain has been very strongly activated. These alarm systems are RAGE, FEAR, and PANIC/GRIEF (see page 29). As a result, your child's arousal system (see page 40) will be way out of balance, with excessively high levels of stress chemicals searing through his body and brain.

CASE STUDY

A tantrum at breakfast

James has a distress tantrum because the family has run out of his favourite breakfast cereal. He is not being naughty, but he is disappointed. He needs to discharge the bodily arousal caused by the frustration, and he needs a compassionate response.

James's dad scoops him up in his arms and uses understanding words that will enable James to start to develop stress-regulating systems. This approach is more effective than trying to reason with a young child.

Distress tantrums happen because essential brain pathways between a child's higher brain and his lower brain haven't developed yet. These brain pathways are necessary to enable a child to manage his big feelings. As a parent, your role is to soothe your child while he experiences the huge hormonal storms in his brain and body. If you get angry with a child for having a distress tantrum, he may stop crying, but this may mean that the FEAR system in his brain has triggered, over-riding his PANIC/GRIEF system. Or he may simply have shifted into silent crying, which means his level of the stress chemical cortisol remains sky high. As we've seen throughout this book, uncomforted distress can leave a child with toxic levels of stress hormones washing over the brain.

Children can't talk or listen well when distressed

The dramatic brain and body changes of a distress tantrum hijack your child's thinking functions and the verbal centres in his higher brain that control the comprehension and expression of speech. It is important to understand this because trying to talk to your child during a distress tantrum, or expecting him to talk about his feelings, is a waste of time. All he can do is discharge his emotions.

A distress tantrum needs sensitive handling

It is important that you take a genuine distress tantrum seriously and meet your child's pain of loss, frustration, or acute disappointment with sympathy and understanding. When you do this, you will be helping your child to develop vital stress-regulating systems in his higher brain (see pages 22–24). Repeatedly getting angry with a child's genuine distress can mean that he never develops inhibitory mechanisms in his higher brain. Picture a man who often loses his temper in a restaurant, or violently kicks a faulty vending machine – in early life he may have missed out on the parenting that would have helped him manage rage.[12]

" Your role is to soothe...the huge hormonal storms in his brain and body. **"**

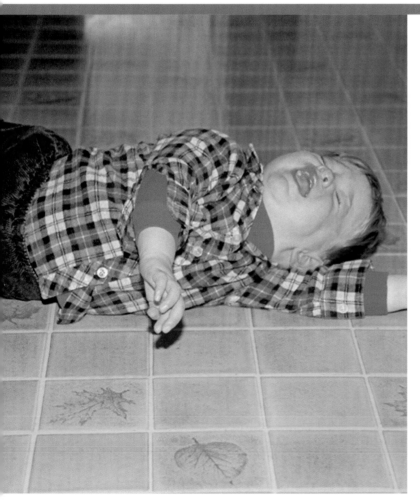

" Life is so terrible **"**

When a child has a "distress" tantrum, you can see real anguish in his face. Two-year-old Ben, writhing on the shop floor because he had set his heart on shoes that did not fit, is in emotional pain. One of his brain's alarm systems has triggered, and stress chemicals and hormones are flooding his body, making him feel dreadful. He needs comfort.

"Help me to handle this"

If your child is experiencing a distress tantrum, she will need your help to quieten down again. If you hold her in your arms, your mature bodily arousal system (see page 46) will help to calm her immature one.

Speak to her softly, using simple, soothing words. Your child will begin to feel very safe as she realizes that you can help her with her big feelings. This will prevent her becoming angry or withdrawing from you.

When your child feels better, try to distract her with something fun, such as a toy, or point out something interesting nearby.

Regulating childhood distress is a key task for all parents, teachers, and other childcarers

Receiving help to manage intense feelings of rage, frustration, or distress means that a child can develop the brain pathways that enable him to calm himself down when under stress. If we don't respond to a genuine distress tantrum and, instead, adopt a fixed approach to all tantrums, we lose a vital opportunity to sculpt a child's brain in a positive way. It is deeply reassuring to a child to know that an adult can calm and understand the volcanic storms that rip through his body and brain. It is most disturbing to a child that when he is in terrible emotional pain his Mummy gets angry or just walks away from him.

How to handle distress tantrums

Your role is to give your child a sense of safety, comfort, and reassurance when he is having a distress tantrum. These techniques can all help to calm your child:

• **Use simple, calm actions** or provide a simple choice. For example, if your child is upset about getting dressed, ask him whether he wants to wear his blue or his brown trousers.

• **Distraction is a wonderful,** often under-used technique. It activates the SEEKING system (see page 30) in your child's lower brain and makes him feel curious and interested in something. It can naturally override the brain's RAGE or PANIC/GRIEF systems. It also triggers a high level of dopamine, a great positive arousal chemical in the brain, which reduces stress and triggers interest and motivation.[13]

• **Hold your child tenderly.** Sometimes it really helps to hold a distressed child, but you must feel calm and in control yourself. Being next to your calm body will bring his over-aroused body and brain systems back into balance and release natural, calming oxytocin and opioids. Say simple words such as, "I know, I know". (Words alone, however, will not strongly release these wonderful chemicals.) If his RAGE system has been triggered as well as his PANIC/GRIEF system, and he is

CONSIDER THIS...

It is very common for children to have nightmares after they have had a distress tantrum during the day. Intense feelings may well be symbolized by monsters in the nightmare.

"We are deeply feeling and deeply biological creatures... we must come to terms with the biological sources of the human spirit.**"**
Professor Jaak Panksepp

TRY THIS...

Getting a young child dressed can be a common area of conflict. Offering your child a choice, or engaging her brain with a distraction, can make the process less stressful for both of you. If you try to hurry a child, a scenario along the following lines is all too likely to occur:

Parent: "Time to get dressed, please."

Molly: "No."

Parent: "Come on. It's time to go out."

Molly: "Shan't! No! No! No!"

The RAGE systems in both the child's and mother's lower brains are triggered as cascades of horrid hormones and stress chemicals flood out. Before this turns into a tantrum, try activating a child's frontal lobe by giving her something to think about. Offer her a choice. So instead of saying, "Time to get dressed", try, "Do you want to wear a dress or trousers today?"

You could also try distraction as you get your child dressed. Point out a toy, or sing a song, using a lovely, playful tone of voice. This engages your child's higher brain and makes the whole process much more enjoyable.

throwing things around the room or hitting or biting, you will need to use the proper holding technique (see page 237).

• **Sometimes a child will feel safe and contained** just by you sitting down calmly next to him and talking gently. Some children find this preferable to being held, as it allows them the freedom to move.

• **Don't use the Time Out technique**. You wouldn't walk away from your best friend or send her to a Time Out room if she was writhing and sobbing on the floor, so this is certainly not appropriate for tantrumming children, who have far fewer emotional resources than adults. Putting a child in distress in Time Out would also mean missing a vital opportunity for rage and distress regulation and establishing effective stress-regulating systems in the brain.

• **Avoid putting a child in a room on his own** during a distress tantrum. Although the child may stop vocal crying, he may continue to cry internally – something that research shows is more worrying.[14] Whereas crying out loud is a request for help, silent, internal crying is a sign that the child has lost faith that help will come. In some people, this tragic loss of faith can stay for life.

• **Remind yourself that a child's distress is genuine.** A two-year-old who is screaming because his sibling has snatched a toy car is not just making a fuss. Research shows that a sense of loss activates the pain centres in the brain, causing an agonizing opioid withdrawal.[15] Because young children have been in the world for only a few years, they don't have a clear perspective on life. As adults, we have a backdrop of events and experiences that tell us that the loss of a toy car is a minor disappointment. But for a young child this loss can mean everything. If a child is repeatedly punished for grief-fuelled tantrums (grief often includes rage), the lesson he learns is, "Mummy cannot manage or understand my grief." As a result, he is likely to cut off from feelings of hurt because they are no longer safe to have. This has consequences for how a child manages his feelings in adulthood.

Q It feels as if I'm giving in when I distract her with a game. Am I "spoiling" her and encouraging more tantrums?

Starting a game of pat-a-cake or launching into a song is a very good way of distracting a toddler who is building up to a tantrum. Research shows that distraction can work very well at this stage, whereas it often doesn't once a child is deep into a full-blown distress state.[16]

Using distraction to avert a tantrum is not "spoiling" your child. Young children do not have an adult perspective on life, and not being able to do or have something they want can activate a full-blown PANIC/GRIEF reaction. Throwing a tantrum is not naughty, but is a result of immaturity. As a parent, you need to use compassion and understanding to help your child manage her feelings.

Little Nero tantrums

The Little Nero tantrum is very different from the distress tantrum in that it is about the desire to control and manipulate. A child having a Little Nero tantrum doesn't experience or show the anguish, desperation, and panic that characterizes the distress tantrum, and he doesn't have stress chemicals flooding his brain and body.

BRAIN STORY

The brain activity during a distress tantrum is very different from that in a Little Nero tantrum. During a distress tantrum, your child can't think or speak rationally because his higher brain functions are hijacked by the primitive emotional systems in his lower brain. By contrast, a child who is having a Little Nero tantrum is using his higher brain to produce behaviour that is calculated and deliberate.

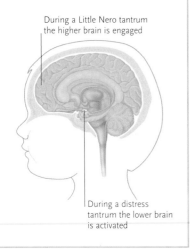

During a Little Nero tantrum the higher brain is engaged

During a distress tantrum the lower brain is activated

A Little Nero tantrum is about a child trying to get what he wants – attention, a particular toy, or food – through bullying his parents into submission. A child who has frequent Little Nero tantrums has learned that shouting and screaming produce results: "If I cry and scream, I know that eventually I'll get that bar of chocolate."

Children who have Little Nero tantrums need to learn that they can't always receive the gratification they want at the time they want it, and that it's not okay to bully or control people to get what they want in life.

The problems of giving in

If you reward frequent Little Nero tantrums by giving in to your child's demands, you are in danger of setting up a trigger-happy RAGE system in your child's brain. This is because the mere experience of rage without the capacity for reasoned thinking can result in rage becoming a part of your child's personality.[17]

Some children, whose Little Nero tantrums have not been handled well, not only win the battle at the age of two, but are still winning at six, eight, and ten years old. They then grow up to be power-seeking, bullying adults who think they can rule the roost at work and at home. Such people are developmentally arrested – Little Nero two year olds in adult bodies – and they can bring abject misery to the people who have to live with them or work with them.

"Give me what I want – now!"

A Little Nero tantrum is very different from a distress tantrum. There is usually an absence of tears and the child is able to articulate her demands, and to argue when you say "no". A child uses this type of tantrum because she has learned that it will get her what she wants. The more you reward this type of tantrum with attention and giving her what she wants, the more she will continue to adopt this behaviour. This can train your child to become a bully in later life (see page 222).

"Well, that didn't work!"

If you ignore a Little Nero tantrum, you are helping your child to develop important social skills. It is essential that you do not humiliate your child, though; he should lose the battle gracefully and with dignity. Reward your child with your attention as soon as his behaviour improves.

Techniques for handling Little Nero tantrums

Little Nero rages need a very different sort of response from a distress tantrum. The following key techniques will help you rather than your two-year-old to be the one in charge.

• **Don't give your child an audience.** A Little Nero tantrum must be a solo performance. If you are absolutely sure your child is not having a distress tantrum, simply walk out of the room. If you ignore a child's Little Nero tantrums, he will stop. It's no fun if there is no-one watching.

• **Don't try to reason, argue with, or persuade** your child. Attention and words reward his negative behaviour.

• **Don't "kiss it better".** This approach gives your child the message, "If you go into a rage, I will give you lots of love."

• **Don't negotiate.** If you do, you are rewarding controlling, angry behaviour. If a child discovers that rage works well in manipulating his parents, he may continue to use it in his adult life. Consider the following nightmare. You've always rewarded your child's wish to control you with attention. Now, at 16, he is still hitting you and kicking doors, but as he's bigger than you, you can't just put him in his room.

• **Give clear, firm "no's"** and try to manage your own rage. No human being likes feeling controlled.

• **Deal firmly with your child's commands.** Give a clear, firm message about commands being unacceptable as a way of getting what you want. For example, if your child is shouting and screaming for a biscuit, try saying, "I'm really happy to talk with you about what you would like when your voice is as quiet as mine." Then get on with what you are doing until your child is calmer and says "please". Pay absolutely no attention to your child while he is using control and dominance as a way of requesting something. Carrying on any conversation with him while he is still issuing you with commands rewards his rage and power-seeking behaviour, and goes one step further towards setting up a hot temper as a personality trait.

• **Give information about social charm.** This works better with an older child, whose higher brain is more developed. You could say, "If you order people to do something, they won't want to help you. So if you want something, can you think of a way of asking that will unlock my kind feelings? If you need help with that, let me know." Or try a really light and clear response, "Hey, Toby, that really won't work for me."

• **Use humour and play when appropriate.** This can deflate a Little Nero's power bubble. Mirror him back to himself. The underlying message is that your child will not get away with a "power over" transaction with you. Try something like, "You really do want to boss me about, don't you? Let's do it together to this can of peas. 'Can of peas – get me that biscuit now! Or, I know, let's boss the toothbrush around... come here toothbrush!'" By now, your child will be looking at you as if you are mad. But the ploy serves to upstage him, stop him in his tracks, move you both into the realm of humour and play (whether he likes it or not), and mirror him back to himself. It will also show that you do not take bullying seriously.

• **Distinguish between a Little Nero tantrum** and a distress tantrum. Sometimes this is difficult because one tips into the other. Obviously, you should never reward statements such as, "Go to the shops to get me white bread NOW," but if he moves into a grief reaction when you say "no" (and you sense the pain is genuine rather than a magnificent act) he will need help with his feelings. The message you need to give your child is, "I don't respond to commands, but I will help you if you are in pain." All mammals, including human infants, are genetically programmed to react with rage if they don't receive an anticipated reward, and do not have the frontal lobe development to override these feelings.

• **Playful parenting is far more effective** than punishing parenting. Punishing parenting triggers stress hormones, which shift children into defensive states of rage, fear, or shame. Playful parenting activates anti-anxiety and anti-aggression hormones, so children are not interested in

CASE STUDY

Out of control Emma

If Emma didn't get her own way, she would scream, kick, cry, and throw herself on the floor. She was often bossy, saying things like, "Don't go out, stay with me." She deliberately damaged her doll because she wanted a new one. Emma's mother tried to reason and plead with her – the worst response to Little Nero behaviour. Emma got worse. When she began to pull light fittings off the wall to make her mother do as she asked, Emma was referred to a therapist. Her mother confessed that although she loved Emma, she didn't like her any more.

Emma was very well-behaved at school. When asked why she was so different at school, she said, "You aren't allowed to be naughty at school." When Emma's mother went to parenting classes, she learned how to set clear boundaries and consequences. At age nine, Emma lost a two-year-long battle – but better late than never!

"Ask yourself if there is enough parent–child play in your house.**"**

fighting with their parents or peers. In family cultures fuelled by repeated criticism and shouting there is never any fun or laughter because RAGE and FEAR systems have blocked the CARE and PLAY systems.[18] Research shows that it is never too late to change a stress hormone family culture into a healthy one, and such shifts often bring about good behaviour far more effectively than techniques such as Time Out.[19]

Feelings and physical states linked to tantrums

As we have seen, certain physical and emotional states are responsible for bad behaviour in general. Similarly, there are well-recognized tantrum triggers. Hunger, tiredness, and tension are among the most common. You could also check to see if the following painful states are turning your house into a persistent scream zone.

• **Boredom** If children are suffering from stimulation hunger (see page 179), then screaming and shouting can become very appealing. Ask yourself if there is enough parent–child play in your house. Screaming is common in families who don't play together. A classic example of boredom is the tantrum in the supermarket. If you give your child interesting tasks and activities, the tantrums usually stop (see page 202).

• **Frustration** Children aren't good at finding words for frustration. You may need to help them express their feelings, "It's so hard to share sometimes, isn't it? You just started playing with that toy and your little brother came and took it."

• **Disappointment** Loss and disappointment activate the pain centres in the brain. As adults, we are able to say "never mind" and distract ourselves with something else, but when children are disappointed they find it overwhelming and may burst into tears. Children need help to manage their painful feelings and for you to acknowledge that disappointment can hurt a lot. Ignoring or getting angry with a disappointed child will simply add to his pain.

Understimulation or boredom is a painful state in terms of low bodily arousal. To satisfy the human psychological hunger for stimulation, your child may resort to screaming and tantrums. Learn how to play together as a family, and find your child plenty of rewarding tasks to do.

Key points

- There are six triggers for bad behaviour: tiredness and hunger; an immature brain; unmet psychological needs; intense emotions; parental stress; and a parenting style that activates the alarm systems in a child's lower brain.

- A child having a distress tantrum is in genuine pain and needs lots of calm, compassionate support from you. Ignoring or punishing distress can be damaging.

- Although distress tantrums can be challenging, they present a great opportunity to help your child develop essential brain pathways that enable him to manage stress in the future.

- Little Nero tantrums should be ignored. Children who are rewarded for rage often continue to use it as a technique as they grow older. Rage can become an ingrained personality trait.

the trying times

Focusing mainly on the under-fives, this chapter looks in depth at what is happening in the brains of young children when they are behaving badly. Most parents will be familiar with the common situations covered here – from bouncing on beds and rioting in restaurants to "I want" scenes in toyshops and fighting with siblings. What parents may not know is that such behaviour happens at a stage of development when children's brain systems are not mature enough to take control.

Getting out of control

Adults don't particularly want to jump up and down on beds or run around shops. Why not? It's because the frontal lobes of our brains are mature enough to naturally inhibit our "motoric impulses" – urges to run, jump, and climb. Young children have not yet developed such controlling mechanisms, and so simply asking them to comply with adult behaviour is unlikely to work.

CONSIDER THIS...

In children, the brain's dopamine and noradrenaline systems are slow to mature. These systems are vital for concentration and sustained, focused attention. This is why your child is often:

- easily distracted
- impulsive
- unable to focus
- unable to filter out distractions
- prone to lots of manic behaviour.

When they just say "won't"

While we need to give a child clear boundaries, rules, and consequences for unacceptable behaviour, we also don't want to damage her will. A child's strong will is a great life resource. Saying "won't" at two or three years of age is the precursor for the capacity to stand up for yourself, the passion to know what you want in life, and the drive to follow it through. Children who move into total compliance at the toddler stage often suffer in later life from not having developed a separate self. They may be very skilled at adapting to the needs and feelings of others, but with little or no notion about what they want and feel. This can happen with over-strict parenting where an infant is too frightened to protest, or with parenting that employs all manner of subtle forms of withdrawal of love and approval to get obedience. The latter happens with parents who delight in the placid, dependent baby, but then can't allow the stroppy toddler to have any autonomy or protest. A parent's love and approval is a basic need for a child, and if the price of that is total obedience, the toddler may decide, well so be it.

If you have a toddler who often asserts her will in very trying ways, give yourself credit for the fact that while you obviously need to be clear about boundaries, you have not moved into obedience training. As parents, we need to think very carefully how to respond to a child who says "no". This chapter offers many resources and ways forward.

Trying times when they bounce about

Bouncing on beds and running about is not being naughty. Unless under-fives have been frightened by obedience training, which triggers a freeze response on naturally spontaneous behaviour, they will find it extremely difficult to put the brakes on their behaviour. This is because their higher brain (frontal lobes) has not yet formed key pathways that connect to their lower brain. These pathways will naturally inhibit the urge to bounce about. Also, infants have very immature noradrenaline and dopamine systems in their higher brain, which also results in impulsive "can't sit still" behaviour.[1] The answer is to find a channel for their energy.

   If you are worried about your bed or sofa, give your child something else; for example, provide a trampoline in the garden, or take her to the local playground. There is no need to lose your temper; just say in a gentle voice, "We can't jump on the bed, but what we can do is go outside and do jumping". If your child still won't get off the bed, pick her up gently, and take her outside.

Trying times in public places

Because of your child's uninhibited impulses, it's wise to consider carefully which public places you can visit. Young children and five-star restaurants are, by and large, a very bad mix. Parents can get very angry and disappointed when their child's brain can't act like an adult's, and an outing is ruined. If they think of places to go to that cater well for a young child's motoric impulses, they will probably have a great time.

Find a space to run around

If you are visiting a public place such as a gallery, restaurant, or hotel, look around for a large outdoor space where your child can run about. The fewer other people around the better, then your child can be as noisy as she needs to be.

CONSIDER THIS...

In one sense, all young children have ADHD (attention deficit hyperactivity disorder, see page 111), which means impulsive behaviour and poor concentration on one thing for any length of time. Instead, they run around, climb, move constantly, and fidget. This is a natural developmental stage and the result of an immature brain. It is also considerably harder for boys to sit still than girls because the maturation of the higher brain (frontal lobes) is slower in boys than in girls.

   Young children need a lot of time in the day for running about. If they don't get it, they tend to be highly active at times that don't always suit you.[2]

"I just can't keep still!"

If children understood their own brain processes and had the powers of sophisticated speech, they would explain that they simply haven't got the brain wiring yet to curb their physical impulses. They might impress on you the need for some space to let off steam, such as a trip to a soft play centre. The novelty of a fresh environment and new toys will activate calming dopamine in their frontal lobes (higher brain).

After running about to her heart's content, she will be more inclined to behave quietly again inside.

Boredom often breeds bad behaviour in cafés and restaurants

Consider the following scenario. Mia, aged two, has been taken to a café for tea, and she's getting bored. So she bangs her spoon loudly on the table, causing heads to turn. She starts to spurt her blackcurrant drink over the table and dabbles her fingers in it. Then she pours sugar everywhere and plays at dive-bombing her mother's cup of coffee. What is going on in Mia's brain?

Mia isn't being naughty; the immature systems in her brain are making her act like this. She's been told to sit quietly but, like any young child, she's bored stiff by the adult conversation going on over her head. Mia's boredom means she is in a state of low arousal, which can activate painful stress chemicals in her brain, making her behave in an even more trying way. Her behaviour at the table is her attempt to satisfy her stimulation hunger and discharge the physiological stress of boredom. Coupled with this are Mia's motoric impulses, which her brain is too undeveloped to be able to inhibit naturally.

Of course, a toddler messing about like this is very trying. Parents may at this stage move into punishment. (Out of ignorance about a child's developing brain, some parents will lash out at children at such times.) But there is a way forward.

If we give Mia a toy to play with or a colouring book, it is very likely to engage her higher brain in a coordinated way with her lower brain's SEEKING system.[3] This system releases dopamine and opioids, brain chemicals that will enable Mia to focus on the activity, and in so doing, naturally calm her motoric impulses. If we don't bring things for children to do in cafés and restaurants, it is very likely that they will make their own entertainment by spilling the sugar across the table or climbing all over the seats.

> **"**Of course, a toddler messing about is very trying. But there is a way forward.**"**

The cafe is boring and Mia needs something to lock her attention onto – otherwise the outing may well end in tears.

❝Sitting with nothing to do is extremely stressful for children.❞

Turn the shopping trip from hell into an exciting treasure hunt

A long trip to the supermarket with nothing to do is often too hard to bear for a young child. To avoid a trying time, it is important to engage your child in what is going on. Without an activity such as a task-focused game, a child can feel very bored, with unmet structure and stimulation hungers (see pages 179–180). She will also experience low bodily arousal

❝I'm fully engaged❞

We need to provide entertainment for a child when visiting public places or immaculate homes where children are not always made welcome. If you don't give a child alternatives, such as a fascinating toy or a drawing book, he will find his own entertainment, such as playing with cutlery, blowing bubbles in his drink, and exploring where he shouldn't.

states, which, as we have seen, can trigger pain centres in her brain. This means that you are right on target for a shopping trip from hell, with your child running up and down the aisles and crashing the shopping trolleys.

Before all this happens, move into the playful part of your brain for a moment or two, and think up a game for you and your child to enjoy together while shopping: a "let's do something together" game. This will satisfy her stimulation and structure hungers. A good example is "Champion Shoppers", which can go something like this:

"Let's play a game. Have you heard of 'Champion Shoppers'? No? Well, here is how it works. When we get to each aisle, I will whisper in your ear an item of shopping we need for the trolley and you can go and look for it. When you've found it and brought it back, I'll whisper something else. If you find everything, you are a Champion Shopper and deserve a Champion treat. You can choose it yourself!"

TV Supernanny Jo Frost has a really creative version of a "let's" game for supermarkets. At the beginning of each shopping trip, the children are given a board with pictures of foods they have to find. The boring shopping trip is instantly turned into a treasure hunt.

Trying times on train and car journeys

Sitting with nothing to do is extremely stressful for children. If a child has to sit in a car or train or other form of transport for a while, her motoric impulses will become very strong, leading to fidgeting and restlessness. As adults, our mature frontal lobes inhibit such impulses, so we are happy to keep still, especially with a book or conversation to occupy us.

To enjoy a journey, give your child something interesting to do to engage her frontal lobes

If you engage a child's frontal lobes you engage the SEEKING system, which will naturally calm those primitive impulses to run about. You could initiate a guessing game, or give her

Neil, aged four, has been given the task of looking for items of shopping. He's become helpful instead of rioting. The structured activity has engaged his higher brain and his lower brain's SEEKING system, which will dramatically improve his ability to focus and concentrate. When a child's higher brain is not engaged because there is no structured activity on offer, his bodily impulses to run wild, shout, and scream can have a field day.

"If you forget to bring something to play with, don't be surprised if you have a stressful journey."

some paper and crayons. The more you join in with your child's play – for example, by initiating a game that involves you both or paying attention to her drawing – the more your mature brain and body systems will be emotionally regulating her immature systems.[4] Your calmness will have a direct, calming effect on her. You can increase her settled state by letting her sit on your lap and cuddling her. This will release oxytocin in her brain, which is a calming anti-stress chemical.[5]

By taking on board these simple facts about brain science, and fully catering for your child's immature brain systems, you can turn a potentially difficult journey into a delightful time together. If you forget to bring something to play with, or to come up with some creative activities to engage her higher brain, don't be surprised if you have a stressful outing.

"We're bored and stressed in the car!"

Sitting in the back of a car for ages is very stressful for children. It activates negative arousal chemicals in the brain. To change this painful brain chemistry, children will find their own amusement.

Kicking your sister (which is what happened here) seems like a good activity to fill the time. And if your sister cries or hits you back, then you have live entertainment to lift you out of your boredom.

To inhibit their motoric impulses, give them something to read, make, or draw. This will shift negative to positive brain chemistry, enabling them to lock their concentration onto more peaceful activities.

Take a break from the road

If you are on a long car journey, find time to pull off the road and head for the nearest playground or open space. This will give your child a much needed chance to let her motoric impulses rip for a while.

Trying times with meals

Why does your child prefer to play games at the table, swooping like a seagull or a bomber pilot, rather than sitting nicely and eating her food? If she's excited about something, her highly aroused body (the autonomic nervous system, see page 44) will be suppressing her appetite. An excited child is not being naughty because she's refusing to eat her food properly. It's just that human bodies are genetically programmed to have no interest in eating when in a state of high excitement. Once again, you will have a trying time if you attempt to fight against these facts about your child's bodily arousal system.

Some parents can get into a very negative pattern at mealtimes, trying to make an excited child eat. This can cause considerable relational stress for the child, which is bad for her developing brain. If you wait until her high arousal level has come down again and she is calm, she will start to feel hungry again.

Similarly, if a child is anxious or fearful, she will lose her appetite. Some parents get very agitated around mealtimes, and the child picks this up and doesn't want to eat. The more uptight the parent gets, the more anxious the child becomes, and the less interested in her food. The more laid-back a parent can be around eating times, the better.

Benjamin has been on the train for half an hour and his impulses to move are very strong. His natural brain and body responses are urging him to clamber all over the seat rather than sit on it.

If a child has become anxious about food, undo any negative associations between eating and place

In all mammals, high levels of stress or fear can block hunger and close down natural digestive processes. So if your child picks up on your anxiety about her not eating enough, or

TRY THIS...

If your child has got into an anxious lock with food because she has picked up on your anxiety about eating, try the following suggestions:

• Change where your child eats, in order to undo any negative associations between eating and place.

• Cook together, so your child becomes interested in food. Let her do some playtime with foods where she can explore new textures with her fingers and make a mess with food.

• Don't punish poor eating. Ignore it if you can. Instead, reward good eating and sitting well at mealtimes. Use stickers and stars when your child eats properly. Give the sticker immediately so there is a clear association in the child's mind between nice feelings and eating well at a table.

• If a child isn't eating well, and you are convinced it's not because of your anxiety, make sure there aren't lots of super little snacks available so she's quietly grazing throughout the day.

about the mess she is making (you can give this away by madly wiping away any mess round her mouth or spills), she may not want to eat. Parental anxiety and intrusive feeding can be a major cause of eating problems in children. When you worry about your child not eating enough, her right frontal lobe, which is very sensitive to emotional atmospheres, will pick up on your anxious facial expression, agitated voice, or tense body in milliseconds. So, try to activate your child's lower brain PLAY system at mealtimes, so she starts to associate food with fun instead of fear. Give her patterned plates, and allow her to play with food to explore new textures and colours.

Trying times with making a mess

The house has gone strangely quiet. You go to look, and then you discover the mess. The children have laid waste to the bathroom, making a river out of toilet rolls. What do you do? You can let it trigger the RAGE system (see page 19) in your lower brain, or you can pull yourself back from the brink and think of how to make your response a positive, rather than negative, relational experience for your child. The important thing is to avoid squashing your child's wonderful creativity and imagination. Imaginative, cooperative play is a real developmental achievement for young children, and it helps to develop their higher brains (frontal lobes).[6]

Cooperation, planning, thinking about what to do next, and listening to each other's ideas can form all manner of new neural connections and pathways in your child's higher brain. Such activities must be applauded and encouraged, not punished. That said, it is also important not to give your child the message that she can create whatever havoc she likes all over the home and expect you to clear it up.

Make tidying up into a game

With a young child, try making tidying up a "let's" game. Say, "Let's see who can put the most toys away in the box. I bet

I can beat you… ready, steady, go". Let your child win!
Afterwards say, "Wow, you are a champion toy tidier."

If your child refuses to tidy up, you may need to move
into the technique called "choices and consequences" (see
page 229). Not only does this stop the nagging, it also
activates the decision-making part of your child's higher
brain. Take her hands, look calmly into her face, and say,
"There's a rule in this house that whoever makes a mess clears
it up, so you have a choice. You can tidy up your toys now or
I can tidy them up. But each toy I tidy, I will take away from
you and keep in a box until you have shown me you
understand the tidying. Let me know what you've decided."
With lots of children, this will be enough for them to start
tidying. If the child ignores you, avoid nagging or persuading
and just carry on as you said you would. Tidy up the toys and
take them away. She can earn them back by helping you tidy
up something else in the home.

Trying times and toy wars

Why do children get so heated about possession of a toy?
There are several brain factors involved here. First, emotional
attachment to an object releases opioids in a child's brain.
These give the child a sense of well-being when she is playing
with a toy. But if the toy is taken from her, she may move
into a state of opioid withdrawal in her brain, which causes
emotional pain,[7] hence the distressed crying.

Furthermore, to a child, the toy is her territory. Any
animal is likely to respond with rage to an invasion of its
territory; it is an instinct triggered in the ancient reptilian
core of our brain. The brain chemical vasopressin, which is
linked to aggression, is released when animals guard their
territory. Together the pain and the rage and the territorial
brain chemicals can cause your child to descend rapidly into
primitive fight behaviour. As your child is in real pain and
her brain and body are awash with strong hormones, she
needs help and compassion when having to share a toy,

"What a mess!"

The bathroom has become a river made
from eight rolls of toilet paper, and the
mess and waste are appalling. You could
let your RAGE system take over, but you
could also control the situation (and
keep the creativity going) by saying
something like:

"Let's see if we can find a better way
of making a river without lots of paper.
Help me tidy up and we'll see what's
in the garden."

"If children come up with a solution, give them masses of praise, because negotiation and compromise are sophisticated human skills. **"**

and not an angry response. The good thing is that the pain can be short-lived, especially if you are skilled at distraction.

Who gets the toy? Help children to find a solution

If your child's higher brain (frontal lobes) is not yet developed enough for solution-finding, you need to find a solution for her. Use a calm voice, and never punish a young child for the immaturity of her brain. With older children, whose frontal lobes are better developed, give them support as they try to negotiate. You could teach them about trading or taking turns, "So you both want to play the dragons game at the same time? Shall I help you to take it in turns?" You can help them to say something to the other child like, "I'll trade you time with my boat for time with your car." You

"This toy is all mine!"

Sonia has taken possession of the rocker at nursery. Two of her playmates would like to join in, and grab the handles. There's plenty of room for all of them.

Sharing the rocker doesn't suit Sonia at all. She wants it all to herself and because she sees the plaything as her territory, she defends it passionately with screams of rage.

A carer steps in. She explains about sharing, providing vital emotional regulation. Sonia, now calm, can re-engage her higher brain and her anger is short-lived.

could also devise some family rules over sharing toys. If the behaviour becomes "reptilian" again, take away the toy and say something like "Okay you two, I am taking this away until we have found a way to share the time with it." If the toy is no longer there, children can often move from intense feelings to thinking. If they do come up with a solution, give them masses of praise, because negotiation and compromise are sophisticated human skills.

If a child throws a tantrum or cries after losing a game, it is down to her immature higher brain

If a child cries or rages because she has lost a game, you have to ask whether it is fair, at her age, to put her through an experience when she might lose. In terms of a child's underdeveloped brain, losing a game can be very painful, so it is unfair to punish her or accuse her of being a bad loser.

Young children are not good at putting things into perspective. The memory store in a young child's brain is still relatively empty, so she has no layers of experience from which to realize the relative insignificance, in the grand scale of things, of losing a game. Also, a child can throw a tantrum on losing because she may have anticipated feeling the delight of winning. All mammals (including humans) experience anger or rage at the frustration of anticipated rewards. At the thought of winning, dopamine, a positive arousal chemical, can be activated in the brain, whereas with losing, there can be a decrease in levels of dopamine. This decrease can bring about a low mood state in adults and crying in infants. So if your child goes into distress or rage states at losing a game, think of choosing cooperative games until she is a bit older and so able to get the whole thing more in perspective. It's far kinder.

Trying times and wanting something

Imagine your child in a toyshop. First, she won't leave, and then she runs out of the shop, and tries to take a toy with her.

CONSIDER THIS...

Allocate a shelf for toys that siblings are not ready to share. The child is allowed to put a limited number (you decide what the number is) of toys on this shelf. They cannot be shared without the owner's permission. This can also develop ownership skills and care of special things, which is particularly great if your children share a bedroom.

A child aged over five has more mature frontal lobes and will respond well to choices. Introducing her to pocket money is a vital part of this development. You can say, "You have a choice here. You can use your birthday money to buy the toy or put it towards the bicycle that you want." This engages her higher brain.

Toyshops can activate the SEEKING system in the child's lower brain. This system, which is to do with curiosity, exploration, will, drive, expectancy, and desire, activates optimal levels of dopamine and glutamate, making your child extremely aroused and focused. If you do not let her have the toy she wants, her desire is deeply frustrated, so her RAGE and PANIC/GRIEF systems can be triggered. A child's higher brain (frontal lobes) is not developed enough to moderate these powerful lower brain systems naturally, hence her tears and rage.

Managing under-fives in a toyshop means taking a firm stance

A good strategy is to pay no attention whatsoever to any pleading. Give a clear "no", accompanied by an empathic response to all that desperate yearning; for example, "I really hear how much you want that doll, but we have no money for it today." Then walk straight out of the shop with absolutely no further comment or discussion. Your child is highly likely to follow you because of the strength of her attachment to you. If you prefer, just pick her up and carry her out, and distract her as soon as you can. "Oh, look at that over there!" Don't try to reason with your child, along the lines of, "You have so many toys at home." This is trying to engage the child's higher brain when it's her lower brain that is in the driving seat.

Children over five years old will respond well when given a choice

With over-fives, their higher brain should have matured enough for you to use a technique involving decision-making: you can offer them a choice. Start by saying, "If you want something special, you've got to do something special." Ask your child whether she would rather give up the toy or help you with some task to earn the money to buy it. Once her higher brain is engaged in decision-making, it will naturally calm all that lower brain intensity. What's more, reflecting like this is so good for developing new pathways in your child's higher brain.

When she won't listen to a word you say

There will be times when your child won't come when you call or jump to it when you ask her to do something. This is because key chemical systems in her brain are undeveloped, making her unable to shift attention from one thing to another as easily as an adult can. If your child has locked her attention onto an activity, it is truly difficult for her to respond to you.

So give your child some slack. One thing you can do is to build in a clear disengagement strategy, such as the following: "In five minutes' time I am going to ask you to pack up your toys and to go and clean your teeth." When five minutes are up, say, "I will now count from five to one." If your child does

> **"** Walk straight out of the shop with absolutely no further comment or discussion. **"**

" I'm not leaving without it **"**

Jessica (aged six) is refusing to leave the toyshop without the furry animals she has found. Her brain is flooded with chemicals that increase her longing for the toys.

Her mother is left managing a storm in the toyshop! The best way out of this situation will be to engage Jessica's higher brain into thinking about the options.

Here, Jessica and her mum have a conversation about pocket money and choices. This breaks the deadlock of "I want" and moves on to "I will think about it".

" If a child has locked her attention onto some activity, it is truly difficult for her to respond to you. **"**

TRY THIS...

Humour and fun can be very creative ways of managing some of the trying times. For example, if a bored child has moved into horrid screaming around the house, turn the noise into a game.

"Hey, Billy, I've just had an idea! Let's do a BIG NOISE contest! Let's go up to the loft or down to the shed. We each choose to be an animal with a big roar, then we can see who has the biggest roar."[8]

The game can be developed into a story about, say, a dragon or a lion, and you can start to have lots of lovely one-to-one times, playing with your child instead of telling him off. These intense relational times also have real brain-developing powers for your child, as his immature brain systems are emotionally regulated by being in strong contact with an adult's mature brain systems.

as you ask, give her lots of praise. If she doesn't, simply pick her up and carry her to the bathroom to clean her teeth. Be consistent. Don't move into asking her lots of times to clean her teeth; she will start to desensitize to nagging.

Different rules apply when you need your child to stop immediately

Make it very clear what the rules are when you are out and about. Your child should not run off when you say "stop", and she must come back when you call her. You could say, "If I need you to come back to me, I will call your name and count from five to one. When I get to 'one' I want you to be back by my side."

If your child ignores you, you could respond, "I can see that you are not quite ready yet for me to let you run around, because you did not come when I called." Then put her in her buggy or use long reins fixed to your wrist – and explain why. There is no need for a raised voice or anger. Your actions will give a clear message to your child that you will not be caught up in her behaviour. Next time you are out, practise this method again until your child understands. Every time she comes back well, praise her hugely, saying, "Well done. That was great. You did so well at stopping/coming back when I called." This response is likely to produce a lovely cascade of dopamine and opioids in her brain and make her feel pleased with her actions.

Trying times with selfishness

"Our four-year-old is so selfish. She won't share her toys with the little ones and she never thinks of us. I am sure there is something wrong with her. Maybe it's bad genes." The selfishness of children can be infuriating, but we shouldn't punish them for their lack of consideration. This is because the capacity for concern is largely a sophisticated higher brain function and, as we have seen in previous chapters, children are born with very unfinished higher brains. The capacity to feel and think deeply about another person's emotional pain or stress levels develops slowly over time. Only after many hours of showing your concern for them can you expect your children to feel empathy with you. Sadly, some children have been on the receiving end of so little kindness and concern that they never develop this higher brain function.

Telling tales and name-calling

For a child, telling tales is often far too delicious a proposition to forgo. Child psychologist and author Adele Faber suggests saying something like, "Well I'm not interested in what Sally's doing right now. But I'd love to talk about you."

Help your child to express anger and resentment in healthier ways. For example, say, "You know we don't have name-calling in this family. If you have a problem with your sister, tell her what it is."[9] If a child is hurt by another child's behaviour, empathize with her pain: "It was mean of Sally to call you that and it must have really hurt your feelings. It's not true, so ignore her. But how smart of you to come and tell me instead of being mean back."

CONSIDER THIS...

Camilla and Shannon are playing cooperatively here, but they are not always so amicable when it comes to wanting the same toy. Parents often see refusal to share as selfishness, not realizing that having to share toys with a sibling can sometimes trigger deep feelings of having to share a parent. Children don't usually have the words to express this, unless you help them. If you think that asking your child to take turns with a toy is causing a huge amount of pain that can't be stopped with distraction techniques, it may be worth talking to her. Ask her whether she thinks she is getting enough time on her own with Mummy or Daddy (see page 122).

Children at war

When children have an impulse to lash out and fight, your creative parenting can enable them to learn how to reflect and negotiate instead. The wrong reaction from a parent can strengthen the wrong responses in the primitive brain. Shout at children who fight, or ignore them, and they may still be hitting people with words or fists when they grow up.

CONSIDER THIS...

Over time, if a child continues to be attacked by her sibling on a regular basis, without parental intervention, her brain can start to adjust some of its key systems to survive in an aggressive world. The FEAR and RAGE systems can be hard-wired for overactivity, commonly leading to problems with anxiety or anger in later life.

Many parents believe that their children fight more than other children, but the truth is that it is normal for siblings to fight. One study found that 93 percent of seven year olds fought their siblings, and 24 percent of these fought a lot.[10]

That said, fighting can be an uncomfortable reminder that humans do indeed have a primitive, reptilian core to their brains (see page 17). What's more, because of a young child's underdeveloped higher brain, this reptilian core is often in the driving seat. Parent power is so influential that if you treat fighting the wrong way, it can actually strengthen the primitive responses in the brain. If you treat fighting a better way, it will develop the higher brain and naturally inhibit reptilian impulses in your child to lash out when she is feeling competitive, territorial, or threatened in some way.

In short, you have the power to influence whether your child learns how to hurt harder and to be more devious in her physical attacks, or whether she develops and masters those sophisticated human skills of negotiating, planning, and clearly communicating what she needs and wants without using tactics of power and control.

Why do fights happen?

Fights happen because one, or more, of your child's psychological hungers is not being met (see page 179). A child may fight with another child because she is bored and is trying to top up her stimulation levels. She might simply be hungry, which makes her aggressive (see page 175). Overstimulation may result in physiological hyperarousal, which she relieves by biting, kicking, and hitting. She may be angry, frustrated, upset, or bottling up emotions, and because she doesn't have the words to express her feelings she uses her fists. Or perhaps she is being hit by a sibling, or smacked by a parent, and is modelling her hitting behaviour on what she knows at home. She might be being bullied at school, an experience that all too easily moves a child into her own primitive fight-or-flight behaviour in other areas of life.

How should you respond to fighting?

You need to make sure that the child's higher brain, not the reptilian brain, is activated. There are some vital do's and don'ts involved in this strategy:

Don't meet violence with violence

Don't scream, shout, or smack when you see siblings fighting. Such tactics may shock them into temporary obedience or submission, but this response is modelling using rage in

❝A child may fight with another child because she is bored.**❞**

❝This isn't funny!**❞**

What started out as a game can very quickly end in lost tempers – these little boys are not sure their play is fun any more. Parents cannot always tell when to intervene, but children's facial expressions are often the clue. Smiles show that the rough-and-tumble is good-natured. Clenched teeth and an increase in energy usually mean that it is time for parents to step in.

" Children need us to protect them from the hurtful actions of others. "

challenging, stressful situations. It could lead to the fight-or-flight part of the brain being hard-wired for an overactive response. The child could also grow up with an explosive temper, or start internalizing her anger, and as a result suffer from stress-related illnesses.

Meeting a child's violence with an angry response will also do nothing to help her to develop her higher brain. Rather, fighting is a time for you to help her regulate her overly high levels of bodily arousal, and to calm her down. So your tone of voice in response to the fighting is very important; you should sound firm but calm.

Don't take sides or reward tale-telling

Unless you witness an unprovoked hurtful act, don't take anyone's word for it. Some children are good at play-acting, putting on a show for their parents, clutching their tummies, and rolling on the floor. If you do take sides, children soon get the idea that if they constantly complain about the "abuse" of a sibling, they earn your loving attention. And, naturally, they delight in seeing their rival punished.

If your child is having a "too big" feeling, help her with it; don't leave her with it

Putting a raging child in a Time Out room might give you a breathing space and perhaps your child might think twice about biting her sister again. But it will not help your child find better ways of dealing with her anger, as there is absolutely no parental emotional regulation when she's in Time Out. Instead she's more likely to use the time to plot her revenge.

Research shows that if children are helped to put words to feelings, it can develop new pathways in the higher brain (frontal lobes), which naturally calm and inhibit their impulses to hit, lash out, or bite.[11] For more on this subject see pages 238–39.

Keeping children safe

Children need to have their hurtful actions stopped and they also need their parents and carers to protect them from the hurtful actions of others. Many adults say that as children they did not have enough protection from aggressive siblings – their parents would respond to fights with something like "they're only playing" and not realize that rivalry had deteriorated into abuse.

Children should have the freedom to resolve their own differences, but only if they are capable of doing this. Some situations are so emotionally charged that children can't resolve them on their own.

TRY THIS...

What should you do and say in response to fighting that's hurting? Here are some suggestions:

• Separate the two parties, as you would in a dog fight. Say, "Stop now. Separate rooms, please."
Or, "Hold it right there. People are not for hurting. That looks like real fighting. It's not safe for you two to be around each other right now. Sally, go to the kitchen. Jamie, go to the living room."

• Pay attention to the injured party and not the aggressor. Say to the aggressor something like, "Bad choice, Toby, for hitting Sam. I'll now spend time with Sam. You stay here and think about how you could have let Sam know you were angry in a better way."

• Give the children options on how to express their anger. Try, "Hey Jamie, let your sister know with words how angry you are."

• Often, anger is fuelled by hurt, so giving a child a language for hurt is a real gift. Say, "You wish he wouldn't snatch. Seems like you are really cross with him and really hurting because he knocked over your castle."[12]

TRY THIS...

Make sure you have some clear family rules about quarrelling and fighting and read through them with your children. The rules could include the following:

• There is zero tolerance in this home on fighting that hurts.

• Play-fighting is fine, but it has to be agreed by both of you that it really is play that you both enjoy.

• Fighting over a toy means the toy gets taken away until you agree a way of sharing. Ask a grown-up for help with this if you get stuck.

• If you really want to hit out because you are so frustrated or angry, go to a grown-up for help with your feelings.

• Name-calling is not allowed in this family. Go to a grown-up to help you find a really good way of telling your sister/brother what you would like her/him to do differently.

A lot of bullying in schools comes from children who have been hit by siblings

Unless parents intervene when appropriate, hitting can spread like wildfire. Many children who have been hit repeatedly by their siblings, without their parents stepping in every time, start bullying other children at school (see page 222). Nearly half of all schoolchildren say they have experienced bullying at some time.

Calling a family meeting about fighting

If hurting-fighting is clearly becoming an established activity in the home, call a family meeting to discuss it. Make it an occasion that will be marked in the children's minds and show them a clearly written statement of rules about fighting (see panel, left). Family meetings give vital psychological messages that feelings can be thought about rather than discharged with fists and teeth. This is also in line with the brain research that shows that putting very strong feelings into words can naturally inhibit the primitive RAGE system in the lower brain.[13] Meetings need ground rules and structure to stop them becoming a free-for-all. A good formula for successful meetings is based on Circle Time – an effective emotional literacy intervention used in primary schools, originated by Jenny Moseley. No-one can speak unless they are holding the little teddy (or equivalent). This ensures that children listen to each other and don't interrupt.[14]

If the children are too young to discuss ideas, you can provide the solutions. Even if a child is not happy with a decision, this process will make her feel safe, knowing that you have taken the time to listen, and that you are strong enough to take charge.

Key points

• Trying times with under-fives are often the result of immature brain systems.

• It is never okay to punish a child for exasperating behaviour that is due entirely to undeveloped brain systems.

• Before going on an outing, think how you will engage your child's higher brain in an interesting activity, so that her motoric impulses and primitive lower brain systems don't ruin the day.

• If your child is to grow out of primitive impulses to lash out in rage, she needs lots of one-to-one time with you to help her manage her very intense feelings and for you to find words to help her to think about them.

• Cater for your child's structure hunger, stimulation hunger, and recognition hunger and you will have a great time.

all about discipline

Discipline is a real art. If you get it right, it becomes far more than simply managing behaviour. It will develop your child's social, moral, and emotional intelligence. If you get it wrong, it can blight a child's life, leaving him with a heightened level of fear or anger in response to the world. So it's vital to use discipline techniques that activate your child's higher thinking brain, instead of triggering his lower brain to react as if under threat or attack.

Children often behave badly because they are not very good at speaking about painful emotions. If you spend time listening to your child in order to help him with his feelings, and if you work to improve the health of your relationship, your child will often stop being interested in behaving badly.

How not to raise a bully

Over the history of mankind, the way children have been disciplined has played a major role in the perpetuation of human misery. This is because for centuries, the disciplining of children has been built on an assumption that a sense of morality is achieved through harsh punishment. Both psychological and neurobiological research has now found this assumption to be entirely wrong.

CONSIDER THIS...

In the UK, in 2011 children were suspended from school on more than 80,000 occasions last year for attacking teachers and classmates.[1] In the same year, seven of out of ten teachers who left the profession gave the presence of violent and disruptive pupils in the classroom as the reason.[2] Studies published in 2011 also indicated that up to 20,000 children carry knives for their own protection.[3] In 2012/13 about 100,000 children and young people (aged 10–17) were convicted of, or cautioned for, an indictable offence in England and Wales.[4]

Sculpting the brain of a bully

The risk of bringing up a bully is largely determined by the type of parenting a child receives. Well-meaning parents don't realize that disciplining through criticism and commands may actually change stress-response systems in the child's brain. This can make the child oversensitive and render his RAGE or FEAR systems over-reactive. This sort of discipline also teaches a child about submission/dominance, and he can all too easily move into this behaviour himself in the form of bullying others, especially if he is smacked as a form of punishment. A report on parental behaviour in the UK, published in 2012, found that 41.6 percent of parents had physically punished or smacked a child; 67 percent had threatened to smack a child; 77 percent repeatedly shouted or screamed at a child; and 44 percent had told a child he was stupid or lazy.[5] The UK government has still not outlawed the hitting of children by their parents. Smacking teaches your child it is okay to hit out when he's frustrated. He may then hit his sibling, or kick the cat, or hit other children at school.

Let's be clear, we're not talking about occasional episodes of shouting at children

Some commands are inevitable and essential, such as shouting "Stop!" to a child who is running into the road or about to put his finger into an electric socket. But if criticism and commands form the bulk of parent–child interactions, it will guarantee for both parent and child a horrid time living together. The child learns all about relationships based on power and control, and all too little about relationships based on warmth, kindness, and cooperation.

When a child lives on a daily basis with the stress of a parent's repeated shouting and angry explosions, the tension from the feelings he is left with can be so awful that it must be discharged. Hitting or bullying another child is a common way of doing this, or for a younger child, shouting, screaming, biting, hitting, or breaking something. Such children love war games, and are often obsessed with violent computer games.

If a child is repeatedly on the receiving end of criticism, commands, and threats, it will not help his higher brain to develop in ways that are essential for reasoning, planning, and reflecting. What is more, this type of parenting can also hardwire the RAGE and PANIC/GRIEF systems in the brain to be over-reactive.[6] These children then live their lives on a very short fuse. People don't warm to children whose way of being in the world is ruled by the fight-or-flight mechanisms in the reptilian part of their brain, and so their negative view of the world is reinforced.

The over-disciplined child can learn to put someone down as she has felt put down, to give orders as she has felt commanded, to shame as she has been shamed, to hit with words as she has felt hit with words.

Discipline through empathy not shame

The science of childrearing makes it clear that you need to take the stress out of everything. The hardest thing for some parents is taking the stress out of discipline because, as children, they were disciplined through shame and anger, so they are under-resourced in terms of other options.

So why does this matter so much? The science of verbal aggression studies show that if you repeatedly discipline with angry words and tone of voice, the effects on your child can include vulnerability to depression, anxiety, or other psychiatric disorders in later life.[7] Verbal aggression can also damage the auditory processing part of the brain, leading to lower verbal IQ, which affects comprehension skills.[8] Furthermore, the fact that you are lovely and affectionate with

" Many world leaders who have been disciplined through anger and cruelty go on to treat their own people abominably, or go on to bully other nations. "

CASE STUDY

Julie's lost children

Julie is having a miserable time as a parent and resorts to frequent criticism, commands, and lectures to discipline her two children. The methods don't work all that well, but she had little first-hand experience in her own childhood of the potency of warm touch, hugs, and interactive play.

Mary, aged four, is frightened of her Mummy's shouting. Her sister, Sam, aged 12, seems to cope better. When Julie shouts at her, she shouts back, but she is a very angry young girl.

The way Julie has disciplined her children may have had enduring effects on both children's brains. The FEAR system in Mary's brain over-reacts to the slightest stress, and there is a danger that she will grow up to be fearful and lack social confidence. Sam has an over-active RAGE system in her lower brain. This may be a real problem in her adult work and social life, as she is likely to explode at the smallest frustration.

your child for the rest of the time does not negate the damage caused by repeated shouting, shaming, and criticizing.[9] The same is true if one parent is regularly verbally aggressive and the other parent is warm and praising; the damage from the "hurtful" words can't be mended with praise and warmth from the other parent. Also, discipline that shames a child triggers very high levels of cortisol, which is toxic to the developing brain[10] and leads to what is known as "shame proneness" in later life. As well as causing vulnerability to depression[11] this has other life debilitating effects, such as, lack of belief in yourself; internalizing shaming voices in your head; and not daring to apply for that job, or to approach or confront someone – all out of fear of being shamed. In contrast, children who experience discipline with empathy, over time do better socially, emotionally, and academically, and their body arousal system is very well balanced, which brings about both emotional and physical health.[12]

Putting it into practice

You need to empathize with your child when he is furious with you for putting down a boundary, rather than criticizing him for his anger, too.[13] Here is an example. When five-year-old Tom says a really mean thing to his little brother, breaking the house rule of no unkind words, his mum's response is to say, "I'm afraid your meanness means you can't play with your favourite computer game today." Tom is very cross and says, "I hate you, I hate you. You know I love playing that game." Mum, "I know Tom, but sadly you made a bad choice by being so mean to your brother." Tom, "I am sorry. Why are you so mean to me Mummy? I hate you." Mum, "Tom I know it's so hard that I said no computer game tonight. I can see you are really hurting about that." But Tom continues, "I hate you, you are the worst Mum." Mum, "I need you to learn that it is not right to hurt people's hearts with mean words, but I can also see that you are furious." By now Tom may not feel so bad as he realizes that his anger is acknowledged.

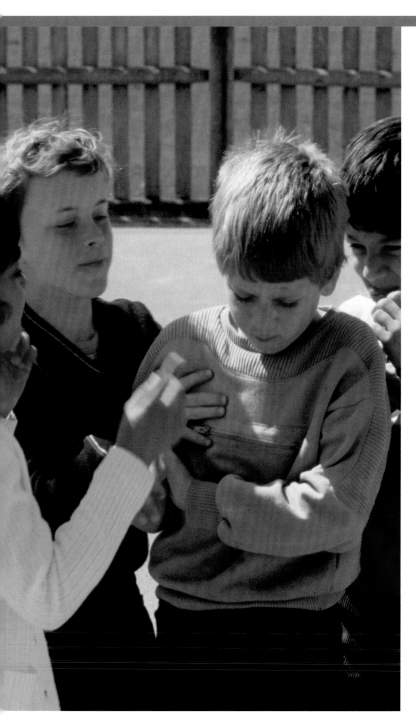

"I hate playing this game"

Children model their behaviour on the many influences they are exposed to. Violent scenes on TV have been shown to have an effect, but also the way parents choose to correct a child's behaviour can lead him to act in mean or cruel ways. It has been shown that children who have been hit at home are, by the age of four, playing either victim or persecutor roles in their games. On the other hand, children who have not been disciplined harshly tend to play with kindness and cooperation.[14]

Boundaries and behaviour

We have already described how harsh discipline actually hinders socialization, and is far more likely to result in a child becoming a thug than growing up to be a moral citizen. But what of the parents who fail to impose much discipline at all? Society is also peopled with children whose provocative behaviour makes their parents' life a misery.

CONSIDER THIS...

Some parents are frightened to say a firm "No" because they fear that their child won't like them if they do. It is, however, vital that children are given clear "No's" if they are ever to develop morally and socially. The child who rarely meets a firm "No" in a parent often ends up feeling more powerful than, and disrespectful towards, his parent. But it is also frightening to a child if he feels that the grown-ups in his life are not in charge. What's more, the lack of parental boundaries over unacceptable behaviour gives the child a very worrying message, that, "It's okay to hurt people, take things from them, swear, treat your mother as a piece of rubbish. Nothing much happens if you do."

The challenge is how to communicate very clearly to children that something is absolutely not acceptable, in ways that engage his higher brain and not the primitive systems of FEAR or RAGE, dominance or submission, deep in the ancient parts of his brain.

Some parents find it difficult to lay down any boundaries at all. Often these are parents who have themselves suffered the legacy of very strict or punitive teachers or parents when they were children. As a result, they are adamant that they will never be like that with their own children, so they swing to the opposite extreme. When the child acts in a way that clearly needs a firm boundary, and an immediate consequence imposed, the parent may say something like, "Please don't do that dear. It's not nice," but fail to take any action. The irony is that out of fear of being a bossy, controlling parent, you can get a bossy, controlling child. If there are no immediate consequences for antisocial behaviour, you will get antisocial behaviour.

Here is what can happen if you set no boundaries with your child

Your child can learn that he can control you, rather than seeing you as being the one in charge. See it from his point of view – if nothing much happens when you hit Mummy or kick the door, why should you want to stop releasing your anger in this way? It can be exhilarating and make you feel very powerful. If you never set clear limits for unacceptable behaviour, your child won't know where the limits are.

The worry of this is that neuroscientists have found that the mere experience of emotion without reflection can result in it becoming an ingrained personality trait.[15] When a five-year-old thug reaches, say, nine or ten, he can be just too big to control physically, for example by being carried into another room. At this age, he can seriously hurt you and other family members.

Children need to learn early on that they can't control you

Children need a model of discipline that is assertive, carries conviction, and is firm and clear, without being angry or shaming. They need to feel absolute conviction in your voice and body movement when you want something to stop, and an immediate consequence if they overstep your boundaries. There should be no discussion. If your voice is flat or weak, your child won't believe you mean it.

Children are not born socialized and considerate of others. They need your help with the raging or controlling impulses in the more primitive parts of the brain, and this chapter is all about giving you the techniques to do it.

When to be emotional...

The first rule is to be very emotional with good behaviour. For example, if your child is playing cooperatively, be lavish with your praise, "Wow, that was great when you let your brother share the toy. Well done for being so kind!".

When to be matter-of-fact...

By contrast, be very matter-of-fact and not at all emotional with bad behaviour. For example, if a five-year-old splatters his pudding all over the table, say in a really low-key voice, "Hey, bad choice. That means you can't watch your DVD today. I hope you choose better next time." Then stick with your decision.

It's very easy for parents to get this the wrong way round, because bad behaviour is usually much more attention-grabbing than good behaviour. They get very emotional when a child is being defiant or irritating, and are matter-of-fact or

" My Daddy just can't control me "

You need to be able to decide when to tread softly and when to take swift action. You can safely ignore or deal lightly with most things that are not dangerous, damaging, or hurtful. Firm discipline is needed when your child is in danger of causing damage to himself, to others, or to property. You need to be consistent in this from an early age to avoid future problems.

fail to notice when the child does something good, kind, generous, or creative. Using low-key responses for provocative behaviour will help to keep your child calm. If you "lose it" with your child, you are in danger of triggering the primitive reptilian parts of his brain, which in the long-run may be damaging to his developing social brain.[15]

Ignore attention-seeking behaviour

Ignoring is the appropriate response for things like kicking a chair leg or stomping down the stairs very loudly. These attention-seeking misdemeanours generally happen when a child is suffering from stimulation or recognition hunger (see page 179), perhaps because he feels he is losing your attention to a sibling, your smart phone, or a TV programme. Or he may not be getting enough positive attention from you, such as praise and lovely warm touches.

If you don't manage to ignore minor misdemeanours, a child soon learns that he gets masses of attention for provocative small acts. Often, the clue is the way that your child watches your face expectantly for a delicious display of angry parental feelings! To a child this means a whopping dose of attention in the form of "stop that" or "how dare you". So try not to meet his eyes, and pretend not to see and hear. Instead, think about how to satisfy his stimulation or recognition hunger in creative ways.

Have a clear set of family rules

A clear set of family rules is a key way of satisfying your child's structure hunger, and will also engage his higher brain. Not having rules, or rewards for keeping to them and penalties for breaking them, is quite frankly crazy. Rules, in both family and society, make children and adults alike feel safe, whereas a lack of them can lead to anarchy and mayhem. Rules help our higher brain to keep in check aggressive feelings and dominating instincts that can so easily be triggered in the old mammalian and reptilian parts of our

CONSIDER THIS...

If you give some control to a child in the form of offering him a choice over unimportant things like what to wear, he is less likely to fight you to get some control. For example, instead of shouting, "Put your coat on right now. I will not tell you again," if you ask light-heartedly, "Do you think this jacket will be warm enough, or should we find your big coat?", he is more likely to get ready happily, rather than start a fight.

brain (see pages 16–17) – and the lack of them often leads to family members getting hurt, psychologically and physically. Rules lift everything out of the personal and into the objective.

Rules are all about fairness, and people calm down when they feel things are fair. So make a list of rules and put them up in the home, where all can see – on the fridge for example. Rules may include items such as no hitting, swearing, or damage to property; respect for others; asking for help when you are hurting inside, instead of taking it out on someone else. Children need to know what the consequences are for breaking a rule, whether you use Time In (see page 233), the thinking stair or chair (see page 235), the confiscation of a favourite toy, withdrawal of an activity such as screen time, or simply imposing a household chore.

Use simple, clear words for young children

As your children get older, they can appreciate explanations about certain behaviours in terms of fairness, the importance of respecting others, and developing a culture of generosity instead of meanness. But until their higher brain has developed enough, you are wasting your time. So with under-fives, you need to give simple instructions. Get down to their level. Use a clear, authoritative (not angry) voice and say simply, "No", "Stop", "I mean it", and "If you do that again, the consequence will be…". If your under-five child is hyperaroused and out-of-control, pick him up and hold him (see page 237). With high levels of physical arousal, he won't be able to focus on what you are saying, however simply it is expressed.

Use choices and consequences

This is a tried-and-tested way of disciplining children, developed by Foster Cline, whose method of engaging the child's higher thinking brain and not activating the FEAR or RAGE systems in the lower brain, has proved highly successful even with the most destructive and anti-social of children. It is suitable for children aged five and over.[16]

TRY THIS...

Don't reward rude, provocative, or attention-seeking statements with an angry outburst. Be calm and show yourself to be absorbed in whatever else you are doing at the time. This will give a child's statement minimum not maximum impact, and therefore not reward it in any way. For example:

Child, "Your hair is stupid."

Parent, "No kidding" (said with a really low-key voice and with your attention focused elsewhere).

" Children need to know what the consequences are for breaking a rule. **"**

TRY THIS...

Make family rules based on the finest human qualities – goodwill, give and take, a culture of generosity, and respect for others.

Make sure rules have a point and are appropriate; for example, pocket money and privileges have to be earned. Make sure rules are fair – children will be acutely aware of those that are not.

Giving older children a say in family rules is a good idea, and most will be able to make a real contribution to the conversation. But offering premature democracy to under-fives won't work because they don't have the brain maturity to make these types of decisions. Children of this age group tend to see things in black-and-white and move into gruesome punishments for minor sins. For example, when asked by his parents what they should do after baby Eddie had bitten his nanny, Simon (aged five) said, "Put him in the rubbish".

Remember to praise your children when they keep the rules, rather than simply watch out for when they break one.

Providing choices and consequences goes something like this. William is jealous of his sister's new birthday doll. He tries to spoil the doll by stamping on it. His mum says that the consequence for William's actions is to help with jobs in the home in order to earn pocket money to buy another doll. This teaches William that there is a consequence to his behaviour. Alternatively, William's mum could offer a choice: William can choose to do jobs to buy another doll, or give his sister his own favourite toy – an exchange that William's little sister would be delighted with. William's mum refuses to enter into any debate; this strategy avoids giving William masses of attention and rewarding his bad behaviour. Thinking about the choice moves William into his higher thinking brain. Eventually he chooses to do the jobs.

Don't feel you have to come up with an appropriate choice or consequence on the spot. If you pressurize yourself to think quickly, your choices (and the consequences) may end up being crass, pointless, or something that doesn't suit you. So give yourself time. For example, say, "I will have to think up a consequence for what you have done. I'll let you know when I have." However, make sure consequences for behaviour happen on the same day. Young children don't care about the future; they can't really hold it in mind. So avoid choosing a consequence like, "No cinema trip at the weekend."

Reward good behaviour.

Stickers, point systems, and privileges are all types of reward techniques that will engage and develop your child's higher thinking brain, because they involve weighing up the pros and cons of behaving in a certain way. Families who have no clear reward systems sometimes fall into giving the child a diet of criticism with all too little praise. Giving lots of attention for bad behaviour results in more bad behaviour. Lots of attention for good behaviour results in lots of good behaviour. It's a simple formula, but very true.

Let's face it, there is arguably no such thing as unmotivated behaviour. This is largely due to the fact that our brain is designed to seek pleasure and avoid displeasure. As adults, we are motivated to get up to go to work because we get the pleasure of money, job satisfaction, and social contact. So the next time you're surprised that your child doesn't leap at the idea of doing the washing up, remember he is acting normally because he may not see much of a reward in it for himself.

Enjoying doing something for the good of others (for example, contributing to the effective running of the home) without needing a tangible reward is a developmental stage. So give your young child a break! At first, he may need rewards, such as a sticker or a point. For others, a big smile

> " Lots of attention for good behaviour results in lots of good behaviour. It's a simple formula, but very true. "

" Why should I tidy up? "

Mum has asked Susie to tidy before they go to the cinema, but Susie is not interested. She thinks Mum will probably give in and do it if she ignores the request.

Mum says that if Susie does not tidy up, the trip to see the film is off. Hence, in a low-key, but clear way, Mum is using choices and consequences.

There has been no shouting, hitting, or cajoling, but Susie has tidied up. Now Mum is ready to take her to the cinema.

TRY THIS...

A change of emphasis involves changing threats into promises. So instead of saying in an angry voice, "If you don't tidy your room, there will be no screen time," say in a warm voice, "I promise that if you tidy your room, you can watch your DVD." This simple, but vital shift can make all the difference between a family spoilt by endless nagging and highly motivated, helpful children.

and "Well done" from Mummy will be enough. As a child gets older, he will move into more sophisticated forms of motivation, such as pleasure from the sense of achievement gained from cooking a meal for the family, or at an even later developmental stage, the pleasure of doing something out of love, which becomes a far greater pleasure than receiving a gift oneself.

If you want to reward certain behaviours, such as acts of kindness or the ability to share toys well, give the sticker as soon afterwards as possible, so that there is a real connection between what a child did and the pleasure of the reward. The accumulation of stickers for a bumper reward is very effective. Making a chart and putting it up on the wall enables your child to see how many stickers he has earned, and is a visual prompt to you to keep praising him for what he has achieved. A good idea for a special treat is something like staying up a bit later at the end of the day, or a special outing to the park with Dad, or a little surprise gift.

For older children or adolescents, rewards can work just as well, but this time points translate into cash. Your child

"Look what I've done!"

Stickers are great for encouraging and rewarding good behaviour. Let your child put the stickers on a chart so he can see his progress. You could paint a series of different-sized trees on a chart and make a "magic carpet" marker. Each time your child earns a "sticker", the carpet moves up to a higher tree. When the carpet reaches the tallest tree, your child gets a treat.

will learn that if he wants pocket money, he must earn it and be careful not to lose it. Earning pocket money is a great practice ground for learning to operate well in the adult world. He may be able to earn points by doing chores, and by keeping well to family rules over a period of time, or for acts of kindness. There are also clear penalties for losing points. If the child goes "broke", important items such as his tablet will be taken, but he can then earn them back.

Use thinking words

When trying to instil socially acceptable behaviour, some parents make the mistake of using fighting words. These are likely to overactivate primitive alarm and stress response systems in a child's lower brain, which, as we've seen, can lead to personality problems with anger and/or anxiety in later life. Fighting words demand obedience but often incite in the child the opposite: namely, defiance and disobedience.[17]

In contrast, thinking words engage the higher brain. Faced with screaming Little Nero behaviour (see pages190–94), for example, you might use the following thinking words, "Well, it looks like things aren't going so well for you right now. When you get yourself to the point of being able to ask nicely, I'll be glad to listen." At this point, walk away with not another word. Fighting words would be, "Just another of your bad moods. If you knew what we did for you and we never get any thanks!". The former will make him think about what has happened; the latter is likely to trigger the RAGE system in his lower brain even more.

Try some Time In

Time In is taking the time to sit with your child after a bout of bad behaviour, to talk together about why he is behaving this way. Time In is not giving attention to bad behaviour, it is giving attention to the feelings that underlie the bad behaviour, so that these can be resolved. Time In acknowledges the fact that so much bad behaviour results from a child having painful

<aside>
BRAIN STORY

Using choices and consequences with a defiant child will help to develop his frontal lobes' capacity to reflect, consider, negotiate, and weigh up options. It is important not to use shouting and commands, and to use a calm, quiet voice. Developed frontal lobes have the capacity for:

• reasoning, planning, reflecting, and thinking before acting
• linking and connecting
• negotiation
• problem-solving.

Commands are often an attack on the child's dignity, leaving him feeling shamed or humiliated. Commands teach a child about submission and dominance – the sort of training that can create a bully (see page 222).
</aside>

CONSIDER THIS...

A child who is helped with Time In learns that his parent isn't afraid of his big feelings and knows how to handle them. If we don't use Time In, we are in danger of withdrawing from our children when they are most in need of adult understanding. The development of a child's social brain includes the ability to be sensitive to others, empathize, and accurately imagine another person's emotional experience. Children can only develop their social brain if they have had social experiences where someone has been emotionally sensitive to them.

feelings that he is not able to manage himself or to describe to you in words. You may need to find a creative way to encourage your child to talk about his feelings (see page 118).

In contrast, Time Out (the technique of putting a child in a room on his own behind a closed door when he has been naughty, for a minute for every year of his age – so a six-year-old gets six minutes), may stop the bad behaviour, but it does not give you, as a parent, the opportunity to find out what is making your child behave badly. Instead, the painful feelings that may have triggered the behaviour often go underground.

Weininger (an originator of the Time In technique) says about Time Out, "We are in danger of withdrawing from a child just at the very time they need help with their feelings." Over time, using Time In with your child can help him to change from angry, attention-seeking behaviour to a more thoughtful and reflective way of being in the world.[19]

Why Time Out is never appropriate.

Time Out is never appropriate for punishing children. Most children under five have their moments and will, from time to time, throw themselves on the floor in distress. Little ones may scream when they are being dressed (see page 182), or if another child takes a beloved toy. Loss like this when you are only young will activate the alarm systems in the brain, so it is sheer cruelty to put a child in a distressed state into Time Out. If you do, you move into a double failure: you fail to comfort his distress, and punish him for having perfectly natural feelings of pain and loss. A child who experiences Time Out is receiving the following very worrying psychological messages:

• **Passionate and painful feelings are not acceptable**. Mummy or Daddy will punish me if I have them. I am only acceptable if I have mild feelings.

• **I should not ask for help** from Mummy or Daddy when I am struggling with a painful feeling; they might get cross.

We want to train children out of bad behaviour, but we must be careful in doing so that we don't train them out of their passionate emotions, and so out of the capacity to feel life fully. Using Time Out is also very worrying in terms of developing brain systems. The distressed cries of loss, disappointment, and rage need your emotional regulating capacities as a parent. Research shows that if a child is left in a distressed state like this (for example, when taken and left in a Time Out room), high levels of stress chemicals can wash over his brain. He may stop crying, because you are getting angry with him, but research shows that his cortisol levels can remain sky high.

The Thinking Stair or Chair technique

This technique involves providing a place where your child can think about why what he has done is not okay. As well as helping the child to calm down, this technique activates his

"Time Out is simply about stopping the behaviour, so the painful feelings that may have triggered it can go underground.**"**

"No one understands me**"**

Consider Time In not Time Out. If you spend time listening to your child, you may be able to resolve the areas of conflict that lead to bad behaviour before it occurs again.

higher thinking brain. It is a form of Time Out, but it is not as severe, because your child is not left behind a closed door. There is less of a feeling of isolation for your child, as he is separate, but not removed from the general hubbub of the house. This is less distressing than being confined to a room, but it can be difficult to manage if your child keeps leaving the stair or chair. A typical scenario might be dealt with like this:

• **The first stage is a warning**, delivered in a firm, strong voice and bending down to his level. Say something like, "Sam, there's no swearing in this house. So if you swear again you will have to go and sit on the thinking chair."

• **If he carries on with the bad behaviour move into action.** Gently take him to the thinking stair or chair.

"Why did I do that?"

To use the Thinking Stair or Chair technique, choose a place to sit that is boring, such as a quiet, unused room. The child needs to face the wall. This low level of stimulation offers a boundary to her. Ask your child to spend time thinking about her actions. Explain that she will stay there for, say, eight minutes (one for each year of age), and you will collect her at the end of this time. If she tries to leave the chair or stair, ask her to sit again.

• **After the allotted time, come back.** Ask your child if he is ready to talk nicely. If he says yes, then bring him back to play. If he repeats the behaviour, repeat the technique.

• **If your child moves off the stair or chair**, keep putting him back. With young children, you can calmly but firmly hold them in the chair, but saying nothing while you do so.[20]

• **With an older child, consider Time In** instead (see page 233) and take the opportunity to talk about the reasons behind his actions.

Try using the Holding technique.

Holding your child when he is out of control in order to calm him down is not restraint. Rather, it entails providing him with the strong, safe, calm blanket of your enveloping arms. The primary function of Holding is to give your child a sense of there being someone big and calm enough to be able to manage their intense feeling storms. When children are feeling "full of wildness that cannot be tamed"[15] and are not helped with their out-of-control hyperaroused states, it can be terrifying for them. Holding is appropriate for situations when a child is in danger of hurting himself, another person, or property, and when a clear "Stop!" isn't working. The child is in such a high state of arousal that he can't hear your words because the verbal centres of his brain are not registering. Under these circumstances, teachers in the UK are legally able to use this technique.[22]

Only use holding if you are calm yourself.

Holding is done with kindness and firmness. Just as a baby is soothed by being next to your calm body, your child will be calmed, too. Your mature bodily arousal system will regulate the child's immature system.

Never use this technique if you are seething with anger, otherwise you will not be able to calm your child. Also, your child will feel punished and become more hyperaroused by your stress, rather than calmed.

BRAIN STORY

• **Thinking words have** many developmental benefits for your child because they develop your child's higher thinking brain. Research shows that when a child is helped by a thoughtful adult to link words to feelings, brain pathways will form from his higher brain to his lower brain.[23] These pathways are vital for his ability to manage strong feelings or stress well in later life. A vital part of emotional and social intelligence is the ability to find solutions for the stressful times in life when we are thrown into intense states of emotional arousal.

• **Fighting words are bad** for a child's brain because they demand blind obedience but often activate disobedience. If the FEAR system is activated a lot in the name of discipline, a child can suffer from anxiety disorders and social phobias in later life (see page 29).

Demanding blind obedience will teach children about submission/dominance. For some, it will activate the RAGE system in the lower brain. When this happens, a child can be seen to comply at the time, but his RAGE system is like a time-bomb; it can go off at any time in his life. For some, it goes off in the playground and a child can move into bullying. Others contain it until adolescence, when it may manifest itself in self-harm or violence.

TRY THIS...

If you have tried firm "No's" with your child and he is in danger of hurting himself or someone else through his behaviour, then consider using the Holding technique. Holding should be done when you are able to offer real calmness, so your child can benefit from your emotionally regulated body and brain system.
A hyperaroused child can take 20 minutes to calm down. Let him lie in your arms for a while afterwards.

Only use Holding with children who are smaller than you. It is no good for either of you if, in his wild state, a child hurts you or manages to get out of your arms. He will not feel contained and safe if he does. If there is any danger of this, don't use the technique.

There is a clear technique to Holding so that the child feels very safe and "emotionally held". If you improvise, you or your child could get hurt, or it just won't calm him down.

• **Find a place against a wall or sofa** where you can get support. Sit on the floor. Make sure you remove your watch and any jewellery that could hurt your child as he struggles. Take your shoes off.

• **Visualize yourself as a lovely warm, calm blanket.** Fold your child's arms in front of you and fold your arms on top of his. Gently, but firmly, hold his arms still. Bend your legs at the knees and fold them over his legs. This way he cannot kick. In this enveloping blanket, your child will feel safe, but not in any way hurt or gripped. If you are doing the technique correctly, you will, after a while, feel very calm too, almost in a meditative state. Give yourself plenty of time.

• **Say to the child, "I am just going to hold you here until you are calm again."** If a child is very out of control and if you are worried about being head-butted or bitten, put a cushion against your chest, or between his chin and your arms.

• **Children may try all manner of things** to get you to let go, saying, "I am going to wet myself" or "I need a drink." If he goes into panic or genuine distress, let go. Otherwise, don't be fooled. If you have been, you'll soon know, as he'll go off grinning and triumphant. If he does, just haul him back.

• **Give your child enough time** to reach a state of calm.

Step-by-step discipline

The problem with the way most discipline is applied is that it happens on the spur of the moment when parents are enraged by what they see their child doing. Without thought, they may move straight to the top level of censure. A better way is to begin with a low-level boundary, and only move to a stronger one if the one before isn't working:

• **Boundary One.** Parent, "James, please keep the paintbrush on the paper." For a lot of children this is quite enough. James respects the boundary and keeps the paintbrush away from the carpet. But what if he doesn't? Then James is looking for a bigger boundary than this.

• **Boundary Two.** Parent, "James, I really mean it. You must keep the paintbrush on the paper". The mother also puts her hands on James's shoulders, "James. Do you understand?" For a lot of children this is quite enough. James doesn't do it again. But imagine James is looking for a bigger boundary than this and begins to paint on the wall.

• **Boundary Three.** Parent, "James, go and sit in the thinking chair please. After eight minutes, I will come and ask you how you will make up for what you have done." James goes to sit in the chair. He then says he will clean the wall.

• **Alternative Boundary Three.** Parent, "You'll now have to clean the paint off the wall and spend some time with me cleaning the kitchen cupboards." However, this time James is looking for a bigger boundary still and flies into a rage, with paint flying everywhere.

• **Boundary Four.** Parent moves into Holding technique. "You seem very intent on making me angry. So I will hold you until you have calmed and are ready to tell me how you will make up for what you have done." James kicks and screams. The parent keeps on holding him. Eventually James and his parent agree that he will wash the wall and then help in the kitchen to say he is sorry. Such behaviour would also benefit from some Time In after it has passed.

But why do some children repeatedly look for such a strong boundary?

It can happen because the child has been winning battles early on at age two and three because of weak or no boundaries. All young children need to lose this battle

CASE STUDY

Don't resort to Time Out

Time Out can damage parent–child relationships. For example, a six-year-old who is always being put in Time Out for the slightest offence may start to prefer it to the company of her repeatedly critical mother. One day, Martha was put in Time Out for refusing to finish an over-large portion of spaghetti. As her mother closed the door, she heard Martha say, "Thank goodness; time away from my Mummy who is bad to me."

When her mother opened the door after six minutes to say, "You can come out, Martha." Martha replied, "I don't want to, thanks." She had found some string and was happily making it into a spider's web.

❝ Children want to know that the adults in their life are in charge. Then they can feel safe. **❞**

gracefully because if they win, they can feel more powerful than their parents. On one level this may feel very exciting indeed, but it is also very frightening to them. Children like this begin to test you out more and more. They are looking for stronger and stronger boundaries, because they want to know that the adults in their life are in charge. Then they can feel safe.

If you feel that you have tried everything and your relationship with your child is troubled, then discipline techniques may improve his behaviour, but they won't heal your relationship. A great way forward is to see a parent–child therapist or a family therapist.

How should you respond to conflicts in your relationship with a child?

You need to regulate anger and handle conflicts in gentle, positive ways.[24] Acknowledge that whatever the child is feeling towards you is real for them at that moment, even if to you it feels unjust or irrational. For example, if 12-year-old Susan, angry with her father, says, "Dad, you never listen to me. You just nag me. I hate you for that," a defensive response from her dad could be, "Yes I do listen, I am always listening to you." However, for an empathic response he should acknowledge Susan's perception and respond with, "So it feels like I have not been able to hear the most important things you need me to know – as if I have been deaf to you somehow. No wonder you are cross with me if you feel that. Will you let me listen to you now, Susan?".

With younger children often the best thing to do is to cross the transaction with humour. For example, if an angry toddler says, "Go away", don't respond with "How dare you tell me to go away." Instead try, "Ah, we have a problem because I am a hungry tiger who likes eating toes!" and proceed to pretend to do so with a funny voice and funny movements.

Key points

• Correcting behaviour with anger, criticism, and commands can lead to over-sensitive RAGE and/or FEAR systems in your child's lower brain.

• Ignoring your child's bad behaviour, and giving him lots of attention when he behaves well, always gets a good result.

• Time In helps you understand why your child is behaving badly.

• Family rules and clear boundaries help children to feel secure.

• Choices and consequences engage your child's thinking brain instead of activating FEAR and RAGE systems in his lower brain.

• Disciplining your child in ways that uphold his dignity is a great gift in terms of his future mental health and his social and emotional intelligence.

the best
relationship
with your child

Research shows that special relationship times are as important for an eight-year-old as they are for an eight-month-old. So how can parents have the best possible relationship with their children? In this chapter we show you show how to make the most of the precious time you have with your children. There's a whole host of practical and fun-packed ideas – all backed by brain science – designed not only to enrich parent–child relationships while children are young, but to be an investment for life.

How to make the best connection

The best relationships form from making the best connections and communicating right from the outset. But how do you do this? There is evidence that on average mothers have an hour a day quality parent–child time with their children, and fathers a little over half an hour.[1] Good communication is vital not only for bonding, but also for a child's brain development. You can start connecting with your baby before she is born, and continue as she grows.

DID YOU KNOW...

• For most families, the average amount of parent–child quality time is about one hour a day for mothers and 35 minutes for fathers.

• More than a third of parents think they don't spend enough time with their children.

• Sixty-five percent of parents say they play only occasionally with their children.

• One in six fathers say they do not know how to play with their child.

• One third of fathers say they don't have the time to play.

• Two-thirds of conversations between parents and children are about daily routine.[5]

Make connections in pregnancy

Mothers-to-be often gently rub their abdomen to try to soothe and regulate a kicking fetus. Many parents-to-be also talk and sing to their unborn child. These are all forms of communication, yet you may wonder, "Is there any point? Does it benefit my child?"

The answer is "yes". We know that very young fetuses have a social need and social interest. Research has shown that twins communicate with each other from around 14 weeks of gestation, with movements specifically aimed at each other.[2]

Maternal voice and touch (through rubbing the abdomen) are powerful stimuli that produce definite responses from a fetus that can be seen in arm, head, and mouth movements – these are more obvious in older fetuses (third trimester) than younger ones (second trimester). A fetus's auditory system is functional at 25 weeks' gestation, but only with some frequencies. Scans show fetuses smiling at calming music or songs and scowling or grimacing at loud raucous sounds: they clearly hate loud, discordant music and enjoy soothing music.[3] Babies have been shown to recognize a melody months after the birth following extensive exposure to it in the last trimester.[4]

Communication benefits the mother, too

Communicating with your baby via gentle stroking of the abdomen is good for you, too. A woman's mood is better after an abdominal massage, and what's good for her is good for her baby.[6] Massage in pregnancy has many benefits, see right, as does massage during labour, preferably from your partner. Labours were on average three hours shorter with less need for medication when partners massaged a woman's back and legs from a sideways position during the first 15 minutes of every hour of labour. Newborns whose mothers were massaged had lower cortisol levels than babies of women who weren't.[7]

The best connection with a newborn

Research shows that mother and baby skin-to-skin contact immediately after birth offers the infant the best first meeting. In Sweden, it is now routine for hospitals to facilitate this. Skin-to-skin contact stimulates the sensory nerves in the skin, which triggers the release of the hormone oxytocin (see page 87). As a result:

• Mother and child feel a deep sense of well-being.
• Mother–baby bonding and attachment is improved.
• Babies cry less.
• Mothers are less anxious and more attentive and attuned to their baby's needs.
• Babies breathe more easily.
• Babies are able to leave hospital sooner.
• Quality of breast milk improves.[8]

Infants who had skin-to-skin contact within two hours of birth were found to be far calmer, more emotionally regulated, and better at socializing by the age of one, than those who didn't. Amazingly, by the of age 10, children who as premature infants had skin-to-skin contact after birth were still showing lower stress hormone levels, had a more regulated bodily arousal system (ANS), slept better, had better cognition, and had a better relationship with their mothers than babies only cared for in incubators.[9]

CONSIDER THIS...

Massage in pregnancy is great for you and your relationship with your baby. Research shows that just 20 minutes a week for five weeks can have the following benefits for women and babies (although I would suggest one hour per week):

• Decreased depression and anxiety.
• Less leg and back pain.
• Lower maternal cortisol levels.
• Decrease in excessive fetal activity.
• Fewer antenatal complications.
• Seventy five percent lower prematurity rate.
• Labours were on average three hours shorter with less need for medication.
• Incidence of low birth weight was 80 percent lower.
• Babies had lower cortisol levels at birth.
• Newborn babies performed better on the Brazelton Neonatal Behavioral Assessment.
• Mothers enjoyed better bonding with their babies. [8]

Delivery by Caesarean section can follow a period of labour or, in the case of an elective Caesarean, bypass labour altogether. Sadly, in neither situation will you enjoy the natural release of oxytocin (the bonding hormone) that occurs during a vaginal birth when the baby's head is pushing against the cervix. In addition, epidural pain relief blocks the nerves that trigger oxytocin, which means that mothers who have epidurals will have lower levels of oxytocin during labour.[10] So the "best connection" can be missing in these circumstances. As a result, some parents just don't fall head over heels in love with their baby, and then worry about that.

However, don't despair. Once you start breastfeeding, oxytocin begins to flow and your levels will soon be the same as those in women who had a natural childbirth. Research also shows that immediate or early skin-to-skin contact after a Caesarean section can help initiate breastfeeding, reducing time to the first breastfeed, which helps bonding and maternal satisfaction, and reduces newborn stress.[11]

There seems to be a vital, but very short, developmental window of opportunity after delivery.[12] Most importantly, if a full-term baby is placed on her mother's chest within one or two hours of birth, she won't need to be "put on the breast"; these babies find the breast themselves and instinctively attach to it.[13] Sadly too few women know this and many become very stressed trying to get their baby to latch on and feed because they missed this very precious window of opportunity.

Best conversations with a newborn

I don't need to state the obvious that the more you talk to your new baby the better. But, of course, with all of today's technology it's very easy to fall prey to the allure of music via earphones, or social media contact via a smart phone or tablet, while you are feeding your baby, for example. This is just at a time when a baby's frontal lobes need optimal stimulation from relationship interactions in order to bring about the best possible social, emotional, and cognitive functions. At birth, babies can see only 20–30cm (10–12in) away. Get out a ruler – that's the distance from your breast to your face. However, they can hear well. Talk to your baby

To make the best connection at night – ditch the pyjamas. Oxytocin is triggered by skin-to-skin contact. If you both wear clothes in bed they form an insulating layer or barrier between you, which blocks the skin's sensory nerves, counteracting the effect of the closeness. The same is true if you co-sleep with a toddler (see page 74).

whenever she's awake, whether she's in your arms, her cot, or her pram or buggy (see right).

Conversations with your older baby

Talking to your baby really helps language development. Poor language is linked to behaviour problems even in young children; two out of three language-delayed three-year-olds have behaviour issues.[14]

For the best conversations, try baby signing

You can start when your baby is between six- and nine-months old and continue right up to age three and beyond if your child is enjoying it. Baby signing uses a combination of manual signs and gestures to support speech – many of these are pictorial images of the words they represent. Unlike conventional signing, which uses signs without speaking, you say the word at the same time as making a sign. Your baby will watch your signs, and start to use them.

• **What the research says** Baby signing has implications long after a child has stopped using it. Infants who sign speak in sentences earlier than non-signers and it improves language and cognitive ability. By the age of three, signers were talking as well as children a full year older, and by the age of eight they scored significantly higher in IQ tests than non-signers.[15]

• **Using baby signing** If you wearily think, "Oh, not another thing to do", don't worry. You only need to have about 20 key words to sign effectively; importantly, these must include "sad" and "happy". Learn basics such as, "please" and "thank you" and "more", and then words for the important events in your child's life, such as "eat", "drink", "all gone". Use some feeling words and phrases such as: "I love you", "cuddle", "sorry", "pain", "hurt", "cross", and "scared". Many tantrums happen because children simply don't have words for their feelings. Always say a word as you sign it, speak slowly, and show delight when your child attempts to sign back.

Communication strategies

As shown in Chemistry of love & joy (see pages 84–125), it's so easy to be too intrusive or too withdrawn in our interactions with infants. As a result, children don't want to make eye contact and often close off. It can be hard to get a baby to re-engage as she loses trust in your ability to offer her a really sensitive attuned response. Research shows that mis-attunement in early parent–child relationships can even show up 12 years later in too high cortisol levels, particularly in boys.[17]

CASE STUDY

Avoid questioning or leading

Molly's mother makes some very common mistakes when playing with her baby: she choses the toys and leads the play, which activates stress hormones for the child

Mum: "Look Molly what is this? It's a red block. Put it with the red ones. What is this? A blue block. Now put the blue block with the other blue ones. Come on Molly, you try, like this. You try now."

Molly feels intruded on and expected to perform. She bursts into tears and throws the blocks across the room.

Key ways to connect

There are several possible strategies to connect with young children – or re-engage if you need to. Each one is designed to support the best communication with under fives to ensure the most sensitive attunement.[18] A key technique – observe, wait, and listen, known as "Owling" (see opposite),[19] ensures that you attune to your infant in the best way possible. "Copying and commenting" where you comment and track your child's play, is also effective.

Communicate through copying and commenting

Let your child choose the toy she wants to play with from the selection you have put out. Then observe, wait, and listen. When she engages with a toy, meet her delight – see opposite. If an older child is painting, a possible communication could run like this, "Can I play with you? What would you like me to do?" If she hands you a brush or sponge, gently touch her back or pat her foot occasionally as you play. A commenting strategy would be to say something like, "Ah, so you are putting the red paint on the sponge now. And now you are drawing some lovely lines on the paper." Always praise her, "Wow, what a beautiful picture. Thank you so much."

• **Copying strategy** means using sounds or movements while she's playing. So if she is hitting two toy ducks together, you pick up two toy ducks and do the same.

• **Comment on what your child is doing** – do not ask questions. Don't just parrot her back, though; gently build on the length of her sentences. Track her play and don't question any of her actions; use playtime to help language development. If a child speaks in single words, for example, "water", respond in two or three word phrases, so say, "water in bucket". If she talks in two-word phrases, respond with longer ones. So if she says "water falling", you can respond with "Yes. Water falling on Denice's hands". If she moves to a different activity, follow her and continue to comment. This way you are not only sustaining her interest in an activity, which is vital for her self-esteem, but you're also creating a feeling of "I can make good things happen in the world – what I am doing is so important, Mummy is commenting on it." Research shows that a parent's verbal attention-focusing behaviour in play increases the child's sustained attention, exploratory and social skills, language skills, and symbolic play competence.[20]

> **"** Use play to help language development by gently building on the length of a child's sentences. **"**

"Observe, wait, and listen"

Mum offers Stanley (aged six months) a wooden spoon to play with and places it on the table in front of him. Mum sits at the table opposite Stanley and observes, waits, and listens (or OWLs).

Stanley thinks about it – remember, thought processes and therefore decision processes are far far slower in infants than in adults. Mum leaves her hands on the table and waits. No pressure Stanley – take your time.

When Stanley goes for it, Mum still observes, waits, and listens. When he engages with it she praises him, meeting him in intense arousal state with her voice!

How to have the best conversations

Professionals often use a programme called the "parent–child game", to ascertain the emotional health of a family culture or parent–child relationship. Research shows that in troubled parent–child relationships, which can result in badly behaved children, commands are often a common mode of interaction. By this I mean that their "conversation" includes frequent orders – "do this", "don't do that", and lots of "no" and "stop". Commands trigger a child's RAGE, FEAR, or PANIC/GRIEF systems. Many commands also shame the child, releasing high levels of cortisol.

If you ensure that you give your child quality moments every day through praises and play, and keep commands and criticisms to a minimum, his brain habituates to optimal levels of anti-agression and well–being chemicals. As a result, he'll rarely need disciplining because he just won't be interested in fighting with you.

Avoid commands at all costs

Overall, you can't have "best relationships" in a house of repeated commands as the biochemical basis of commands will eventually make everyone miserable. With a household where interactions are about commenting, choices, and playful parenting there will be lots of laughter. In addition, the more "commands" a child gets, the more oppositional and defiant they can become. [21]

Use comments and choices instead

Parents who transact mainly through commands often do so because that's how their parents interacted with them when they were children. Sometimes they are simply short on resources for alternatives. When parents are helped to interact in other ways, for example, using "comments" (psychologist Sue Jenner refers to these as "attends") or choices, the biochemical basis of the entire family culture can change and the best relationships can result (see also page 130).

• **The difference between commands and comments** Three-year-old Maisy comes to the table clutching her favourite frog puppet, asking for the frog to be fed, too. A command-led parent might say, "Put your frog down, Maisy. We are eating now," with the result that Maisy cries. In contrast a comment response would be, "Ah! You are bringing frog to the table. Hello frog!!! How are you today? You're hungry too I hear!".

• **Enjoy conversations through child-led play** Commands can blight parent–child playtime, too. In parent-led play, commands, control, and criticism figure greatly. This is likely to de-activate opioids in the child's brain, making her feel miserable. This can result in the troubled or withdrawn behaviour often found in family cultures with lots of commands and criticism. On the other hand, child-led play (see page 248) means following the child, not teaching her, and your attention releases well-being chemicals in her brain.

• **Monitor the ratio of commands and criticism to commenting and praise** Sue Jenner has found that if a family culture means six commands/criticism to only one praise or "attend", you are heading for "oppositional–defiant" disorder or other mental health problems in a child. If things suddenly feel tense, miserable, or far too serious at home with no play, watch the number of commands that you use and also pay attention to how other family members, for example your partner or relatives, interact with your child. If they are using too many commands draw their attention to it.

• **Offer "Choices" rather than "No's"** where you can. A "no" can be so shaming for a child and close her down, so keep them to an absolute minimum. They are only necessary for some serious immediate needs, for example to stop a child who is about to run into the road. Remember, the lovely brain chemical dopamine (that enables expansive, curious, and spontaneous feelings) can so easily be blocked by the stress hormones triggered when a child is told off in a critical way.

Use of choices provides a non-shaming way of giving your boundaries while ensuring that you don't blight the child's SEEKING system (see Chemistry of drive & will, pages 126–43). Instead of saying "No" – try, "You can't do that... but what you can do is..." – it will make a difference.

CASE STUDY

A trip to a café goes wrong

Dad and his five-year-old daughter are on a treat to a café together. Dad manages to give 25 commands to his daughter in just 20 minutes, and no comments, or praise. His commands go like this, "Sit properly on your chair please; Wipe your hands now; Sit up properly; Stop playing with your food – I am not going to tell you again, is that clear?; Don't tap your fork on the table or you will be in trouble; Stop playing with the sugar – I don't want to have to tell you again; If you don't want the ice cream don't ask for it; We won't be coming here again if you behave like this."

When the little girl starts to speak, "Daddy, Daddy – oh um ah – I've forgot what I wanted to say", the response is "So just say what you want to say!" and she falls silent. By this time tearful, she says, "But Daddy, I'm not doing anything wrong, I am just sitting down." And she is absolutely right...

The dad wanting the best relationship with his child would bring a toy or puppet with him to satisfy his daughter's stimulation-hunger (see page 179) during the meal. Boredom triggers stress hormones in children, which they can't manage without some form of physical release (fidgeting, climbing on the seat, going under the table). Then congratulate her for sitting well and praise her for eating. Tell her she can come here again because she's showing great big girl behaviour.

Quality time

Every parent wants the best quality time with their children. Parents know intuitively what it means to have a relational moment with their child, and also know when they have had a day without any because they have been caught up in other activities. It is not only a sad loss for the child, but it's sad for the parents, too.

DID YOU KNOW...

Attachment play triggers laughter.
Laughter is a physiological response that activates reward pathways in the brain. It is known to improve immune function; lower blood pressure; reduce stress; and trigger opioids.[1] Research has found that people laugh 30 times more when there are other people around than when alone. As American neuroscientist Robert Provine said, "The essential ingredient for laughter is not a joke, but another person".[23]

You may well feel guilty if this happens to you, but give yourself a break. Juggling all the pressures between work and home life, it's amazing any parent manages any quality time with their child at all. In fact statistics show that women with children under three years of age work an average of 90 hours per week when the demands of the job, household chores, and childcare are counted up.[22]

Attachment play for best quality time

The good news is that attachment play (where you usually sit or stand opposite each other for optimum eye contact) guarantees plenty of relational moments between you. Attachment play can be any activity where your relationship is the absolute focus, and it can happen over short periods of time. I am not saying that attachment play is better, say, than spending the day together on a trip to the zoo or park – your child needs both. It's good to think in terms of "quality moments" not just "quality time".

How does attachment play help?

Attachment play helps brain development as it activates two of those powerful systems in your child's lower brain: the CARE (attachment) system and the PLAY system (see page 29). The play might include toys, but only to facilitate fun in the interactions between you – your games should involve deeply intimate face-to-face times.

This type of play optimizes the chances of "real" moments of meeting between a parent or carer, and a child. It brings

together many of the ways in which we connect joyfully – through touch, music, rhythm, humour, and imagination. It includes the key factors that make people feel connected, such as eye contact, touch, being attuned and listened to, warmth, interested facial expression, open posture, and a playful tone of voice.

Attachment play is vital for positive self-esteem – seeing you are lovely in the eyes of the other – which can only be attained through relational moments. It also helps develop a child's capacity for spontaneity and her trust in human relationships. Your reaction to her says: you have my full attention; I delight in being with you; and you are delightful.

Why can't my child just play with friends, or on her own? Can't I just give her good toys?

I am not saying it has to be one or the other – every type of play has different benefits. However, research shows that attachment play offers emotional regulation and so enhances higher brain functioning and habituates the brain to optimal

Let your child lead the game. Sit so that you are at your child's level, that way you can really make eye contact and respond to each other. Attachment play provides amazing moments of meeting and connecting joyfully.

"I look into your face and find myself as delightful there."

Babies love clapping and action games. You can play a variety of games together – babies love to copy your actions, and it's how they learn, too. Sing along to nursery rhymes and clap out the rhythm – comment on what your child is doing at the same time as it helps sustain her interest. If your baby can't clap yet, hold her hands in yours and carry out the rhythm movements for her.

" When [*children*] see their specialness reflected in your eyes, they see it in themselves. **"**

Helen Reiss

levels of the well-being chemicals – opioids and oxytocin (see Your child's brain in your hands, pages 14–33). While children are good playmates for each other, they just don't have the frontal-lobe maturity to be able to offer each other the emotional regulation that an adult can provide in attachment play. Emotionally regulating a child in high-arousal positive states helps her long-term capacity for spontaneity, exuberance, and true expansiveness.

So what are good attachment play activities?

Sit on the floor or a bean-bag cushion or put your child on your lap. It is important that you can both make eye contact.

• **Clapping games** such as "A sailor went to Sea, Sea, Sea" are fun for infants and young children.

• **Lap games** are great for under fives. With infants, try nursery rhymes where you can lift them in the air. Lay an older child across your lap and say, "I've got a jelly on my knee that goes wobble, wobble or roly poly."

• **Face-to-face play** develops that attachment relationship. When parents are good playmates, infants naturally engage in face-to-face play, but with older children try the "sticker on the nose" game. Ask "Can I have a red sticker on my nose? Can I have a blue one on my chin?" then swap. Or make face noises: make a bleep sound when the child presses your nose.

• **Play games that stimulate imagination.** Use bubbles (see who can pop them with different body parts); or balloons (count how long you can both keep one up in the air). Keep a puppet in your bag that you can play an attachment game with on a boring bus journey. If you make your voice interesting, under fives will enter into the fantasy. Choose puppets with moveable mouths because they are more expressive.

• **Music attachment play** triggers the nucleus accumbens (a small area deep in the brain), which engages the emotion processing parts of the brain, triggering reward chemicals so you will both end up feeling good together.[24] Babies and young children really enjoy playing with pots and pans and spoon band games (play background music, too). Over fives find these fun if set to funky music. For older children, use a large gathering drum and take it in turns to bounce a ball on the drum and then catch it in a person's hat.

DID YOU KNOW...
Why drumming together is so powerful?
Drumming activates the caudate nucleus, which triggers warm pro-social feelings towards other people. I have found that drumming attachment play between parent and child is hugely popular at any age. When you look at what drumming together (not a child drumming on her own) does to the brain it's not hard to see why – it has been shown to:
• Induce relaxation
• Enhance theta-wave patterns in the brain
• Lower blood pressure
• Reduce stress
• Trigger the release of calming chemicals
• Boost the immune system
• Increase cancer-killing cells.[25]

Research shows that after drumming together, children were:
• Less withdrawn
• Less hyperactive
• Less oppositional–defiant
• In addition, their attention was improved as there was a marked improvement in social and emotional behaviour.[26]

Golf umbrella houses Each person makes a cosy house with cushions and snacks. One taps "rain" on the other person's umbrella and is invited in. Alternatively, he puts on a duck hat saying he's a duck, then both players do a duck dance around the umbrellas. Then swap roles.

Activities that release well-being brain chemicals

It's important to acknowledge when things are not good between the two of you. Maybe you had a disagreement or work is stressful, so you are too sharp with your child or too emotionally unavailable. There might be just too many stress hormones floating about, making one or both of you irritated, "shouty", and/or stressed. If you start to think "brain biochemically" you'll know that you have the power to change your biochemical state in support of your relationship with your child.

By opting for an activity that triggers well-being chemicals you can change your mood and/or your child's, healing any relationship rupture. Pick activities that support you both biochemically – those that lower too high stress hormone levels and trigger the release of oxytocin and opioids.

"We can choose activities and pursuits that release the oxytocin stored in our own inner medical cabinet... This natural healing nectar provides an antidote to the negative effects of a fast-paced lifestyle marked by stress and anxiety.**"**

Kersten Uvnäs Moberg

Offer to give your child a foot massage or back rub

Parents wanting the best relationships should carry on giving their child massages way past the baby-massage stage. Research at the University of Virginia, USA, found that even holding hands with someone you love can stop the stressful reactions in your brain.[27] It has also been shown that massage triggers oxytocin, which not only reduces anxiety and fear, but also builds a person's desire to be near to and relate to others.[28]

• **Massage is always best on bare skin** as sensory receptors in the skin communicate to the brain, triggering well-being chemicals and so calming body and mind (see pages 46–47). Recent research has found that so called "C-tactile fibres" in the skin respond to soft and caressing strokes given at medium pressure and medium speed. They activate a part of the brain called the insula that triggers feelings of well-being, happiness, empathy, and trust.[29]

Go in warm water together

Those sensory nerves in the skin are also stimulated by heat. Have a bath together or, if your child is over five years old, you could try a jacuzzi or hot tub provided it's set at a safe temperature. It makes me cross that hotel and public pools are usually for "adults only"; they just need to turn the temperature down to 36–37°C (96.8°F–98.6°F) to allow children access. Hot tubs and jacuzzis are never safe for under fives.

Try a sensory room or tent

Sensory rooms or tents are perfect for the release of well-being chemicals in your and your child's brains. These small dark spaces have beautiful soft lighting and calming music – the lights and music activate oxytocin.[30] You can buy them (have a look on the internet), or make your own by throwing a sheet of black-out material over a few chairs.

Play in a sensory room stimulates well-being chemicals. If you have room for one, set it up away from the normal play area (perhaps in a shed or garage). Add extra light-up toys to it. Keep a sensory room for special mummy-me or daddy-me time only, as that way it keeps its specialness; novelty triggers production of the reward chemical dopamine.

A daddy-me (or mummy-me) trip to the park can benefit both you and your child. Add in some attachment play together and you both benefit from the quality time with real relational moments.

Go for an outing together in a green space

Mental fatigue from stressful family life and urban environments can be calmed by venturing with your child into green spaces, such as the park or out into the country. If it's summer, go for a special daddy-me or mummy-me picnic. Research has revealed improvements in a child's attention and concentration levels after being in nature for only 20 minutes. Green-play settings were found to be as good as, or better than, medication for children with ADHD even after as little as 20 minutes' exposure. There is also evidence that a walk together in green space:

• **Calms the body** (lowering blood pressure and cholesterol levels for example) and lowers cortisol levels.

• **Impacts positively on brainwave patterns**, bringing about higher meditative states and lower frustration levels.

• **Calms the bodily arousal system**.

• **Is associated with a lower frequency of stress** symptoms including digestive illnesses and headaches.[31]

Key points

• Make the best connections from the very beginning by communicating with your baby during pregnancy.

• Avoid commands at all costs. Offer your child lots of playful parenting every day and avoid asking questions as she plays.

• Offer your child lots of adult-accompanied play; sit opposite her at her level, comment on what she is doing, and copy and attune to the sounds and movements she makes.

• Think "brain biochemically", by choosing quality-time activities that support the activation of well-being chemicals.

• Make some time every day for activities where your relationship together is the absolute focus.

looking
after you

Parenting is one of the most stressful jobs there is. Alongside the wondrous, delightful, and profoundly fulfilling times, you will also experience broken sleep and extreme tests of your patience and temper. Your job is to help your child with a whole range of feelings, from tantrums and rage to excitement and joy. In order to be a calm, loving, and empathic parent you need to take good care of yourself. This means recognizing when you're feeling low and seeking the support and the time you need to restore mental and physical balance.

Stress-free pregnancy

It's important to look after yourself emotionally as well as physically when you are pregnant. Your emotional state can affect the development of your unborn child's brain. You'll need special support if you are pregnant and feeling stressed, depressed, or anxious.

CONSIDER THIS...

An unborn baby is particularly vulnerable to high levels of maternal stress hormones during the last three months of pregnancy when there is a major growth spurt in its brain. Get as much relaxation and emotional support as you can during this time. Pregnancy massage has been shown to decrease anxiety and stress hormone levels.[2]

From seven weeks onwards, pleasure-inducing opioids can be found in the unborn baby's bloodstream. What a great start in life! However, we also know that if the mother is repeatedly very stressed in the last three months of pregnancy, excessively high levels of stress chemicals (cortisol and glutamate) can be transmitted through the placenta into the brain of the unborn baby.

Some research shows that unborn babies who are subjected to overly high levels of stress chemicals can go on to have a reduced capacity to deal with stress as children and as adults. High levels of stress during pregnancy is one of the risk factors for the child for depression and vulnerability to drug-seeking in later life.[1] A baby who has been stressed before birth can be a very unsettled baby after birth, and parents may have to work extra hard to regulate their child's painful emotional and physical states. If a stressed baby receives plenty of calming and soothing parenting – of the type described in this book – his ability to handle stress can improve.

In some cases, too much stress during pregnancy has also been shown to affect the genetic unfolding of key emotion chemicals and hormones in the unborn baby. This means that certain key genes don't do what they are supposed to do; they don't move to the right place in the brain. In the male fetus, for example, overly high levels of stress in the mother can change the impulses of the hormones testosterone and oestrogen. Research with other mammals shows that male infants may be born with a feminized brain, which can have implications for future sexuality.[3]

Alcohol, drugs, and smoking

If you are highly anxious or stressed out during pregnancy, take a break. A head or foot massage is a good idea. Don't be tempted to resort to drink or drugs (other than any that are prescribed by your doctor). Taking drugs such as cocaine, ecstasy, or speed, or drinking alcohol can change the development of an unborn child's brain. Alcohol also raises the level of cortisol in an unborn child. Research shows that children of alcoholic mothers can have an over-reactive stress response system (see HPA axis, page 40) when they are born. Brain scans of children with mothers who drank a lot of alcohol in pregnancy often show a smaller cerebrum (higher brain), with fewer folds. There can also be damage to the cerebellum (which controls coordination and movement),

" If you are highly anxious or stressed out in pregnancy, try a head or foot massage. **"**

" I would like a break "

Feeling tired during pregnancy can have an impact on your existing children. Everyday activities such as work, shopping, and visiting friends can tire you more than you expect and leave you short-tempered. Try to minimize non-essential tasks; consider shopping online and sharing childcare with family and friends.

and to the brain stem (responsible for basic processes such as breathing and body temperature). The brain of a child with FAS (fetal alcohol syndrome, caused by the mother's excessive drinking) does not fully develop, resulting in mental and emotional difficulties. Alcohol consumed during the first three months is more dangerous to the unborn child than alcohol consumed later in pregnancy. The UK Chief Medical Officer advises that women who are pregnant or trying to

"I can feel a connection with my baby already"

Celebrating pregnancy can have a profound effect not only on you and your unborn child, but also on the rest of your family. Your sense of well-being will be transmitted to the people around you. And when your baby is born, he is more likely to be calm and easier to settle.

conceive should avoid alcohol altogether. Indeed research by Professor Peter Hepper at Queen's University, Belfast, has found that consuming just one glass of wine suppresses fetal behavior and, worse still is that the effect continues even after the alcohol is out of the woman's system.[4]

If you smoke during pregnancy, you are subjecting your developing baby to harmful nicotine, tar, and carbon monoxide

You are also reducing your baby's oxygen supply. Research shows that smoking in pregnancy can also lead to altered structures in some parts of the baby's brain and altered brain functioning, putting the baby at risk of developing behaviour problems and learning difficulties. Pregnant women who smoked more than ten cigarettes a day were significantly more likely to have a child who developed a conduct disorder. Children with mothers who smoked in pregnancy also had a higher risk of alcohol or substance abuse, and of depression, in later life. So make every effort to stop.[5] Mothers who smoked during pregnancy are also advised not to co-sleep with their baby (see page 74).

Falling in love with your baby... or not

If all goes well during and after delivery, your brain will naturally release high levels of oxytocin (see page 86). This can make you feel blissed out, deeply at one with your baby (and deeply in love), and deliciously lacking in stress. In postnatal depression, the release of early bonding chemicals is blocked, but with professional help you can get them flowing again. If not treated, postnatal depression can in turn adversely affect a child's stress hormone levels, sleep, eating, and immune system. Postnatal depression affects about one in every ten mothers, and anti-depressants and/or counselling usually work very well. These get your positive arousal and mood-stabilizing chemicals working properly again and lower stress hormone levels.[6]

Research shows that breastfeeding is great for a mother's mood because it calms the stress response system in her brain. Because the mother feels calm and relaxed, this helps her to calm and soothe her baby. Breastfeeding also gives the baby essential polyunsaturated fatty acids, which can enhance the production of key brain chemicals in the higher brain, namely dopamine and serotonin. However, some studies have shown that both breastfeeding and bottle-feeding, when holding the infant next to your calm body, lower stress hormones, with no significant differences between the two methods.[7]

Now you have children

Along with the joy of parenting comes lots of hard work. Your job is to care not just for your child's physical needs, but also for his emotional and psychological ones. Being constantly on duty can take its toll on you. Responding to the signs of stress in yourself is an essential parenting skill.

After several hours of caring for young children, you may long for peace. If you have a few spare minutes, make an effort to do something that feels self-indulgent. Re-fuelling like this can enable you to stay calm and able to empathize with your children.

A day in the life of a parent

Imagine a typical day of looking after your three-year-old child. He has just got a new toy – a big red bus – and you enthusiastically amplify his delight in it. Then he jumps on top of you and wants 10 minutes of rough-and-tumble play. You know that this kind of play is great for his brain, so how can you refuse? Next, you give him a biscuit and he is distressed when he breaks it. He bursts into tears because he wants you to mend it. When you explain that you can't, he throws a cup of milk on the floor. Now you need to find a good way to tell him that this isn't acceptable behaviour.

Later, you help your child to come to terms with the fact that he can't bring his pet frog into the living room. You also stop a kicking fight with his brother. You are starting to feel weary, but your child wants you to watch him press the "toot toot" button on his yellow lorry. He looks at you expectantly, waiting for you to say "wow", and when you do, it brings a big grin to his face. That smile is lovely for you too, but when he asks you to watch him for the eighteenth time, it's starting to feel a bit wearing. Despite this, you know that attention and praise is so good for establishing positive chemical arousal systems in your child's brain, so you do it again and again. At bedtime, you have to help your child manage his rage about going to bed. And, in addition to all of this, you may also have other children who need you in similar ways.

After several hours spent with young children, you long for peace. So what's happening to you? Well, you can only regulate your child's brain for so long without needing some emotional regulation yourself. In neuroscientific terms, you are biochemically "dysregulated". Your bodily arousal system (see page 44) will also be out of balance, adding to your feelings of stress.

Are you dysregulated?

Feeling frazzled, angry, and potentially explosive when your child does something naughty is a sign that you are biochemically dysregulated. Rather than using your higher brain to reflect on the best response, your RAGE system in your lower brain keeps getting triggered. Your higher brain is flooded with stress chemicals and, as a result, you lose the skills of empathy and clear thinking. You feel like screaming!

" Feeling frazzled, angry, and explosive is a sign that you are biochemically dysregulated. **"**

" I know I have to stay calm **"**

Your role of emotional regulator is to help your child to cope with his unmanageable emotional intensity in order to make it tolerable for him. In so doing, you will be helping him to establish pathways and systems in his brain that will enable him, eventually, to do this on his own. When children have not received effective emotional regulation, later life can be very hard.

Food to enhance your mood

Some of the key chemicals that influence your emotions are manufactured from the food you eat. By eating specific foods, and avoiding others, you can help to control or enhance the way you feel, both physically and emotionally. Eating regularly also helps to control your mood and sense of well-being.

Eating a varied, balanced, nutritious diet is important for everyone, especially busy parents. Certain foods are essential for the production of key brain chemicals, and without them, you may feel miserable and tired.

If you know which brain chemicals are manufactured from which foods, it can really add to your potency as a parent. For example, when you find yourself over-reacting to your child's behaviour, ask yourself, "Is my child annoying me because of a stressful situation, or am I short of some key vitamins?"

Emotion chemicals work in symphony, but it's a very sensitive symphony. If one chemical is a bit low, it can affect the others, making you feel miserable. You can make positive changes to the chemical balance in your brain by eating specific foods.

Eating to keep your mood stable

Serotonin is responsible for improving mood, emotional stability, and sleep quality. When people have a low serotonin level, they can feel depressed, aggressive, and anxious.

Tryptophan is the building block from which serotonin is made, and it comes from food. You can make sure you get enough tryptophan by eating plenty of bananas, bread, pasta, and oily fish, such as salmon and mackerel. You can also take fish oil supplements.

For the brain to manufacture serotonin effectively you also need to eat foods that contain vitamins B_6 and B_{12}, and folic acid (B_9). Good sources include bananas, avocados, fish, vegetables, baked potatoes, chicken, and beef. You can also take vitamin B supplements (the B vitamins all work as a group, so take a supplement that includes B_1, B_2, B_6 B_{12}, and folic acid). Vitamin B_6 is especially important in serotonin production – just one milligram too little, per day, can badly affect your emotional state. Research shows that when some depressed people take enough of vitamins B_6 and B_{12}, their depression goes. Sleep quality improves, too. As you get older, you need more of vitamins B_6 and B_{12} because you absorb these vitamins less well with age. The B vitamins also contribute to the manufacture and release of GABA, which is a key anti-anxiety chemical in the brain (see page 44).[8]

Food to keep you motivated as a parent

An optimum level of dopamine, in combination with other brain chemicals, is key to ensuring that you have the necessary psychological drive to want to engage fully in life and with your children. When dopamine is strongly activated in your brain, it can counteract the negative impact of the minor stressors that are an inevitable part of bringing up children. When dopamine is not optimally activated in your brain, you can feel lethargic, irritable, and depressed, with a lack of motivation to organize interesting things for your children to do that you would also enjoy.

To make dopamine, the brain needs tyrosine, which is present in protein foods such as fish, meat, nuts, and cheese. You also need essential minerals and vitamins. While food can't actually strengthen the activation of dopamine in the brain, it is vital to sustain optimal levels.[9]

Food to help you stay stable under stress

Oily fish contains an omega-3 fatty acid called docosahexaenoic acid (DHA). DHA is a very powerful player in brain chemistry. It forms about half of all the fat in brain cell membranes. It is needed to build and preserve pliable brain cell structures so the brain can work effectively, and so that chemical messages can be sent throughout the brain with ease. DHA has been shown to improve mood by boosting serotonin levels. Once again, DHA is obtained only from your diet. Research on fish oil consumption in different countries

CONSIDER THIS...

If you feel exhausted, consider whether it is just the broken sleep, or are there other causes? Have you eaten properly? If you don't have a steady supply of glucose to the brain, and enough of the protein needed to form positive arousal chemicals in your brain, you will feel tired.

Have you been indoors all day? A change of environment – being with stimulating, energized people; taking a walk; or doing something interesting to activate your brain's SEEKING system (going to a lively coffee bar or a film) – can all raise your dopamine levels.

Don't go to bed stressed. If you do, the high levels of cortisol may wake you up in the early hours. Have a relaxing bath or cuddle with your partner.

❝Non-breakfast-eaters are twice as likely to feel depressed and four times as likely to be anxious.❞

has shown that as fish oil consumption goes up, depression rates go down.[10] In fact, the lower your DHA level, the more severe your depression may be. Many people's diets are badly lacking in DHA. So when you eat oily fish or take DHA supplements, the brain is likely to grab most or all of it.

Sardines, salmon, tuna, mackerel, and cold-pressed linseed oil or flaxseed oil are rich in DHA. You can take DHA in the form of a fish oil supplement, but read the label before you buy anything because some supplements contain only eicosapentaenoic acid (EHA). You need more DHA as you get older. Also, DHA levels are depleted by alcohol and smoking.

❝I need breakfast❞

A protein-rich breakfast will boost your tyrosine levels, and improve your concentration and problem-solving skills. People who eat a full breakfast are far more effective and creative throughout the day.[11] Milk and yogurt, for example, are good sources of protein.

The type of carbohydrate that you eat is also important. Wholemeal bread is preferable to white bread, which supplies energy for only about an hour. After this you'll experience a slump in your mood and energy levels. Complex carbohydrates such as oats make your blood glucose levels rise slowly for a few hours, which provides you with sustained energy and can stabilize your mood.

Feeling good throughout the day

Not eating properly or making poor food choices can have a dramatic effect on your day. If you skip meals, or rely on caffeine or sugary snacks to keep you going, you will feel anxious, irritable, and lacking in energy around your children. The following rules make good sense:

• **Eat a good breakfast and lunch** Research shows that non-breakfast-eaters are twice as likely to feel depressed and four times as likely to be anxious as people who eat at the start of the day.[12] Not eating breakfast means that your blood glucose level remains low. Your brain can't function well in this state, and your adrenal glands respond by releasing high levels of adrenaline and cortisol, which can make you feel anxious and on edge.

• **Avoid sugary snacks and drinks** Eating biscuits or chocolate, because you haven't had time to feed yourself properly, is the worst thing you can do. After the initial release of pleasure chemicals in your brain, it's downhill all the way. On an empty stomach, sugary food sends your blood sugar levels really high. Your body then releases insulin to drop them down again, but this often means sugar levels fall to a level far lower than before you ate the food. This can make you feel tired and irritable with the children, with all those negative feelings commonly triggered by hypoglycaemia.

• **Snack on fruit or protein** To give you (or your children) an energy boost, eat some fruit instead. Fruit has a different sugar in it, called fructose. This does not trigger the insulin release. Carry a banana in your bag as this snack will boost your levels of tryptophan, the substance needed to make the mood-stabilizing chemical serotonin, and will offer you a slow release of sugar into the blood, keeping you going for a while. Nuts can be a good snack, too, activating tyrosine, which is key to the manufacture of the positive arousal brain chemical dopamine.

• **Eat carbohydrate foods in the evening** This activates tryptophan in the brain, a key component in serotonin.

A protein-rich lunch of meat or fish helps your body to make tyrosine, which will sustain optimal levels of dopamine in your brain. This can make you alert and focused for the rest of the day. If you have a carbohydrate-rich lunch, you may feel sleepy during the afternoon.

Optimal levels of serotonin help regulate sleep. If you want yourself and your children to feel sleepy, avoid high-protein bedtime snacks. They can keep you awake.

• **Drink six glasses of water a day** Water is vital to flush out waste products. If you don't drink enough, the waste products stay in your system, making you feel tired, sluggish, and lethargic. Don't use thirst as a barometer of when you need water; by this time, you are already dehydrated.

• **Consider supplements** It can be difficult to ensure that your diet has enough of the minerals and vitamins essential to the manufacture of mood-stabilizing and positive arousal brain chemicals – so vital for managing the stress of parenting. As one researcher states, "It would take 46 cups of spinach a day to reach your optimum level of vitamin E, or 8 cups of almonds". In various parts of the world, including the UK, the daily diet is often lacking in the vital trace element selenium. Low selenium levels are strongly linked to anxiety, low energy, irritability, depression, and fatigue.[13]

Co-enzyme Q_{10} helps convert food into energy. We have lower levels as we get older, so supplements, used carefully, are sometimes necessary. Stress also depletes vital minerals and vitamins.

• **Drink camomile tea** Camomile is a mild sedative. It acts on the benzodiazepine receptors in the brain, producing a calming anti-anxiety effect. It is ideal for drinking before bedtime and throughout the day, instead of caffeine drinks such as coffee.

What else will help to improve my mood?

Go for a walk in the sunshine. Grey skies are linked to low levels of serotonin in the brain, which can make people feel depressed. Also, reduced exposure to light may result in a deficiency of dopamine; hence you can be less alert, lack get-up-and-go, and suffer from poor concentration. Vitamin D from sunshine is absorbed through the skin, so it is useful to walk outside each day. Low Vitamin D contributes to feelings of depression, and levels can plummet in the winter.

Is coffee a bad idea? I need at least four cups a day.

Your child has woken at 6.30 am and you feel tired, so you reach for the coffee to try to feel at least half-human. Caffeine, found in coffee, tea, fizzy drinks, and some painkillers, is one of the most popular mood-altering drugs. Caffeine can raise your mood and makes you feel more alert, motivated, and energized, because it stimulates noradrenaline, adrenaline, and dopamine in the brain and raises glucose levels. It blocks adenosine, a brain chemical that makes you feel sleepy and helps you to sleep. Caffeine tolerance varies from person to person and in terms of the time of day. Drink it with food and, in moderation, it can give you a lift. Drink it on an empty stomach and there can be real problems. After the initial high, there will be a drop in glucose levels, leaving you feeling tired, depressed, or easily irritated. Also, the more caffeine you drink, the more you require just to feel normal. It's called "down-regulating".

Why re-fuelling is necessary

Emotional re-fuelling is necessary to bring your brain and body's stress chemicals back to base rate. If you don't emotionally re-fuel, and instead just keep going without a child-free break, you can end up feeling chronically stressed and bad-tempered. This will have a knock-on effect for your children, who will feel stressed by your stress, which can lead to bad behaviour.

Take regular breaks. If you don't take time out for yourself, you may end up feeling irritable, moody, anxious, and prone to anger most of the time. Stress can also damage the quality of your sleep, making you feel tired during the day.

Re-fuelling means quality child-free time doing something relaxing and enjoyable just for you, rather than quick, short-term fixes with side effects, such as alcohol or cigarettes. Any parent, however skilled, who moves into a stoic "soldier-on" mode, without emotional re-fuelling, will end up with a negative brain chemistry and body hyperarousal. Key signs that you need re-fuelling include finding yourself increasingly irritated and short-tempered with the children, with less and less inclination to play with them, spontaneously cuddle them, and praise them. Rather than seeing them as a delight, you start to experience them as a set of demands. With practice you can become skilled at recognizing the signs of biochemical dysregulation in your brain; namely, the rise of stress chemicals and the lowering of positive and mood-stabilizing chemicals such as dopamine and serotonin.

What is emotional re-fuelling?

There are two main types of emotional re-fuelling: auto-regulation and interactive regulation. Auto-regulation means you do something by yourself to change your brain chemistry, such as reading a book, going out for a walk, or relaxing in a lovely warm bath. Interactive regulation means spending quality time with other people, such as your partner or your friends. If we are to stay emotionally healthy as human beings, we need lots of both of these on a regular basis.[14]

Why quick fixes don't work

Some people turn to harmful ways of dealing with the stress of parenting, such as drinking alcohol and smoking cigarettes. Although both of these habits may offer an immediate solution, they can have serious long-term consequences.

So why do we find drinking alcohol and smoking so alluring?

Alcohol activates GABA (see page 44), an anti-anxiety system in the brain. It also briefly boosts serotonin and dopamine, so you can feel more socially confident, alert, and relaxed. But too much alcohol can soon lead to the opposite of the desired effect. When you drink too much, your oxytocin, DHA, tryptophan, and glucose levels all fall, so with low blood sugar and low serotonin, you can plummet into a very low mood.

After a few drinks, alcohol can start to seriously deactivate higher brain functions such as our speech and emotion-regulating functions. When this happens, the lower, or mammalian, brain is left in the driving seat; so it is easy to see how people who drink too much can become angry, violent, or depressed. It is this takeover by the lower brain that accounts for the fact that much domestic violence and child abuse is alcohol-influenced.

Smoking triggers acetylcholine (an excitatory brain chemical) and dopamine, and stimulates the adrenal glands, activating adrenaline

As a result, you feel more alert, motivated, and clear-headed. It also activates niacin, which supports GABA, so you feel less anxious. It slows the heart rate and helps muscles relax. Some research also indicates that the sucking motion of smoking activates oxytocin, just as a child's sucking on a dummy does.

But of course, both these quick fixes come with a life-threatening price tag, so you need to find a method of emotional re-fuelling that is not actually bad for your physical or mental health.

CONSIDER THIS...

Getting out of your home for a break can be rewarding for the whole family. Fresh air, sunshine, and space can calm both parents and children. There are many studies showing that physical exercise can release endorphins and dopamine. Exercise also brings down high levels of the stress chemicals adrenaline, noradrenaline, and cortisol. Aerobic exercise can make you feel more alert due to more oxygen to the brain. One study found that sedentary people were more depressed than people who exercised regularly, and had lower levels of endorphins and higher levels of stress hormones.[15]

Restoring balance

You've recognized the signs of stress, low mood, and a negative brain chemistry. Your children are starting to get on your nerves and you feel like exploding at things you normally take in your stride. Now it's time to take action. Here are the activities that can bring down your stress chemicals.

Activities that calm you down

When you find an activity that calms you down and makes you feel relaxed, it means that your brain is probably releasing the wonderful anti-stress chemical oxytocin. The scientist Uvnas Moberg, who has written extensively about oxytocin, says, "We can choose activities and pursuits that release the oxytocin stored in our own inner medical cabinet. We have this wonderful healing substance inside us and need only to learn the many ways we can draw upon it. This natural healing nectar provides an antidote to the negative effects of a fast-paced lifestyle marked by stress and anxiety".[16] Research shows that oxytocin can:
- Have an anti-anxiety effect
- Lower blood pressure and pulse rate
- Prevent the bloodstream from being flooded with stress hormones
- Help the body digest food efficiently
- Reduce agitation
- Increase sociability.

Once you have found an activity that makes you feel calm, make a point of doing it on a regular basis. For example, have a weekly massage rather than a once-a-month massage, or set aside time for yoga every weekend. This will keep your oxytocin at optimum levels. Alternatively, choose an activity such as sitting in a beautiful garden or park, which will lower bodily hyperarousal and activate the calm and centred branch of your autonomic nervous system (see page 44).

"I feel calm and relaxed"

Yoga can lower blood pressure. Yoga movements calm the body by activating the vagal nerve system (see page 45). Research shows that yoga releases an anti-anxiety chemical GABA (gamma-aminobutyric acid) so enables us to feel a real sense of calm.[17]

Meditation can lower blood pressure, anxiety, and cortisol levels in long-term meditators. It can also calm the overactive stress response system in the brain, by calming the amygdala (the system in the lower brain that detects threat).[18]

One of the best ways to lower stress levels is to spend time with emotionally warm adults

It can be easy to focus on the chemical changes you can get from particular foods or activities, and forget about the ultimate mood changer – being with lovely people. A stimulating conversation with the right person can lower your stress chemical levels and activate optimal levels of dopamine and noradrenaline. Time with a loved one in whose company you feel very safe and at ease can also strongly activate the opioids in the brain, giving you a wonderful feeling of well-being. If it's a physically affectionate relationship, these opioids will have an even deeper effect on you, because of the sensitizing effects of oxytocin on the opioid system. This chemistry is arguably the most emotionally replenishing of all, as we know from the sheer bliss that can come from

"Time with a loved one in whose company you feel very safe can give you a wonderful feeling of well-being."

❝ A crucial skill is to recognize when you are frazzled. ❞

CONSIDER THIS...

It's important to work out who are the people in your life who emotionally dysregulate you; in other words, who activate high levels of stress chemicals and send your body into a state of hyperarousal. People who commonly emotionally dysregulate other people are those who "talk at you" in lengthy monologues, or who are very anxious or agitated, or who offer little reciprocity in their interactions with you. They rarely, if ever, ask you how you are, or show any curiosity about your life, or they use you as their emotional regulator (or worse, as a therapist), but never show you any empathy for the problems in your life.

luxuriating in the arms of someone we love. So take time to have a comforting phone conversation with a friend, a long lie on the sofa with a loved one, and lots of exchanges full of warmth and laughter. You will be able to meet the most challenging of child behaviour calmly and with the capacity to think well under stress.

As a parent, a crucial skill is to recognize when you are frazzled and emotionally dysregulated (see page 267) and so are in need of the emotionally replenishing qualities of adult company. Every parent needs other adults around if they are to remain calm and in control. Don't wait until you feel isolated, depleted, exhausted, and depressed before you start seeking adult company.

However much you enjoy the company of your children, it's only emotionally aware adults who can give you the emotional regulation you need

This is because emotionally aware adults have developed the higher brain functions of compassion, empathy, and concern and the ability to find the words to express these. Such adults may also have developed good vagal tone (see page 45), which means their bodily energy and physical presence is calming to be around, too. In parenting, emotional regulation must always be a one-way process, so it is never appropriate to treat your child as your little confidante or counsellor. It takes children all their time to manage their own feelings without having to manage yours as well.

Sometimes your nearest and dearest are not the best emotional regulators for you

They may be people who are biochemically dysregulated for much of the time, because of lack of sufficient emotional regulation in their childhood and no counselling or therapy to change this. As a result, they may be anxious, angry, or depressed for much of the time, so being in their company will not activate the chemicals in your brain which promote a sense of emotional well-being. It's a question of identifying which people in your life can calm and soothe you, and then making sure you get enough time with them.

You'll need special support if your child's strong feelings trigger your own childhood pain
Some parents successfully manage to cut off from painful feelings about their own childhood. Then, when they have

" It is never appropriate to treat your child as your little confidante or counsellor. "

" It's good to talk to you "

If you are mostly alone with your children, no one is providing you with the vital emotional regulation you need in order to lower your bodily arousal levels. Enjoying time with other adults can change your brain state from stressed to calm; for example, you could join parent groups to meet people.

Cultures in which a family group or whole village bring up a child are very good for the emotional health of both parent and child. The same is true for groups in many animal species.

"A child's intense feelings can trigger emotional pain, which the parent had successfully buried for years."

a child, it all comes flooding back. The child's intense feelings can trigger emotional pain, which the parent had successfully buried for years. If this happens, the child's crying or raging tantrums can make you feel desperate or explosive, or want to lash out with words or physically.

If you feel like this often, first check that your emotional state is not due to one or more of the other causes we have looked at for the disruption of the brain's positive chemical balance, such as tiredness, hunger, poor diet, too much coffee, or too much time on your own. If you are sure it's none of these, it may be a childhood memory. Don't expect to have a clear memory of what's being stirred up in you now. In infancy, the brain can store sense memories (for example, sensations, feelings, and images), but it is not yet wired up to be able to store "event memories" – "Mummy did that to me, or said this to me". So, if as a baby you were left screaming and no one came, you won't remember the "event" of this,

"I can't do this all by myself"

You will need special support as an emotional regulator for your children if you are on your own with them for much of the time. A great number of isolation studies show that spending too much time on your own without human interaction causes a drop in positive arousal chemicals and a rise in stress chemicals. One study found that isolation is more of a health risk than smoking.[19]

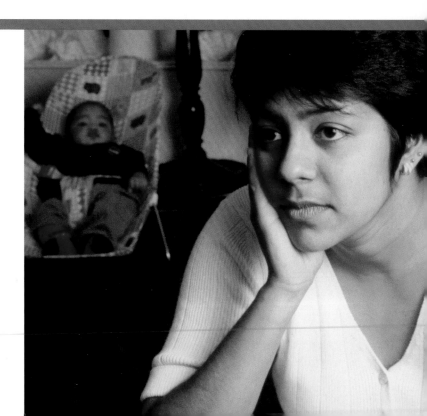

only the sense of desolation and desperation. If you feel like this often, the best thing you can do is seek counselling or psychotherapy (see page 282). If you have labelled your child as "bad" or see him as some kind of enemy with whom you are locked in constant battle, it's also a good idea to get some therapy for you, or parent–child therapy.

You will also need special support if you suffer from depression or postnatal depression

Clinical depression is different from depression as a passing mood that affects most people from time to time. Depression is an illness in which the brain keeps pumping out more and more stress chemicals, and you can't turn the pump off. This then blocks the release of positive arousal brain chemicals. The result is a form of hell-on-earth.[20] The world loses all its goodness. Not even that lovely smile from your child, or your partner telling you he loves you, makes you feel good. You lose interest or pleasure in all or almost all activities. You can have problems sleeping, or you sleep too much. You have feelings of worthlessness, and excessive and inappropriate guilt. You don't enjoy your children and yet you can be plagued by a dread of something awful happening to them. Clinical depression can also block the CARE system and the PLAY system in the lower brain, which robs you of your maternal feelings and your wish to be playful or physically affectionate with your children.

So if you think you might be depressed, don't blame yourself, or suffer alone. Go to your doctor and explain how you are feeling. Research shows that anti-depressants and counselling or psychotherapy in combination are the most effective treatment.

Loss or trauma is another reason for needing special support in your role as a parent

If you are in pain or under a lot of stress in your life at the moment, your feelings will find their way into your parenting.

CONSIDER THIS...

Teachers, like parents, need interactive regulation if they are to emotionally regulate the children in their care. Ideally, all teachers would therefore receive a regular massage and counselling. Also, teaching as part of a team would mean that teachers could bring each other the interactive regulation they need (see page 274).

For many children who haven't received warm, emotionally regulating parenting, school provides a second chance to develop their emotional and social brain. If teachers are chronically stressed, the children in their care don't receive this second chance. These are vital considerations for any government and education system.

Perhaps you are reeling from the effects of losing a loved one, or moving home or job. Research shows that trying to brush feelings about major life events under the carpet won't work.

What's more, like it or not, children are barometers for parental stress and anguish. In fact, the right frontal lobe is so acutely aware that it can pick up on emotional atmospheres and suppressed feelings in another person in milliseconds. A child's unspoken reaction to your stress can come out in bad behaviour, in a neurotic symptom (phobia or obsession), or in a bodily symptom such as sleep, food, or bedwetting problems. Some emotionally eloquent children are able to speak about it. As Gemma, aged six, said, "It's really difficult to have my feelings when Daddy is having his all the time". Research shows that parental emotional baggage can all too easily result in children suffering from depression, anxiety, or problems with anger now or in later life.[21] Again, the solution is for you to go for counselling or psychotherapy.

What can therapy and counselling do?

Psychotherapy is a catch-all term for many different types of talking therapy, all of which help you to understand how your own childhood is still affecting you now. Counselling tends to be shorter term and more problem-focused, but can also involve helping you to understand what you are feeling in terms of how you think about yourself and other people in your present and past. If you did not receive enough compassion, understanding, and consistent emotional regulation from your parents, it's not too late. You can get this from good therapy. The "plasticity" of your higher brain means that it is still able to change, even in adulthood.

Good therapy can offer you powerful emotional interaction through which you can establish effective stress-regulating systems in your brain. It can also put an end to habitual negative emotional states, which have caused you to feel repeatedly anxious, angry, or depressed. For some people, therapy enables them to feel truly calm and at peace with

Q

I find my child's intense emotions really stressful. What can I do?

Some parents find it difficult to bear their child's intense emotions, and may not understand that they are appropriate to the child's age and development. This is usually because of a lack of sufficient emotional regulation in the parent's own childhood, which has left him or her believing that intense feelings are "dangerous". As a result, such parents can find themselves repeatedly wanting their child to have only "nice feelings", punishing developmentally appropriate expressions, and leaving the child to cope with unmanageable feelings by himself. Again, psychotherapy or counselling for the parent is such a gift for the child. It will enable you to manage your child's emotional intensity, rather than giving him the message that passion and excitement are unacceptable.

TRY THIS...

Spend time with people you care about. Warm, meaningful interactions with others bring your brain chemistry and body arousal level back to an optimum state. Hugs and warm, affectionate touches with your partner trigger the release of oxytocin. This gives you a warm, calm feeling.

themselves for the very first time, due to the calming of the amygdala and development of effective stress regulatory systems in the frontal lobes.[22]

People often say, "The past is the past". But when you have suffered an agonizing loss, or if you had a painful childhood, this is exactly what it is not

The past will only go into the past when it is remembered in the present, with someone who can make it safe for you to think about your early life. This is the role of a counsellor or psychotherapist. Research shows that adults who "own" their emotional pain do not re-enact the emotionally inadequate parenting they experienced themselves.[23] You can't usually get this level of emotional regulation from a friend, partner, or relative because these relationships are two-way. A therapist is there for you alone.

Perhaps we should finish with a quote from six-year-old Jamie, whose mother needed therapy after the death of her father. One day Jamie said to his schoolteacher, "Today, I am walking on air with my very happy face." When asked why, he said, "Someone's helping my Mummy with all the bad weather in her heart. It was making my family very cold and wet!".

Key points

• Be kind to yourself when you are pregnant – if you are stressed, your unborn baby will be stressed, too.

• As a parent you spend a lot of time regulating your child's emotions. Remember that you also need emotional re-fuelling, with quality child-free time and interactive regulation from calm, soothing adults.

• Don't be stoic. If you keep going despite feeling stressed, your children will sense your negative brain chemistry and this can affect their behaviour.

• Find activities that trigger the release of the brain's natural calming chemicals. These include yoga, massage, meditation, and lying in the arms of someone you love.

• If you are really struggling, talk to your doctor or to a counsellor or a psychotherapist.

References

Introduction
1 Prescribing and medicines team health and social care information centre (2015) Prescriptions dispensed in the community England 2004- 2014 Health and Social Care Information Centre 2. Sagan C (2005) *Dragons of Eden: Speculations on the Evolution of Human Intelligence,* Black Dog & Leventhal, New York

Chapter 1: your child's brain in your hands
1, 4, 12 Panksepp J, et al (2012) The archaeology of mind: neuroevolutionary origins of human emotion, WW Norton & Co., New York

2 Sagan C (2005) Dragons of Eden: *speculations on the evolution of human intelligence.* Black Dog and Leventhal, New York

3 Pan W, et al (2014) *Identifying the core components of emotional intelligence: Evidence from amplitude of low-frequency fluctuations during resting state.* PLoS One, Oct 30;9(10)

4 see 1

5 Hruby R, et al (2011) *Attachment in integrative neuroscientific perspective.* Activitas Nervosa Superior Rediviva: 53(2) • Hostinar CE (2013) *Future Directions in the Study of Social Relationships as Regulators of the HPA Axis Across Development.* Journal of Clinical Child & Adolescent Psychology: 42(4), 564–575

6 Raine A, et al (2009) The neurobiology of psychopathy: *A neurodevelopmental perspective. Canadian Journal of Psychiatry:* 54(12), 813-823

7 Lieberman A (1995) *The emotional life of a toddler,* Simon and Schuster, New York

8 Schore A (2003) *Affect regulation and the repair of the self,* Norton and Co., New York

9 Gottman J, et al (1996) *Parental meta-emotion philosophy and the emotional life of families: theoretical models and preliminary data.* Journal of Family Psychology: 10(3), 243-268 • Nemeroff CB (2013) *Psychoneuroimmunoendocrinology:* The Biological Basis of Mind–Body Physiology and Pathophysiology, Depression and Anxiety: 30:285–287

10 Dube SR, et al (2003) *The impact of adverse childhood experiences on health problems: Evidence from four birth cohorts dating back to 1900.* Preventive Medicine, 37(3):268-77 • Godfrey KM, et al (2015) *The developmental environment, epigenetic biomarkers and long-term health.* J Dev Orig Health Dis. May: 28:1-8

11 Perry BD, et al (1995) *Childhood trauma; the neurobiology of adaptation and use-dependent development of the brain: how states become traits.* Infant Mental Health Journal, 16: 271-91

12 see 1

13 Perry BD (2002) *Childhood experience and the expression of genetic potential: what childhood neglect tells us about nature and nurture.* Brain and Mind, 3:79-100

14 Bugental D, et al. (2003) *The hormonal costs of subtle forms of infant maltreatment.* Hormones and Behavior, Jan: 237-244 • Walsh ND, et al. (2014) *General and Specific Effects of Early-life Psychosocial Adversities on Adolescent Gray Matter Volume.* Neuroimage Journal: 4:308–318

15 Teicher MH, et al (2006) *Sticks, stones, and hurtful words: relative effects of various forms of childhood maltreatment.* The American Journal of Psychiatry, Jun;163(6):993-1000 • Tomoda A, et al (2011) *Exposure to Parental Verbal Abuse is Associated with Increased Gray Matter Volume in superior temporal gyrus.* Neuroimage Journal, Jan, 54

16 Veenema AH (2009) *Early life stress, the development of aggression and neuroendocrine and neurobiological correlates: What can we learn from animal models?.* Frontiers in Neuroendocrinology: 30:497–518

Chapter 2: crying & separations
1 Panksepp J, et al (1978) T*he biology of social attachments: opiates alleviate separation distress.* Biological Psychiatry Oct 13: 607-18

2 Kitzinger S (2005) *Understanding your Crying Baby,* Carroll and Brown, London

3 Leach P (2003) *your baby & child,* Dorling Kindersley, London: 273
4 Schmid B, et al (2013) *Maternal*

stimulation in infancy predicts hypothalamic-pituitary-adrenal axis reactivity in young men. Journal of Neural Transmission, 2013 Aug;120(8):1247-57

5 Johnson, SB, et al (2013) *The science of early life toxic stress for pediatric practice and advocacy pediatrics 2013,* American Academy of Pediatrics • Bugental D, Gabriela A, Martorella I, Barrazaa V (2003) *The hormonal costs of subtle forms of infant maltreatment,* Hormones and Behavior Jan: 237-244 • Gunnar MR et al (2015) *Parental buffering of fear and stress neurobiology: Reviewing parallels across rodent, monkey, and human models,* Society of Neuroscience 2015 Oct;10

6 Zubieta JK, et al (2003) *Regulation of human affective responses by anterior cingulate and limbic and m-opioid neurotransmission,* Archives of General Psychiatry 60:1145-1153

7 Chester DS, et al (2013), *The interactive effect of social pain and executive functioning on aggression: an fMRI experiment,* Social Cognitive and Affective Neuroscience, 2013, 1-6 • Eisenberger, NI (2012) T*he pain of social disconnection: examining the shared neural underpinnings of physical and social pain,* Nature Reviews, Neuroscience, Vol.13, June 2012

8 Gerhardt S (2014) *Why love matters: How affection shapes a baby's brain:* Brunner-Routledge, Kings Lynn

9 Schiavone S, et al (2015) *Impact of early life stress on the pathogenesis of mental disorders: relation to brain oxidative stress,* Current Pharmaceutical Design. 2015;21(11): 1404-12

10 McEwen BS (1999) Stress and the aging hippocampus, Journal of Neuroendocrinology, Jan;20(1):49-70 • Szyf, M. (2012), Conserved epigenetic sensitivity to early life experience in the rat and human hippocampus, PNAS, October 16, 2012, vol.109, suppl.2: 17266–17272

11 Doom, JR. and Gunnar, MR. (2013) *Stress physiology and developmental psychopathology: Past, present, and future,* Development and Psychopathology 25 (2013), 1359–1373 • Barry TJ, et al (2015) *Maternal postnatal depression predicts altered offspring biological*

stress reactivity in adulthood, Psychoneuroendocrinology, 2015 Feb; 52:251-60

12 Zubieta JK, et al (2003) *Regulation of human affective responses by anterior cingulate and limbic and m-opioid neurotransmission,* Archives of General Psychiatry 60:1145-1153

13 Ludington-Hoe SM, Cong X, Hashemi F (2002) *Infant crying: nature, physiologic consequences, and select interventions,* Neonatal Network, 21 (2) 29–36

14 Moore ER, Anderson GC, Bergman, N Dowswell T (2012) *Early skin-to-skin contact for mothers and their healthy newborn infants,* Cochrane Database Systematic Review 2012 May 16 • Raby KL, et al (2015) *The enduring predictive significance of early maternal sensitivity: social and academic competence through age 32 years,* Child Development, May/June 2015, Volume 86, Number 3

15 Caldji C, Diorio J, Meaney MJ (2003) *variations in maternal care alter GABA, receptor subunit expression in brain regions associated with fear,* Neuropsychopharmacology 28:1950 • Bhansali P, Dunning J, Singer SE, David L, Schmauss C (2007) *Early life stress alters adult serotonin 2C receptor Pre-mRNA editing and expression of the subunit of the heterotrimeric G-protein Gq,* Journal of Neuroscience, Feb 7;27(6):1467-1473

16 Veenema AH (2009) *Early life stress, the development of aggression and neuroendocrine and neurobiological correlates: What can we learn from animal models?,* Frontiers in Neuroendocrinology 30 (2009) 497–518

17 Johnson SB et al (2013) *The science of early life toxic stress for pediatric practice and advocacy,* Pediatrics, American Academy of Pediatrics

18 Stam R, et al (1997) T*rauma and the gut: Interactions between stressful experience and intestinal function,* Gut 1997 • Heaton K (1999) *Your Bowels,* British Medical Association/Dorling Kindersley London • Siobhain M, et al (2010) *Maternal separation as a model of brain–gut axis dysfunction,* Psychopharmacology March 2011, Volume 214, Issue 1, 71–88

19 Bergman NJ (2005) *More than a cuddle: skin-to-skin contact is key,* The Practising Midwife Oct;8(9):44 • Bergman NJ (2014) *The neuroscience of birth - and the case for*

Zero Separation. Curationis 2014 Nov 28;37(2):1-4

20 Jackson, D (2004) *When your baby cries* Hodder-Mobius, London

21 Murray L, Andrews L (2000) *The social baby: Understanding babies' communication from birth,* CP Publishing, Richmond

22 Holt-Lunstad J, Smith TB, Baker M, Harris T, Stephenson D (2015) *Loneliness and social isolation as risk factors for mortality: a meta-analytic review,* Perspectives in Psychological Science 2015 Mar;10(2): 227–37 • Bonnet KA, Hiller JM, Simon EJ (1976) *The effects of chronic opiate treatment and social isolation and opiate reactions in the rodent brain.* In Archer, S et al (Eds) Opiates and endogeous opioid peptides, Elsevier/North Holland, New York: 335–343

23 Eisenberger, NI. (2012) T*he pain of social disconnection: examining the shared neural underpinnings of physical and social pain.* Nature Reviews, Neuroscience Vol.13, June 2012

24 Caldji C, Diorio J, Meaney MJ (2003) *Variations in maternal care alter GABA, Receptor subunit expression in brain regions associated with fear,* Neuropsychopharmacology 28: 1950

25 Chugani HT, et al (2001) *Local brain functional activity following early deprivation: a study of postinstitutionalized Romanian orphans,* Neuroimage Journal Dec: 1290–1301

26 Gunnar MR (2015) T*he effects of early life stress on neurobehavioral development in children and adolescents: Mediation by the HPA axis,* Psychoneuroendocrinology 2015 Nov; 61:3

27 Robertson J, et al (1969) *John – 17 Months: Nine Days in a Residential Nursery,* 16mm film/video: The Robertson Centre. Accompanied by a printed "Guide to the Film" Series: British Medical Association/Concord Film Council

28 Ahnert L, et al (2004) *Transition to child care: associations with infant-mother attachment, infant negative emotion, and cortisol elevations,* Child Development May-Jun: 639-50 • Watermura SE, et al. (2002) *Rising cortisol at childcare; Relations with nap, rest and temperament,* Developmental Psychobiology Jan: 33-42 • Dettling AC, et al (1999) *Cortisol levels of young children in full-day childcare centres:*

relations with age and temperament, Psychoneuroendocrinology Jun: 519-36

29 Hertsgaard L, et al (1995) *Adrenocortical responses to the strange situation in infants with disorganized/disorientated attachment relationships,* Child Development 66: 1100-06 • Gunnar MR (1989) *Studies of the human infant's adrenocortical response to potentially stressful events,* New Directions for Child Development Fall: 3-18

30 Belsky J (2001); *Emanuel Miller lecture: Developmental risks (still) associated with early child care,* Journal of Child Psychology and Psychiatry, and Allied Disciplines Oct: 845-59. • Belsky J, et al. (1996) *Trouble in the second year: three questions about family interaction,* Child Development Apr: 556-78

31 Gunnar MR, et al. (1992) *The stressfulness of separation among nine-month-old infants: effects of social context variables and infant temperament,* Child Development Apr: 290-303 • Dettling AC, et al (2000) *Quality of care and temperament determine changes in cortisol concentrations over the day for young children in childcare,* Psychoneuroendocrinology Nov: 819-36

32 Harlow HF, et al. (1979) *Primate Perspectives,* John Wiley, New York/London • Harlow C (1986) *From learning to love,* Praegar Publications, New York

33 Dimatelis J, et al (2012) *Early maternal separation leads to down-regulation of cytokine gene expression,* Metabolic Brain Disease September 2012, Volume 27 • Leussis MP (2012) *Depressive-Like Behavior in Adolescents after Maternal Separation: Sex Differences, Controllability, and GABA* Developmental Neuroscience 2012;34:210–217

34 Bowlby J (1973) *Attachment and Loss, Volume 2: Separation, Anxiety and Anger,* Hogarth Press, London. • Bowlby J (1979) *The making and breaking of affectional bonds,* Tavistock, London • Bowlby J (1988) *A Secure Base: Clinical Applications of Attachment Theory,* Routledge, London

Chapter 3: sleep & bedtimes
1 Davis KF, et al (2004) *Sleep in infants and young children: part two: common sleep problems,* Journal of Pediatric Health Care May-Jun; 18(3): 130-7 • Hiscock H, et al. (2004) *Problem crying in infancy,* The Medical Journal of Australia Nov 1; 181(9): 507-12 • Lam P, et al. (2003) *Outcomes of*

infant sleep problems: a longitudinal study of sleep, behavior, and maternal well-being, Pediatrics Mar; 111(3): 203-7

2 Frost J (2005) *Supernanny,* Hodder & Stoughton, London • Byron T, et al (2003) *Little Angels,* BBC Worldwide Learning, London

3 Harrison Y (2004) *The relationship between daytime exposure to light and night-time sleep in 6-12 week old infants,* Journal of Sleep Research Dec; 13(4): 345-52

4 Beijers R, et al (2013) *Cortisol regulation in 12-month-old human infants: associations with the infants' early history of breastfeeding and co-sleeping,* Stress. 2013 May;16(3):267-77 • Beijers R, et al (2008) *Sleeping and Biological Imperatives: Why Human Babies Do Not and Should Not Sleep Alone.* Neuropathology, December 21, 2008

5 Morgan BE, et al (2011), *Should Neonates Sleep Alone?,* Biological Psychiatry, 2011, 1–9

6 Bergman, N (2005) *More than a cuddle: skin-to-skin contact is key,* The Practising Midwife Oct; 8(9): 44 • and 15 Jackson D (1999) *Three in a bed: The benefits of sleeping with your baby,* Bloomsbury, London

7 Kramer KM, et al. (2003) *Developmental effects of oxytocin on stress response: single versus repeated exposure,* Physiology and Behaviour Sept; 79(4-5): 775-82. • Hofer MA (1996) *On the nature and consequences of early loss,* Psychosomatic Medicine Nov-Dec 58(6): 570–81 • Buckley P, et al (2002) *Interaction between bed sharing and other sleep environments during the first six months of life,* Early Human Development Feb; 66(2): 123-32

8 Keller M, Goldberg W (2000) *Co-sleeping and children independence; challenging the myths* From McKenna J (Ed.) *Safe sleeping with baby: evolutionary, developmental and clinical perspectives,* University of California Press, California • McKenna J (2000), *Cultural influences on infant and childhood sleep biology and the science that studies it: toward a more inclusive paradigm;* in Loughlin J, Carroll J, Marcus C (Eds.) *Sleep in Development and Pediatrics,* Marcel Dekker, New York: 99–230 • McKenna J, et al. (2005) Why babies should never sleep alone: A review of the co-sleeping controversy in relation to SIDS, bedsharing and breast feeding,

Paediatric Respiratory Reviews 6(2): 134-52.,

9 and 17 Horne J (1985) New Scientist Dec 1985; cited in Jackson D (1999) *Three in a bed: The benefits of sleeping with your baby,* Bloomsbury, London

10 *"Even when asleep, mothers appeared to be aware or sense the presence of their baby in bed with them and at no time was a mother ever observed to roll on her infant, even when sleeping very close together."* Jeanine Young (1998), Bedsharing with Babies: The Facts • Jackson D (1999) *Three in a bed: The benefits of sleeping with your baby,* Bloomsbury, London

11 Gaultier C (1995) *Cardiorespiratory adaptation during sleep in infants and children,* Pediatric Pulmonology Feb 19(2): 105-17

12 Bergman NJ. (2014). *The neuroscience of birth - and the case for Zero Separation,* Curationis. 2014 Nov 28;37(2)

13 Coan JA, Schaefer HS, Davidson RJ (1995) *Lending a hand: social regulation of the neural response to threat,* Psychol Sci. 2006 Dec;17(12):1032-9. Acta Obstet Gynecol Scand. 1995 Aug;74(7):530-3

14 Feldman R, et al (2014) *Maternal-preterm skin-to-skin contact enhances child physiologic organization and cognitive control across the first 10 years of life,* Biological Psychiatry. Jan 1;75(1): 4

15 see 6:2

16, 18, 19, 20 McKenna J (2015) The Mother-Baby Behavioural Sleep Laboratory University of Notre Dame, www.cosleeping.nd.edu

17 see 9

21 Bergman NJ (2014). *The neuroscience of birth, and the case for Zero Separation,* Curationis. 2014 Nov 28;37(2) • Bergman NJ, et al (2011) *Should neonates sleep alone?* Biological Psychiatry. 2011 Nov 1;70(9):817-25

22 Pantley E (2005) *The no-cry sleep solution* McGraw-Hill, New York

23 Zhong X, et al (2005) *Increased sympathetic and decreased parasympathetic cardiovascular modulation in normal humans with acute sleep deprivation,* Journal of Applied Physiology Jun;98(6):2005–32

24 Ziabreva I, et al (2003) *Mother's voice "buffers" separation-induced receptor changes in the prefrontal cortex of Octodon degus,* Neuroscience 119(2): 433–41 • Ziabreva I, et al (2003) *Separation-induced receptor changes in the hippocampus and amygdala of Octodon degus: influence of maternal vocalizations,* Journal of Neuroscience Jun 15; 23(12): 5329–36

25 Levine S, Wiener SG, Coe CL (1993) *Temporal and social factors influencing behavioral and hormonal responses to separation in mother and infant squirrel monkeys,* Psychoneuroendocrinology 18(4):297¬306

26 Adamec RE, et al (1998) *Neural plasticity, neuropeptides and anxiety in animals - implications for understanding and treating affective disorder following traumatic stress in humans,* Neuroscience and Biobehavioral Reviews 23(2):301–18 • Adamec RE, Shallow T (1993) *Lasting effects on rodent anxiety of a single exposure to a cat,* Physiology & Behavior Jul;54(1):101–9 • Adamec RE (1997) *Transmitter systems involved in neural plasticity underlying increased anxiety and defense–implications for understanding anxiety following traumatic stress,* Neuroscience and Biobehavioral Reviews Nov; 21(6):755-65

27 Seltzer LJ, Ziegler TE, Pollak SD (2010) *Social vocalizations can release oxytocin in humans,* Proceedings in Biological Science 2010, Sep 7

28 Panksepp J (2003) *Neuroscience: feeling the pain of social loss,* Science Oct 10; 302(5643): 237–9

29 Field T, et al (1996) *Preschool children's sleep and wake behaviour: Effects of massage therapy,* Early Child Development and Care 120: 39- 44

Chapter 4: chemistry of love & joy
1 Pert CB (1997) *Molecules of emotion,* Simon and Schuster, London

2 Mahler M (1968) *On human symbiosis and the vicissitudes of individuation,* International Universities Press, New York.

3 Douglas AJ (2010) *Baby Love? Oxytocin-dopamine interactions in mother-infant bonding,* Endocrinology, May, 151(5):1978–1980 • Feldman R (2012) *Oxytocin and social affiliation in humans,* Hormones and Behavior, 61: 380–391 •

MacDonald K, et al (2010) *The Peptide That Binds: A Systematic Review of Oxytocin and its Pro-social Effects in Humans,* Harvard Review of Psychiatry, January/February • Mesquita AR, et al (2013) *Predicting children's attachment behaviors from the interaction between oxytocin and glucocorticoid receptors polymorphisms,* Psychiatry Research, 210

4 Jamie L, et al (2015) *Blunted ventral striatum development in adolescence reflects emotional neglect and predicts depressive symptoms,* Biological Psychiatry • Schmid B, et al (2013) *Maternal stimulation in infancy predicts hypothalamic-pituitary-adrenal axis reactivity in young men,* Journal of Neural Transmission, Aug;120(8):1247-57 • Pollak SD (2005) *Early adversity and mechanisms of plasticity: integrating affective neuroscience with developmental approaches to psychopathology,* Development and psychopathology, Summer;17(3):735–52 • Doom JR, et al (2013) *Stress physiology and developmental psychopathology: Past, present, and future;* Development and Psychopathology, 25:1359–1373

5 and 14 Uvnäs-Moberg K, et al (2005) *Oxytocin, a mediator of anti-stress, well-being, social interaction, growth and healing,* Zeitschrift fur Psychosomatische Medizin und Psychotherapie, 51(1):57-80 • Uvnäs -Moberg K (2011) *The oxytocin factor: tapping the hormone of calm, love and healing,* Da Capo Press, Cambridge, MA

6 Barry TJ, et al. (2015) *Maternal postnatal depression predicts altered offspring biological stress reactivity in adulthood,* Psychoneuroendocrinology, Feb;52:251-60 • Bergman K, et al (2007) M*aternal stress during pregnancy predicts cognitive ability and fearfulness in infancy,* J Am Acad Child Adolesc Psychiatry, Nov;46(11):1454-63 • Bhansali P, et al (2007) *Early Life Stress Alters Adult Serotonin 2C Receptor pre-mrna editing and expression of the subunit of the heterotrimeric G-Protein Gq,* Journal of Neuroscience, Feb 7;27(6):1467-1473 • Bremner JD (2003) *Preclinical studies showed that early stress results in long term alterations in the hypothalamic-pituitary-adrenal (HPA) axis,* Biological Psychiatry, Oct 1;54(7): 710-8 • Caldji C, et al (2000) *Variations in maternal care in infancy regulate the development of stress reactivity,* Biological Psychiatry, Dec 15;48 (12):1164-74 • Carrion VG, et al (2007) *Stress predicts brain changes in children: a pilot longitudinal study on youth stress, posttraumatic stress disorder, and the hippocampus,* Pediatrics, Mar;119(3):509-16 • Chen Y, et al (2015) *Towards Understanding How Early-Life Stress Re-Programs Cognitive and Emotional Brain Networks,* Neuropsychopharmacology, Jun, 24

7 Bowlby J (1979) Insecure attachment as "shrinking from life or doing battle with it" a statement from *The making and breaking of affectional bonds,* Tavistock, London.

8 Coan JA, et al (1995) *Lending a hand: Social regulation of the neural response to threat.* Psychol Sci. 2006 Dec;17(12):1032-9. Acta Obstet Gynecol Scand. 1995 Aug;74(7):530-3. Weller A, et al. (2003) *Emotion regulation and touch in infants: The role of cholescystokinin and opioids,* Peptides, 24 (5), 779-788 • Feldman R, et al (2014) *Maternal-preterm skin-to-skin contact enhances child physiologic organization and cognitive control across the first 10 years of life,* Biol Psychiatry, Jan 1;75(1):56-64 • Montagu A (1971) Touching: *The Human Significance of the Skin,* Harper and Row, London • Mörelius E, et al (2015) *A randomised trial of continuous skin-to-skin contact after preterm birth and the effects on salivary cortisol, parental stress, depression, and breastfeeding.* Early Hum Dev. Jan;91(1) • Field T (2014) *Massage therapy Research Review,* Complementary Therapy Clinical Practice, 20(4)

9 Francis DD, et al. (2002) *Naturally occurring differences in maternal care are associated with the expression of oxytocin and vasopressin (V1a) receptors: gender differences.* Journal of Neuroendocrinol. May;14(5):349-53 • Beery AK, et al (2015) *Natural variation in maternal care and cross-tissue patterns of oxytocin receptor gene methylation in rats,* Child Development, May/June, 86(3)

10, 16, 40, 59 Panksepp J, et al (2012) T*he Archaeology of Mind: Neuroevolutionary Origins of Human Emotion,* WW Norton & Co., New York

11 Social Justice Policy Group (2006) *Breakdown Britain: Interim report on the state of the nation,* Centre for Social Justice, London

12 The Bristol Community Family Trust and the Centre for Social Justice, 2011

13 Schore A (2003) *Affect regulation and the repair of the self,* WW Norton and Co., New York

14 see 5

15 Bartal B, et al. (2011) *Empathy and prosocial behaviour in rats,* Science. Dec 9;334(6061):1427–30

16 see 10

17 Kok E (2013) *How positive emotions build physical health: perceived positive social connections account for the upward spiral between positive emotions and vagal tone,* Psychological Science, 2013

18 Birditt K, et al (2015) *Stress and negative relationship quality among older couples: implications for blood pressure,* J Gerontol B Psychol Sci Soc Sci., Apr 7

19 Carter CS (1998) *Neuroendocrine perspectives on social attachment and love,* Psychoneuroendocrinology, Nov; 23(8): 779-818 • Francis DD, et al (2002) *Naturally occurring differences in maternal care are associated with the expression of oxytocin and vasopressin,* Journal of Neuroendocrinology, May;14(5):349–53 • Insel TR (1992) *Oxytocin: A neuropeptide for affiliation,* Psychoneuroendocrinology,17:3–35

20. Cohn J, et al (1990) *Sampling interval affects time-series regression estimates of mother-infant influence,* Infant Behav Dev; 13: 317

21 Beeghly M, et al (2011) early resilience in the context of parent–infant relationships: a social developmental perspective, Current Problems in Paediatric and Adolescent Health Care, 41:197-201 • Tronick E (2007) *Neurobehavioural and Social Emotional Development of Infants and Children,* Norton, London

22 Atzil S, et al (2011) *Specifying the neurobiological basis of human attachment: brain, hormones, and behaviour in synchronous and intrusive mothers,* Neuropsychopharmacology, 36, 2603-2615 • Strathearn L, et al (2009) *Adult attachment predicts maternal brain and oxytocin response to infant cues,* Neuropsychopharmacology, December, 34(13): 2655–2666

23 Musser ED, et al (2012) T*he neural correlates of maternal sensitivity: an fMRI study,* Dev Cogn Neurosci, 2: 428–36 • Noriuchi M, et al. (2008) *The functional neuroanatomy of maternal love: mother's responses to infant attachment behavior,* Biol Psychiatry, 63: 415–23 • Ranote S, et al. (2004) *The neural basis of maternal responsiveness to infants: an fMRI study,* Neuroreport, 15:1825–9

24 Kiel EJ, et al (2013) T*oddler inhibited temperament, maternal cortisol reactivity and embarrassment, and intrusive parenting,* Journal of Family Psychology, Vol 27(3), Jun, 512-517 • O'Connor T (2002) *Maternal antenatal anxiety and children's behavioural/emotional problems at 4 years, report from the Avon Longitudinal Study of Parents and Children,* British Journal of Psychiatry 180:502-8

25 Montagu A (1971) *Touching: The human signficance of the skin,* Harper and Row, London

26 Orbach S (2010) *Bodies,* Profile Books, London

27 Feldman R, et al (2014) *Maternal-preterm skin-to-skin contact enhances child physiologic organization and cognitive control across the first 10 years of life,* Biol Psychiatry, Jan 1;75(1):56-64 • Weller A, et al. (2003) *Emotion regulation and touch in infants: The role of cholecystokinin and opioids,* Peptides, 24 (5), 779-788 • Field T (2014) *Massage therapy research review,* Complement Ther Clin Practice, Nov

28 Haley DW, et al (2003) *Infant stress and parent responsiveness: regulation of physiology and behavior during still-face and reunion,* Child Development, Sep-Oct;74(5):1534-46

29 Panksepp J, et al (2014) *Preclinical modeling of primal emotional affects (Seeking, Panic and Play): Gateways to the development of new treatments for depression,* Psychopathology 2014;47:383–393

30 Burgdorf J, et al (2010) *Uncovering the molecular basis of positive affect using rough-and-tumble play in rats: a role for insulin-like growth factor I,* Neuroscience, Jul 14;168(3):769–77

31 Siviy SM, et al (2011) *In search of the neurobiological substrates for social playfulness in mammalian brains,* Neuroscience and Biobehavioral Reviews, 35:1821–1830

32 Panksepp J (2004) *Affective neuroscience,* Oxford University Press, Oxford

33 Siviy SM, et al (2011) *In search of the neurobiological substrates for social playfulness in mammalian brains,*

Neuroscience and Biobehavioral Reviews, 35:1821–1830

34 Gordon NS, et al (2003) *Socially-induced brain fertilization: Play promotes brain derived neurotrophic factor transcription in the amygdala and dorsolateral frontal cortex,* Neuroscience Letters, Apr 24;341(1):17–20

35 Panksepp J, et al (2003) *Modeling ADHD-type arousal with unilateral frontal cortex damage in rats and beneficial effects of play therapy,* Brain and Cognition 52: 97-105

36 Wohr M, et al (2009) *New insights into the relationships of neurogenesis and affect,* Neuroscience, 163

37 Lyubomirsky S, et al (2006) *The costs and benefits of writing, talking, and thinking about life's triumphs and defeats,* Journal of Personality and Social Psychology, 90(4):692–708

38 Beatty WW, et al (1982) P*sychomotor stimulants, social deprivation and play in juvenile rats,* Pharmacol Biochem Behav. 1 Mar; 16(3):417-22

39 Pellegrini A, et al (1996) *The effects of recess timing on children's playground and classroom behaviors,* American Educational Research Journal, 32 (4): 845-64

40 see 10

41, 43, 44, and 54 Tronick E (2007) *Neurobehavioural and social emotional development of infants and children* WW Norton and Co., New York

42 Schmid B, et al (2013) *Maternal stimulation in infancy predicts hypothalamic-pituitary-adrenal axis reactivity in young men,* J Neural Trans, Aug;120(8):1247-57

43 see 41

44 see 41

45 Moll GH, et al (2001) *Early methylphenidate administration to young rats causes apersistent reduction in the density of striatal dopamine receptors,* Journal of Child and Adolescent Psychopharmacology 11:15-24

46 Panksepp J, et al (2003) *Modeling ADHD -type arousal with unilateral frontal cortex damage in rats and beneficial effects of play therapy,* Brain and Cognition, (Impact

Factor: 2.48). 07/2003; 52(1):97-105
47 Shir A, et al (2011) *Specifying the neurobiological basis of human attachment: brain, hormones, and behavior in synchronous and intrusive mothers,* Neuropsychopharmacology, 36, 2603–2615

48 Kiel E, et al (2013) *Toddler inhibited temperament, maternal cortisol reactivity and embarrassment, and intrusive parenting,* Journal of Family Psychology, Vol 27(3), Jun 2013, 512-517 • Strathearn L, et al. (2009) *Adult attachment predicts maternal brain and oxytocin response to infant cues,* Neuropsychopharmacology, 2009; 34: 2655–66. • McLearn KT, et al. (2006) *The timing of maternal depressive symptoms and mothers' parenting practices with young children: implications for pediatric practice,* Pediatrics, Jul;118(1)

49 Field T (2010) *Postpartum depression effects on early interactions, parenting, and safety practices: a review,* Infant Behav Dev; 33:1–6

50 Laurent H, et al (2012) A cry in the dark: Depressed mothers showed reduced neural activation to their own infant's cry, Social Cognitive and Affective Neuroscience 7: 125-34 Barrett J, et al. (2012) *Maternal affect and quality of parenting experiences are related to amygdala response to infant faces,* Soc Neurosci, 7:252

51 Drevets WC, et al (1997) Subgenual prefrontal cortex abnormalities in mood disorders, Nature, 386:824

52 Schechter DS, et al (2012) *An fMRI study of the brain responses of traumatized mothers to viewing their toddlers during separation and play,* Soc Cogn Affect Neurosci, 7: 969–79

53 Field TM (1994) *The effects of mother's physical and emotional unavailability on emotion regulation,* Monographs of the Society for Research in Child Development, 59;(2-3): 208-27

54 see 41

55 Ashman SB, et al (2002). Stress hormone levels of children of depressed mothers, *Development and Psychopathology,* Spring;14(2):333-49

56 Barry TJ, et al (2015) *Maternal postnatal depression predicts altered offspring biological stress reactivity in adulthood,* Psychoneuroendocrinology, Feb;52:251-60

57 Pilowsky D, et al (2008) *Children of depressed mothers 1 year after the initiation of maternal treatment,* American Journal of Psychiatry 165 (9); 1136-47 • Gerhardt S (2014) *Why Love Matters: How affection shapes a baby's brain,* Brunner-Routledge, King's Lynn

58 Chester DS, et al (2013) *The interactive effect of social pain and executive functioning on aggression: an fMRI experiment,* Social Cognitive and Affective Neuroscience, 1-6 • Eisenberger NI (2012) *The pain of social disconnection: examining the shared neural underpinnings of physical and social pain,* Nature Reviews, Neuroscience, Vol.13, June

59 see 10

60 Goodall J (1990) *Through a window: thirty years with chimpanzees of Gombe,* Weidenfeld and Nicolson, London

61 Glover J (2001) *Humanity: a moral history of the twentieth century,* Pimlico, London

62 Sunderland M (2010) *Helping children with troubled parents,* Speechmark Publishing, London

63 Weninger O (1989) *Children's phantasies: the shaping of relationships,* Karnac Books London

64 Eisenberger NI (2012) *The pain of social disconnection: examining the shared neural underpinnings of physical and social pain,* Nature Reviews, Neuroscience, Vol.13, June

65 Jay Vaughan Family Futures Consortium (2010), personal communication, London

Chapter 5: chemistry of drive & will
1, 5, 7 Panksepp J, et al. (2012) *The Archaeology of Mind: Neuroevolutionary Origins of Human Emotion,* WW Norton & Co., New York

2 and 4 Panksepp J (1998) *Affective neuroscience,* Oxford University Press, New York

3 Brown G (2000) *The energy of life,* Flamingo, London. Full quote: "*Everyone looks for that sparkle in friends and lovers to make things happen. Most of all, everyone is looking for energy within themselves: The motivation, drive and oomph to do something; the endurance, stamina and resolve to carry through.*"

4 see 2

5 see 1

6 *NEET: Young People not in Education, Employment or Training,* House of Commons Briefing Paper, May 21, 2015

7 see 1

8 Kuntsche E, et al. (2006) *Television viewing and forms of bullying among adolescents from eight countries,* J Adolesc Health, Dec;39(6):908-15 • Greenfield S (2015) *How digital technologies are leaving their mark on our brains,* Rider, London • Kousha M, et al. (2013). *Normative life events and PTSD in children: How easy stress can affect children's brain,* Acta Med, Iran • Zimmerman FJ, et al (2005) *Early cognitive stimulation, emotional support, and television watching as predictors of subsequent bullying among grade-school children,* Archives of Pediatrics & Adolescent Medicine, Apr;159(4):384-8

9 Dietrich A (2004) *Neurocognitive mechanisms underlying the experience of flow,* Consciousness and Cognition, 13:746-761

10 Laakso M, et al. (1999) *Social interactional behaviors and symbolic play competence as predictors of language development and their associations with maternal attention-directing strategies,* Infant Behavior and Development, 22(4) • Belsky J, et al (1980) *Maternal stimulation and infant exploratory competence: cross – sectional, correlational and experimental analyses,* Child Dev, Dec 51(4): 1168-78

11 Panksepp J, et al (2011) *Why does depression hurt? Ancestral primary-process separation-distress (PANIC/GRIEF) and diminished brain reward (SEEKING) processes in the genesis of depressive affect,* Psychiatry, Spring;74(1):5-13

12 Institute of Public Policy Research (2006) *Freedom's Orphans: Raising Youth in a Changing World, IPPR,* London

13 Maslow A (1972) *The farther reaches of human nature,* Penguin, London

14 Fox C, et al (2006) *Therapeutic and protective effect of environmental enrichment against psychogenic and neurogenic stress,* Behavioural Brain Research, 175(1) • Sale A, et al (2014) *Environment and brain plasticity: Towards an endogenous pharmacotherapy,* Physiol Rev. 94(1):189-234.

15 Farah MJ, et al (2008) *Environmental stimulation, parental nurturance and cognitive development in humans,* Hurt Developmental Science, 11(5):793–801

16 Rohlfs Domínguez P (2014) *Promoting our understanding of neural plasticity by exploring developmental plasticity in early and adult life,* Brain Res Bull., 107:31-6

17 Gunnell D, et al (2005) *Association of insulin-like growth factor I and insulin-like growth factor-binding protein-3 with intelligence quotient among 8- to 9-year-old children in the Avon Longitudinal Study of Parents and Children,* Pediatrics, 116(5):681-6

18 Johansson BB, et al (2002), *Neuronal plasticity and dendritic spines: effect of environmental enrichment on intact and postischemic rat brain,* Journal of Cerebral Blood Flow & Metabolism, 22:89–96

19 Fred Gage Salk Institute for Biological Studies in La Jolla, California, cited Carper J (2000), *Your Miracle Brain,* Harper Collins, New York

20 Kotloski RJ, et al (2015), *Environmental enrichment: Evidence for an unexpected therapeutic influence,* Experimental Neurology, 264:121–126 • Cao W, et al. (2014) *Early enriched environment induces an increased conversion of proBDNF to BDNF in the adult rat's hippocampus,* Behav Brain Res., May 22

21 Raine, A, et al (2003) *Effects of environmental enrichment at ages 3-5 years on schizotypal personality and antisocial behavior at ages 17 and 23 years,* The American Journal of Psychiatry, Sep;160(9):1627-35

22 Bratton SC, et al (2005) *The efficacy of play therapy with Children: a meta-analytic review of treatment outcomes,* Professional Psychology: Research and Practice American Psychological Association, 36(4):376–390

Chapter 6: your socially intelligent child
1 Steele M, et al. (2002) *Maternal predictors of children's social cognition: An attachment perspective,* Journal of Child Psychology and Psychiatry and Allied Disciplines, 43(7):861-72

2 and 4 Centre for Social Justice (2011) *Strengthening the family and tackling family breakdown,* CSJ, London

3 Centre for Social Justice Policy Group (2006) *Breakdown Britain: Interim report on the state of the nation,* CSJ, London

4 see 2

5 Rodgers B, et al. (1998) *Divorce and separation: the outcomes for children,* Joseph Rowntree Foundation, York

6 Birditt KS, et al. (2015) *Stress and negative relationship quality among older couples: implications for blood pressure,* J Gerontol B Psychol Sci Soc Sci., Apr

7 Holt-Lunstad J, et al. (2015) *Loneliness and social isolation as risk factors for mortality: A meta-analytic review,* Perspect Psychol Sci., 10(2):227-37

8 Bar-on R, et al (2003) *Exploring the neurological substrate of emotional and social intelligence,* Brain, 126(8)

9 Davidson ML, et al. (2008) *Pre-frontal subcortical pathways mediating successful emotion regulation,* Neuron, 59(6)

10 Kana RK, et al (2015) *Aberrant functioning of the theory-of-mind network in children and adolescents with autism,* Mol Autism, Oct 27

11 Faber A, et al (1999) *Siblings Without Rivalry,* Piccadilly Press, London

12 Lieberman MD, et al. (2007), P*utting feelings into words: affect labeling disrupts Amygdala Activity in Response to Affective Stimuli,* Psychological Science, Vol 1 • Lieberman MD (2011) *Why symbolic processing of affect can disrupt negative affect: Social cognitive and affective neuroscience investigations, Social Neuroscience: toward understanding the underpinnings of the social mind,* Published to Oxford Scholarship Online: May 2011

13 Decety J, et al (2013) *The role of affect in the neurodevelopment of morality, Child Development Perspectives,* 7(1):49–54 • Decety J et al (2012) *A neurobehavioral evolutionary perspective on the mechanisms underlying empathy,* Progress, Neurobiology, 98:38-48

14 Ridley M (2000) *Genome: The autobiography of species,* Fourth Estate, London

15 Rosenblum LA, et al (1994) *Adverse early experiences affect noradrenergic and serotonergic functioning in adult primates,* Biological Psychiatry, Feb 15 • Dolan M, et al. (2002) *Serotonergic and cognitive impairment in impulsive aggressive personality disorder offenders: Are there implications for treatment?,* Psychological Medicine, 32:105-17

16 Gottman J, et al (1996) *Parental meta-emotion philosophy and the emotional life of families: theoretical models and preliminary data,* Journal of Family Psychology, 10(3):243-268 • Fainsilber L, et al. (2014) *Parental emotion socialization in clinically depressed adolescents: enhancing and dampening positive affect,* Journal of Abnormal Child Psychology, 42:205–215

17 Gottman JM, et al. (2004) *Parental meta-emotion philosophy and the emotional life of families: theoretical models and preliminary data,* Journal of Abnormal Child Psychology, 32(4):385–398

18 Bader E, et al. (2014) *In Quest of a Mythical Mate,* Routledge, London.

19 Gottman J (2015) *The Gottman Institute,* www.gottman.com

20 Lockwood, PL, et al. (2013*) Association of callous traits with reduced neural response to others' pain in children with conduct problems,* Current Biology, 23(10) • Warneken F and Tomasello M (2006) *Altruistic helping in human infants and young chimpanzees,* Science March 2006 Vol 311 • Chiarella, Sabrina Sarah (2015) *Infants' reactions to the unjustified emotions of a model.* PhD thesis, Concordia University

21 Devinsky O, et al (1995) *Contributions of anterior cingulate cortex to behavior, Brain,* 118(0) • Lockwood PL, et al. (2013) *Association of Callous Traits with Reduced Neural Response to Others' Pain in Children with Conduct Problems,* Current Biology, 23(10)

22 Hughes D, et al. (2012) *Brain Based Parenting,* WW Norton and Co., London.

23 Panksepp J (1998) *Affective Neuroscience,* Oxford University Press, Oxford.

24 Brooks FM, et al (2015) *Video gaming in adolescence: factors associated with leisure time use,* Journal of Youth Studies, Published online: 14 Jul 2015 • Sigman A (2012) *Time for a view on screen time, Arch. Dis. Child,* Nov;97(11):935-42 • Telegraph (2012) http://www.telegraph.co. uk/education/educationnews/9595317/ Children-spend-more-time-watching-TV-than-at-school.html

25 Bar-on Ms (1999) *Turning off the television,* http://www.ncbi.nlm.nih.gov/pmc/articles/PMC1115553/

26 Ronseal (2012) Poll of 2,000 people for Ronseal "Go on, Get outdoors" campaign, http://www.telegraph.co.uk/news/health/news/9398661/Children-spend-10-times-as-long-watching-TV-as-playing-outside-survey.html

27 and 28 Parkes A, et al (2013) *Do television and electronic games predict children's psychosocial adjustment?* Longitudinal research using the UK Millennium Cohort Study, Arch. Dis. Child, doi: 25 March

29 DeBoer M, et al (2015) *Viewing as little as 1 hour of television daily is associated with higher weight status in kindergarten: The Early Longitudinal Study,* Pediatric Academic Societies' Annual Meeting, April 25-28, San Diego.

30 Watt E, et al (2015) *Too Much Television? Prospective Associations Between Early Childhood Televiewing and Later Self-reports of Victimization by Sixth Grade Classmates,* Journal of Developmental & Behavioral Pediatrics, 36

31 Kirkorian HL, et al. (2009) *The impact of background television on parent-child interaction,* Child Dev., Sep-Oct;80(5):1350-9

32 Mar RA (2011) *The Neural Bases of Social Cognition and Story Comprehension,* Journal of Cognitive Neuroscience, 1–17

33 Mar RA, et al. (2009) *Exposure to media and theory-of-mind development in pre-schoolers,* Cognitive Development, doi: 10.1016/j.cogdev.2009.11.002 • Mar RA (2011) The Neural Bases of Social Cognition and Story Comprehension, Journal of Cognitive Neuroscience, 1–17

34 Robb MB, et al. (2009) *Just a talking book?* Word learning from watching baby videos, Br. J. Dev. Psychol. Mar;27(Pt 1):27-45. • Mizuike C, et al. (2010) *Frontal brain activation in young children during picture book reading with their mothers,* Acta. Paediatr., Feb;99(2):225-9. Epub Oct 22

35 http://stakeholders.ofcom.org.uk/binaries/research/media-literacy/media-use-attitudes-/Childrens_2014_Report.pdf

36 Kuhl PK (2004) *Early language acquisition: Cracking the speech code, Nature Neuroscience,* 5: 831-843

37 Mangen A (2013) *Reading linear texts on paper versus computer screen: Effects on reading comprehension,* International Journal of Educational Research, 58:61-68 • *Kerr MA, et al (2006) Computerised presentation of text: Effects on children's reading of informational material,* Reading and Writing, 19(1), 1-19. doi: 10.1007/s11145-003-8128-y

38 Hollingdale J, et al (2014) *The Effect of Online Violent Video Games on Levels of Aggression,* PLoS ONE, 9(11): e111790. doi:10.1371/journal.pone.0111790

39 Murray J (2001) *TV Violence and Brainmapping in Children,* Psychiatric Times, XV111(10)

40 Greitemeyer T, et al (2014) V*ideo games do affect social outcomes: a meta-analytic review of the effects of violent and prosocial video game play,* Pers Soc Psychol Bull., May;40(5):578-89

41 Kim YR, et al. (2012) *Abnormal brain activation of adolescent Internet addict in a ball-throwing animation task: Possible neural correlates of disembodiment revealed by fMRI,* Progress in Neuro-Psychopharmacology and Biological Psychiatry, 39(1):88-95 • Carnagey NL, et al. (2007). *The effect of video game violence on physiological desensitisation to real-life violence,* Journal of Experimental Social Psychology, 43(3), 489-496. doi: 10.1016/j.jesp.2006.05.003

42 Greenfield S (2015) *Mind Change: How digital technologies are leaving their mark on our brains,* Rider, London • Anderson CA, et al (2008) *Longitudinal effects of violent video games on aggression in Japan and the US,* Pediatrics, 122(5)

43 Yuan K, et al. (2013). *Cortical thickness abnormalities in late adolescence with online gaming addiction,* PLOS ONE, 8(1), e53055. doi: 10.1371/journal.pone.0053055

44 Blair RJ, et al. (2005) *Deafness to fear in boys with psychopathic tendencies,* Journal of Child Psychology and Psychiatry and Allied Disciplines, 46(3)

45 wwwnhs.uk and nspcc.org.uk

46 Singer T, et al. (1994) *Empathy for pain involves the affective but not sensory components of pain,* Science, 303

47 Teicher MH, et al. (2004) *Childhood neglect is associated with reduced corpus callosum area,* Biological Psychiatry, Jul

15;56(2):80-5 • Teicher MH, et al. (2010) *Hurtful Words: Association of Exposure to Peer Verbal Abuse with Elevated Psychiatric Symptom Scores and Corpus Callosum Abnormalities,* American Journal of Psychiatry, 167:1464–1471

48 Zhi-Peng Liu, et al. (2014) *Chronic stress impairs GABAergic control of amygdala through suppressing the tonic GABAA receptor currents.* Molecular Brain, 20147:32

49 Teicher M (2015) *Relationships that Hurt Conference,* The Centre for Child Mental Health, July, London

50 Jenkins-Tucker, C, et al (2013) *Association of sibling aggression with child and adolescent mental health,* Pediatrics: Volume 132, Number 1, July 2013, 79

Chapter 7: behaving badly
1 Sadeh A (2012) *Sleep, emotional and behavioral difficulties in children and adolescents* Sleep Medicine Review Volume 16 • Astill, R et al (2012) *Sleep, cognition, and behavioral problems in school-age children: A century of research meta-analyzed,* Psychological Bulletin, Vol 138(6), Nov 2012

2 Knuston K et al (2007) *The metabolic consequences of sleep deprivation,* Sleep medicine reviews June 2007 Issue 3

3 Adolphus K, et al (2013) *The effects of breakfast on behavior and academic performance in children and adolescents,* Frontiers in Human Neuroscience., 8;7:425 • Murphy JM (2007) *Breakfast and Learning: An Updated Review,* Current Nutrition & Food Science, 3(1):3-36(34) • Chaplin K, et al. (2011) *Breakfast and snacks: associations with cognitive failures, minor injuries, accidents and stress,* Nutrients, 3(5):515-28

4 Millichap JG, Yee M M (2012) *The diet factor in attention-deficit/hyperactivity disorder* Pediatrics February 2012 • Teves D et al (2004) *Activation of human medial prefrontal cortex during autonomic response to Hypoglycemia* Proceedings of the National Academy of Sciences of the United States of America *Apr 20*

5 Richardson AJ, et al (2005) *The Oxford-Durham study: a randomized, controlled trial of dietary supplementation with fatty acids in children with developmental coordination disorder,* Pediatrics 1115; 1360-66. • Innis SM (2000) *The role of*

dietary n-6 and n-3 fatty acids in the developing brain, Developmental neuroscience Sep-Dec; 22(5-6): 474-80 • Wainwright PE (2002) *Dietary essential fatty acids and brain function: a developmental perspective on mechanisms,* The Proceedings of the Nutrition Society Feb: 61-69

6 McCann D et al (2007) *Food additives and hyperactive behaviour in 3-year-old and 8/9-year-old children in the community: a randomised, double-blinded, placebo-controlled trial* The Lancet Volume 370, No. 9598, p1560–1567, 3 November 2007

7 NSPCC (2012) Child Abuse and Neglect in the UK Today London

8 See Stewart I, Jones V (1987) *T.A. Today,* Lifespace, Nottingham

9 Fromm E (1973) *The anatomy of human destructiveness,* Cape, London: 31
10 Lieberman, MD, Eisenberger, NI, Crockett, MJ, Tom, SM, Pfeifer, JH, and Way, BM. (2007), *Putting feelings into words: affect labeling disrupts amygdala activity in response to affective stimuli,* Psychological Science, Volume 18—Number 5

11 Christian Poster, C et al (2012) *Regulatory disorders in early childhood: Correlates in child behavior, parent–child relationship, and parental mental health,* Infant Mental Health Journal 2012, 6 March

12 Loman MM, Gunnar MG (2010) *Early experience and the development of stress reactivity and regulation in children,* Neuroscience and Biobehaviorial Reviews, Volume 34, Issue 6, May 2010, 867–876

13 and 18 Panksepp J, Biven L (2012) *The Archaeology of Mind: Neuroevolutionary Origins of Human Emotion:* WW Norton & Co., New York

14 Hennessy, MB (1997) *Hypothalamic-pituitary-adrenal responses to brief social separation,* Neuroscience and Biobehavioral Reviews Jan; 21 (1): 11-29 • O'Mahony SM et al (2010) *Maternal separation as a model of brain–gut axis dysfunction,* Psychopharmacology March 2011, Volume 214, Issue 1, 71–88

15 Eisenberger NI (2012) *The pain of social disconnection: examining the shared neural underpinnings of physical and social pain,* Nature Reviews, Neuroscience, Vol.13, June 2012

16 Pollak SD (2005) *Maternal regulation of infant reactivity,* Developmental psychology, Summer; 17(3): 735–52

17 Adamec RE (1991) *Partial kindling of the ventral hippocampus: identification of changes in limbic physiology which accompany changes in feline aggression and defense,* Physiology & Behavior Mar; 49(3): 443–53 • "The mere experience of an emotion without the capacity for [thinking] may tend to ingrain the aroused emotion as an [emotional] disposition in the brain." Panksepp J (2001) *The long-term psychobiological consequences of infant emotions – prescriptions for the twenty-first century,* Infant Mental Health Journal 22 (1-2) Jan-Apr: 145

18 see 13

19 Jenner S (2008) *The parent/child game,* Bloomsbury, London

Chapter 8: trying times
1 Cozolino LJ (2006) *The neuroscience of human relationships, attachment and the developing social brain,* WW Norton and Co., London

2 Bohn-Gettler CA, Pellegrini AD (2014) *Recess in Primary School: The Disjuncture Between Educational Policy and Scientific Research* Justice, Conflict and Wellbeing Multidisciplinary Perspectives: Eds Brian H. Bornstein BH, Wiener RL

3 Panksepp J, Moskal J (2012) *Dopamine and SEEKING subcortical "reward" systems and appetitive urges* chapter 5 in handbook of approach and avoidance motivation, Ed: Elliot A Psychology Press

4 Laakso M, et al (1999) *Social interactional behaviors and symbolic play competence as predictors of language development and their associations with maternal attention-directing strategies Infant Behavior and Development* Volume 22, Issue 4, 1999, Pages 541–556 • Belsky J, et al (1980) *Maternal stimulation and infant exploratory competence: cross-sectional, correlational, and experimental analyses,* Child Development 1980 Dec 51 (4)

5 Coan JA, Schaefer HS, Davidson RJ (1995) *Lending a hand: social regulation of the neural response to threat,* Psychological Science 2006 Dec:17(12):1032-9. Acta Obstet Gynecol Scand. 1995 Aug;74(7):530-3

6 Diamond A, Lee K (2011) *Interventions shown to aid executive function development in children 4 to 12 years old*

science 19 August 2011: Vol. 333 • Hoffmann J, Russ S (2012) *Pretend play, creativity, and emotion regulation in children,* Psychology of Aesthetics, Creativity, and the Arts, Vol. 6(2), May 2012, 175-184

7 Eisenberger, NI. (2012) *The pain of social disconnection: examining the shared neural underpinnings of physical and social pain,* Nature Reviews, Neuroscience, Vol.13, June

8 *For other ways of dealing creatively and effectively with provocation* see Hughes D, Baylin J (2012) Brain-based parenting: the neuroscience of caregiving for healthy attachment, norton series on interpersonal neurobiology 20 Apr 2012 • Hughes D (2009) *Principles of attachment-focused parenting: effective strategies to care for children,* WW Norton and Co., London

9 and 12 Faber A, and Mazlish E (1999). *Siblings without Rivalry* Piccadily Press Ltd, London

10 Newson J, et al (1970) *Seven Year olds in the Home Environment,* Penguin, London

11 and 13 Lieberman MD, et al (2007), *Putting Feelings into Words: Affect Labeling Disrupts Amygdala Activity in Response to Affective Stimuli,* Psychological Science, Volume 18, Number 5

12 see 9

13 see 11

14 Mosley J (2014) *Circle Time for Young Children* Essential Guides for Early Years Practitioners, Routledge, London

Chapter 9: all about discipline
1 Independent, 2011,http://www.independent.co.uk/news/education/education-news/80000-pupils-suspended-for-school-violence-2038430.html

2 Independent, 2011,http://www.independent.co.uk/news/education/education-news/seven-out-of-10-teachers-want-to-quit-survey-shows-2096257.html)

3 (Youth Justice Statistics, England and Wales 2013/14 - https://www.gov.uk/government/uploads/system/uploads/attachment_data/file/399379/youth-justice-annual-stats-13-14.pdf)

4 http://www.telegraph.co.uk/news/uknews/law-and-order/8523918/Thousands-of-children-carry-knives-

survey-finds.html (again from 2011).
5 NSPCC (2012) *Child abuse and neglect in the uk today* NSPCC report

6 Tomoda A, et al (2011) *Exposure to parental verbal abuse is associated with increased gray matter volume in superior temporal gyrus,* Neuroimage 2011 Jan;54 • Panksepp J, Biven L (2012) *The Archaeology of Mind: Neuroevolutionary Origins of Human Emotion:* WW Norton & Co, New York

7 Teicher MH, et al (2006) *Sticks, stones, and hurtful words: relative effects of various forms of childhood maltreatment,* The American Journal of Psychiatry Jun;163 (6):993-1000

8 Choi, J, et al (2009), *Preliminary evidence for white matter tract abnormalities in young adults exposed to parental verbal abuse,* Biological psychiatry, 2009;65:227–234 • Tomoda A (2011) *Exposure to parental verbal abuse is associated with increased gray matter volume in superior temporal gyrus,* NeuroImage 54 (2011) S280–S286

9 Polcari, et al (2014) *Parental verbal affection and verbal aggression in childhood differentially influence psychiatric symptoms and wellbeing in young adulthood,* Child Abuse and Neglect. 2014 Jan;38(1):91-102

10 Hellman, N, et al (2015) *Depression history as a moderator of relations between cortisol and shame responses to social-evaluative threat in young adults,* Biological Psychology 2015 Jul;109:159-65 • Gruenewald TL et al (2004) A*cute threat to the social self: shame, social self-esteem, and cortisol activity,* Psychosomatic Medicine 2004 Nov-Dec;66(6):915-24

11 Pulcu E, et al (2014) *Increased amygdala response to shame in remitted major depressive disorder,* PLoS One. 2014 Jan 30;9(1)

12 Gottman J et al (1996) *Parental meta-emotion philosophy and the emotional life of families: theoretical models and preliminary data,* Journal of Family Psychology 1996, Vol. 10, No.3 • Gottman J, et al (2004) *Parental meta-emotion philosophy and the emotional life of families: theoretical models and preliminary data,* Journal of Abnormal Child Psychology Vol. 32, No. 4, August 2004, pp. 385–398

13 Hughes D, Baylin J (2012) *Brain-based parenting: the neuroscience of caregiving for healthy attachment* Norton series on

interpersonal neurobiology 20 Apr 2012
14 Troy M, et al (1987) *Victimisation among preschoolers: role of attachment relationship history* Journal of American Academy of Child and Adolescent Psychiatry 2: 166-72

15 Panksepp J (2001) *The Long-term psychobiological consequences of infant emotions* Infant mental health journal 22 (1-2) Jan–April 145 • Adamec RE (1991) *Partial kindling of the ventral hippocampus: identification of changes in limbic physiology which accompany changes in feline aggression and defense,* Physiology & Behavior Mar;49(3):443-53

16 Choi J, et al (2009) *Preliminary evidence for white matter tract abnormalities in young adults exposed to parental verbal abuse,* Biological Psychiatry, 2009;65:227–234 • Tomoda A (2011) *Exposure to parental verbal abuse is associated with increased gray matter volume in superior temporal gyrus,* NeuroImage 54 (2011) S280–S286

17 Fay J, Cline F (2013) *Parenting without the power struggle* NavPress, USA

18 Jenner S (2008) *The parent-child game,* Bloomsbury, London • Forehand R, Searboro ME (1975) An analysis of children's oppositional behavior, Journal of Abnormal Child Psychology, Vol. 3, No.1, 1975

19 Weininger O (1997) *Time-in parenting strategies* Esf Publishers, USA

20 Frost J (2005) *Supernanny* Hodder and Stoughton, London

Chapter 10: best relationship with your child
1 Sevilla A (2014) Economic and Social Research Council, Britain, June, 2014

2 Castiello U, et al. (2010) *Wired to be social: The ontogeny of human interaction,* PLoS One, Oct 7;5(10)

3 Stanley N, et al. (2008) Auditory Development in the Fetus and Infant, Newborn and Infant Nursing Review, volume 8, issue 4, December 2008. *Arch Dis Child Fetal Neonatal Ed.* • Zoia S, et al (2007) *Evidence of early development of action planning in the human foetus:* A kinematic study, Experimental Brain Research 2007; 176: 217-226. PMID: 16858598

4 Partanen E, et al (2013) Prenatal music exposure induces long-term neural effects, PLoS One, Oct 30 (8)

5 *Parent-Play Survey* (2013) Playmobil UK

6 and 8 Field T, et al (2009) *Pregnancy massage reduces prematurity, low birthweight and postpartum depression,* Infant Behav Dev, Dec;32(4):454-60

7 Field T (2010) *Pregnancy and Labor Massage,* Expert Rev Obstet Gynecol, March 2010; 5 (2): 177-181

8 see 6 AND Field T (2014) *Massage Therapy Research,* Complement Ther. Clin. Pract., Nov;20(4)

9 Uvnäs-Moberg K (2013) *The Hormone of Closeness: The Role of Oxytocin in Relationships,* Pinter & Martin Ltd, London

10 Stevens J (2014) *Immediate or early skin-to-skin contact after a Caesarean section: a review of the literature,* Matern Child Nutr, Oct, 10 (14): 456-73.10

11 Feldman R, et al. (2014) *Maternal-preterm skin-to-skin contact enhances child physiologic organization and cognitive control across the first 10 years of life,* Biol Psychiatry. Jan 1;75(1):56-64

12 and 13 Klaus MH (2009) *Commentary: An early, short, and useful sensitive period in the human infant,* Birth, Jun; 36 (2): 110-2

14 The Communication Trust, 2012

15 Goodwyn SW, et al. (2000) *Impact of Symbolic Gesturing on Early Language Development (Abstract),* Journal of Nonverbal Behavior, 24, 81-103

16 Zeedyk S *The Science of Human Connection,* http://suzannezeedyk.com

17 Schmid B, et al (2013) *Maternal stimulation in infancy predicts hypothalamic-pituitary-adrenal axis reactivity in young men,* J Neural Transm Aug;120(8)

18 *Play and Communication Strategies,* with thanks to NHS London Borough of Barking and Dagenham.

19 *It Takes Two to Talk,* The Hanen Program®

20 Laakso M, et al. (1999) *Social interactional behaviors and symbolic play*

competence as predictors of language development and their associations with maternal attention-directing strategies, Infant Behavior and Development, 22(4) • Belsky J, et al. (1980) *Maternal stimulation and infant exploratory competence: cross-sectional, correlational and experimental analyses,* Child Dev, Dec 51 (4) 1168-78

21 Forehand R, et al. (1975) *Mother-child interactions: Comparison of a non-compliant clinic group and a non-clinic group,* Behaviour Research and Therapy, Jun;13(2-3):79-84 • Jenner S (2008) *The Parent-Child Game,* Bloomsbury, London

22 Lieberman A (1995) *The Emotional Life of a Toddler,* Free Press, London

23 Berk L, et al. (2006) *Beta-Endorphin and HGH Increase Associated with Both the Anticipation and Experience of Mirthful Laughter,* The Journal of the Federation of American Societies for Experimental Biology.
24 Cirelli L, et al (2014) *Interpersonal synchrony increases pro- social behaviour in infants,* Developmental Science, Volume 17(6), 1003–1011

25 Kokal I, et al. (2011) *Synchronized Drumming Enhances Activity in the Caudate and Facilitates Prosocial Commitment – If the Rhythm Comes Easily,* PLoS ONE 6(11), November, 6 (11) • Bittman B, et al (2001) *Composite effects of group drumming music therapy on modulation of neuroendocrine-immune parameters in normal subjects,* Alternative Therapies in Health and Medicine 7.1 (Jan 2001): 38-47

26 Ho P, et al (2011) *The impact of group drumming on social-emotional behaviour in low income children.* Evid Based Complement Alternat Med., 250708, Published online, Feb 13

27 Coan JA, et al (2006) *Lending a hand: social regulation of the neural response to threat.* Psychol Sci., Dec;17(12):1032-9.

28 Uvnäs-Moberg K (2011) *The Oxytocin Factor: Tapping the Hormone of Calm, Love and Healing,* Da Capo Press, Cambridge, MA

29 McGlone F, et al (2014) *Discriminative and Affective Touch: Sensing and Feeling,* Neuron, 82(4), 737–755

30 Uvnäs-Moberg K (2013) *The Hormone of Closeness: The Role of Oxytocin in Relationships,* Pinter & Martin Ltd, London

31 Taylor AF, et al. (2009) *Children with Attention Deficits Concentrate Better After Walk in the Park, Journal of Attention Disorders,* March 1, 12: 402-409 • Berman MG, et al. (2008) *The Cognitive Benefits of Interacting with Nature,* Psychological Science, 19: 1207

Chapter 11: Looking after you
1 Glover V (2014) *Maternal depression, anxiety and stress during pregnancy and child outcome; what needs to be done,* Best Practice & Research Clinical Obstetrics & Gynaecology, 28(1):25–35 • Bock J, et al. (2015) *Stress in Utero: Prenatal Programming of Brain Plasticity and Cognition • Biological Psychiatry,* Understanding PTSD: From Mind to Molecules, 78(5)

2 Field T, et al. (2009) *Pregnancy massage reduces prematurity, low birthweight and postpartum depression,* Infant Behav Dev., 32(4):454-60

3 Swaab D, et al (2011) *Sexual Differentiation of the Human Brain: Relation to Gender-Identity, Sexual Orientation, and Neuropsychiatric Disorders,* Frontiers in Neuroendocrinology, 32(2):214-226 • Corsello V, et al, (2011) *Biological aspects of gender disorders,* Minerva Endocrinol, 36:325-39

4. *Can I drink if I am pregnant?* National Health Service, UK, http://www.nhs.uk/chq/Pages/2270.aspx?CategoryID=54&SubCategoryID=130#close • Hepper PG, et al. *Fetal Brain Function in Response to Maternal Alcohol Consumption: Early Evidence of Damage,* Alcohol Clin Exp Res., Dec;36(12):2168-75

5 Cornelius, MD, et al. (2012) *Prenatal cigarette smoking: Long-term effects on young adult behavior problems and smoking behavior,* Neurotoxicology and Teratology, 34(6):554–559 • Longo CA, et al. (2013) *The long-term effects of prenatal nicotine exposure on response inhibition: An fMRI study of young adults,* Neurotoxicology and Teratology, 39:9–18

6 Barry TJ, et al. (2015) *Maternal postnatal depression predicts altered offspring biological stress reactivity in adulthood,* Psychoneuroendocrinology, 52:251-60

7 Ejdebäck M, et al. (2009) *Effects of sucking and skin-to-skin contact on maternal ACTH and cortisol levels during the second day postpartum-influence of epidural analgesia and oxytocin in the perinatal period,* Breastfeed Med. Dec;4(4):207-20 • Heinrichs M, et al. (2001) *Effects of suckling on HPA axis responses to psychosocial stress in postpartum lactating women,* The Journal of Clinical Endocrinology and Metabolism, Oct; 86(10):4798-804

8 Anglin RES, et al (2013) *Vitamin D deficiency and depression in adults: systematic review and meta-analysis,* The British Journal of Psychiatry, 202(2):100-107 • Mitchell ES (2014) *B vitamin polymorphisms and behavior: Evidence of associations with neurodevelopment, depression, schizophrenia, bipolar disorder and cognitive decline,* Neuroscience & Biobehavioral Reviews, 47:307–320 • Bodnar LM, et al. (2005) *Nutrition and Depression: Implications for Improving Mental Health Among Childbearing-Aged Women,* Biological Psychiatry, 58(9):679–685

9 Prasad C (1998) *Food, mood and health: a neurobiological outlook,* Brazilian Journal of Medical and Biological Research, 31(12):1517-27.

10 Tang M, et al. (2015) *Fish oil supplementation alleviates depressant-like behaviors and modulates lipid profiles in rats exposed to chronic unpredictable mild stress,* BMC Complement Altern Med., 17(15)239 • Trebaticka J, et al. (2014) *Psychiatric disorders and omega-3 fatty acids,* Free Radic Biol Med., 75 Suppl. 1:S52

11 Adolphus K, et al (2013) *The effects of breakfast on behavior and academic performance in children and adolescents,* Front Hum Neurosci., 8;7:425

12 Murphy JM (2007) *Breakfast and Learning: An Updated Review,* Current Nutrition & Food Science, 3(1):3-36(34) • Chaplin K, et al. (2011) *Breakfast and snacks: associations with cognitive failures, minor injuries, accidents and stress,* Nutrients, 3(5):515-28

13 Pasco JA, et al. *Dietary selenium and major depression: a nested case-control study,* Complementary Therapies in Medicine, 20(3):119–123

14 Coan JA (2010) *Adult attachment and the brain,* Journal of Social and Personal Relationships, 27(2):210–217 • McEwen BS (2012) *Brain on stress: How the social environment gets under the skin,* PNAS, May:1-6

15 Lucassen PJ, et al. (2010) *Regulation of adult neurogenesis by stress, sleep disruption, exercise and inflammation: Implications for depression and antidepressant action,* European Neuropsychopharmacology, 20:1–17

16 Uvnäs-Moberg K (2011) *The Oxytocin Factor: Tapping the Hormone of Calm, Love and Healing,* Da Capo Press, Cambridge, MA • Uvnäs-Moberg K (2013) *The Hormone of Closeness: The Role of Oxytocin in Relationships,* Pinter and Martin Ltd, London.

17 Streeter CC, et al (2007) *Yoga Asana Sessions Increase Brain GABA Levels: A Pilot Study,* The Journal of Alternative and Complementary Medicine, 13(4): 419-426.

18 Takahashi T, et al. (2005) *Changes in EEG and autonomic nervous activity during meditation and their association with personality traits,* International Journal of Psychophysiology, 55(2):199-207.

19 Holt-Lunstad J, et al. (2015) *Loneliness and social isolation as risk factors for mortality: A meta-analytic review,* Perspect Psychol Sci., 0(2):227-37

20 Johnstone T, et al. (2007) *Failure to Regulate: Counterproductive Recruitment of Top- Down Prefrontal-Subcortical Circuitry in Major Depression,* The Journal of Neuroscience, 27(33):8877-8884 • Panksepp J, et al. (2011) *Why does depression hurt? Ancestral primary-process separation-distress (PANIC/GRIEF) and diminished brain reward (SEEKING) processes in the genesis of depressive affect,* Psychiatry, 74(1):5-13

21 Fainsilber K, et al (2014) *Parental Emotion Socialization in Clinically Depressed Adolescents: Enhancing and Dampening Positive Affect,* Journal of Abnormal Child Psychology, 42:205–215 • Ashman SB, et al. (2002) *Stress hormone levels of children of depressed mothers,* Development and Psychopathology, 14(2):333-49

22 Tronick E, et al (2009) *Infants of Depressed Mothers,* Harvard Review of Psychiatry, 17(2):147–56 • Halligan SL, et al (2006) *Maternal depression and psychiatric outcomes in adolescent offspring: A 13-year longitudinal study,* Journal of Affective Disorders, 97(1-3):145–5

Useful addresses

4Children
Tel: 020 7512 2112
www.4children.org.uk
Gives information on afterschool and out-of-school care in England, Wales, and Scotland.

Association for Family Therapy and Systemic Practice
Tel: 01925 444 414
Web: www.aft.org.uk
Gives information about family therapy and how to find a therapist in your area.

Association for Post Natal Illness
Tel: 020 7386 0868
www.apni.org
Email: info@apni.org

British Association for Counselling and Psychotherapy (BACP)
Tel: 01455 883300
www.bacp.co.uk
Email: bacp@bacp.co.uk
UK's professional association for counsellors and psychotherapists. Use to find a counsellor or therapist in your area.

Bullying UK
www.bullying.co.uk
Tel: 0808 800 2222
Gives information and advice to those affected by bullying.

The Centre for Child Mental Health (London)
Tel: 020 7354 2913
www.childmentalhealthcentre.org
Gives information and lectures on neuroscientific and psychological research in child mental health for parents, teachers, and childcare professionals.

Childline
Tel: 0800 1111
www.childline.org.uk
Provides a free 24-hour helpline and support for children and young people.

Cry-sis
Tel: 08451 228 669
www.cry-sis.org.uk
Email: info@cry-sis.org.uk
Parents helpline – crying/sleepless children.

Family Lives
Helpline: 0808 800 2222
www.familylives.org.uk
Operates a national freephone helpline to support parents and carers of children.

Gingerbread
Helpline: 0808 802 0925
www.gingerbread.org.uk
Self-help body for single-parent families.

Grandparents' Association
Helpline: 08454 349585
www.grandparents-association.org.uk
Advice line on all aspects of grandparenting.

Home-Start
www.home-start.org.uk
Email: info@home-start.org.uk
Provides support and self-help network for parents of under-fives. Enter your postcode on the site for local assistance.

Institute for Arts in Therapy and Education
Tel: 020 7704 2534
www.artspsychotherapy.org
Offers nationally recognized Masters degree in Integrative Child psychotherapy; also Diplomas in Emotional Literacy for Children and in Parent–Child Therapy.

Institute of Family Therapy
Tel: 020 7 391 9150
www.ift.org.uk
Email: therapy@ift.org.uk
For young people and families with anxiety, depression, and behavioural problems.

Kidscape
Tel: 020 7730 3300
www.kidscape.org.uk
Protects children from bullying or abuse.

National Society for the Prevention of Cruelty to Children (NSPCC)
Helpline (24 hr): 0808 800 5000
www.nspcc.org.uk
UK's leading child protection charity. Helpline gives advice to anyone concerned about a child at risk of abuse.

One Parent Families Scotland
Tel: 0808 801 0323
www.opfs.org.uk
Email: info@opfs.org.uk
Support for lone parents and their children.

Relate
Tel: 0300 100 1234
www.relate.org.uk
National network of counselling centres for marriage and family relationship needs.

Twins and Multiple Birth Association (TAMBA)
Tel: 01252 332 344
Web: www.tamba.org.uk
Email: enquiries@tamba.org.uk
Provides information and mutual support for families of twins, triplets, and more.

Young Minds
Helpline for parents: 0808 802 5544
Web: www.youngminds.org.uk
National charity for improving children's mental health. Parents' advice line.

Index

Acknowledgments

Over my 17 years of studying the neuroscience of parent-child interactions, resulting in the first and second edition of this book I wish to express my gratitude to the following people:

Professor Jaak Panksepp who for many years has been correcting the text of this book and in the nicest possible way, ensuring that I properly represent the science. It has been a great privilege and honour to learn from such an eminent scientist, whose work is key to the emotional well-being of children.

Elaine Duigenan, an extremely talented photographer working in London and New York, who took many of the photos in this book. Elaine has a gift to fully enter into a child's experiencing of the moment, powerfully representing the full range of their feeling states from intense joy to intense pain. She shows children just as they are, rather than looking through a sugar-coated lens, and in so doing reassuring parents about the normality of those inevitable testing times as well as the delight.

Russ Parrett at Redshark TV for the additional photography for the new edition.

Professor Allan Schore (University of California at Los Angeles, David Geffen School of Medicine). It is only right that I declare that I am not the first to make the "Everestian climb" into this vast area of scientific study. Allan is! In his many books, he has integrated an awesome mass of brain research on parent–child interaction, brilliantly applying it to psychopathology and psychotherapy. At the start of my journey I received some vital tutoring from him, and this book owes a lot to his groundbreaking psychoneurobiological models.

Eleanore Armstrong-Perlman, Past Chair of the Guild of Psychotherapists and Fairbairnian psychoanalytic scholar. I thank her for her invaluable help on the chapter, "Chemistry of Love & Joy", and for her outstanding empathy for the suffering of children. She has helped me to speak for the babies.

Dr Dan Hughes (author: *Building the Bonds of Attachment*), who appears from time to time through the lines of this book. I've gained such a lot from him both personally and professionally. It is always a profoundly moving experience to watch him reaching unreachable children with his neuroscientifically grounded PACE model (play, acceptance, curiosity and empathy).

The late Sue Fish, a key founder of Integrative Child Psychotherapy in the UK. Her capacity for high intensity relational moments with both children and adults are testimony to all the studies in this book about the long-term brain benefits of human warmth, shared play, compassion and touch.

All those at The Centre for Child Mental Health: Charlotte Emmett, Ruth Bonner, and latterly Eleanor Cole, whose work on this book has meant it was largely a high dopamine experience of togetherness, rather than an isolated slog!

Brett Kahr, Senior Clinical Research Fellow in Psychotherapy and Mental Health and **Sir Richard Bowlby,** President of the Centre for Child Mental Health, who both bring so much richness and inspiration to our work in disseminating the latest child mental health research.

Professor Martin Teicher for his brilliant research on the impact of adverse parent-child interactions on the brain.

My mother Muriel Sunderland, whose love of knowledge, psychology and education has inspired my own.

Graeme Blench (Co-Director, Centre for Child Mental Health) for his unending support to me both personally and professionally.

And finally I want to thank all the scientists and psychologists referred to in this book, whose findings will help us to move towards a better world for our children.

PUBLISHER'S ACKNOWLEDGMENTS

DK publishing would like to thank:

Vanessa Bird for the index. Claire Cross and Anna Davidson for proofreading and editorial assistance.

Illustrator: Joanna Cameron

The children and parents who have acted as models for photography. We wish to point out that names have been changed and captions, quotations and case histories bear no relation to the actual children and adults, pictured in this book.

Original 2006 Edition: Senior Editor Esther Ripley, **Senior Art Editor** Anne Fisher, **Project Editors** Becky Alexander, Ann Baggaley, Kesta Desmond, **Designer** Jo Grey, **DTP Designer** Sonia Charbonnier, **Production Controller** Elizabeth Cherry, **Managing Editor** Penny Warren, **Managing Art Editor** Marianne Markham, **Picture Research** Myriam Megharbi, **Jacket Editor** Adam Powley, **Publishing Director** Corinne Roberts

Picture credits
The publisher would like to thank the following for their kind permission to reproduce their photographs:

(Key: a-above; b-below/bottom; c-centre; l-left; r-right; t-top)

123RF Stock Photo: anyka 157tl; **Aflo Foto Agency:** 275; **Alamy Images:** Finn Roberts 36cl, 202; **BananaStock:** 165; **Hal Beral:** 17clb; **Andy Bishop:** 266; **blickwinkel:** 153; **Brand X Pictures:** 124; **Brandon Cole Marine Photography:** 159; **Rolf Bruderer:** 272–73; **Scott Camazine:** 41; **cbp-photo:** 133; **CNRI:** 179; **Curious Fox Company:** Baby Deluxe Treasure Box: 142; **Scott Camazine & Sue Trainor:** 152, 167tc; **Harry T. Chugani:** M.D. Children's Hospital of Michigan, Wayne State University, Detroit, Michigan, USA: 52l; **Corbis:** 75, 94, 100–101, 220; **Jim Craigmyle:** 136; **Goupy Didier:** 20cl; **Kevin Dodge:** 148; **Pat Doyle:** 154; **Dorling Kindersley:** John Davis 271tr; **Elaine Duigenan:** 10, 11t, 12b, 17crb, 25t, 26, 29, 31t, 34, 37, 42, 43t, 46, 51, 55t, 59, 60tl, 84, 86, 90, 99, 108, 109, 110, 112–13, 114, 115, 125, 132, 134, 135, 139, 151, 156, 226, 164, 174, 177, 178, 180, 181, 182br, 183, 184, 191, 192, 193, 195, 196, 200, 201, 203, 204, 207, 208, 211, 213, 223, 231, 235, 236, 238, 239, 240, 267, 269, 274; **Laura Dwight:** 182br, 232; **Elvele Images:** 167br; **Jim Erickson:** 188tl; **Fotofacade:** 214; **John T. Fowler** 210t; **Garry Gay:** 40bl; **Françoise Gervais:** 169; **Tim Graham:** 282–83; **Getty Images:** Walther Bear: 194cl; **Jane Goodall:** 50; **Ghislain & Marie David de Lossy:** 172; **Onur Guentuerkuen:** 7t; **H.F. Harlow:** 58; **John Henley:** 30t, 168; **iStock:** Silvia Jansen: 122; **Gavriel Jecan:** 70; **Johansson and Belichenko, 2002:** 140; **John Powell Photographer:** 186, 228; **Christina Kennedy:** 123; **Ronnie Kaufmanf:** 96; **Gavin Kingcome Photography:** 89; **Tim Kiusalaas:** 260; **Pete Leonard/zefa:** 64; **Elyse Lewin:** 51; **Bob London:** 187tr; **Simon Marcus:** 230t; **Medical-on-Line:** 280; **Gideon Mendel:** 222; **Bill Miles** 78cl; **Motoring Picture Library:** 263; **Sidney Moulds** 40cra; **Jeffry W. Myers:** 74; **Tim O'Leary/zefa:** 103; **Tim Pannell:** 284; **Pegaz:** 216; **Photick - Image and Click:** 119; **Photofusion Picture Library:** 215; **Photo Network:** 185b; **Profimedia.CZ s.r.o.:** 209; **ROB & SAS:** 2–3, 241; **Reflections Photolibrary:** 225; **Royalty Free Images:** Alamy Images: 49tr; **George Shelley:** 8t; **Ariel Skelley:** 9b; **Sovereign, ISM:** 106; **The Image Bank:** 166bl; **thislife pictures:** 182bc, 276; **Tom Stewart** 32t; **LWA-Dann Tardif:** 91tr; **University of Southern California:** Susan Lynch, Brain and Creativity Institute, University of Southern California / Dr Antonio Damasio, Professor of Psychology, Neuroscience and Neurology, and Director, Institute for the Neurological Study of Emotion, Decision-Making, and Creativity, University of Southern California: 24; **Kennan Ward:** 17cb; 88; **Westend61** 147; **Janine Wiedel Photolibrary:** 120, 121; **Larry Williams:** 104; **Claude Woodruff:** 4–5; **Yellow Dog Productions:** 131.

All other images © Dorling Kindersley
For further information see: www.dkimages.com